Grace Chatt

The Ancestor Syndrome

In *The Ancestor Syndrome*, Anne Ancelin Schützenberger shows how, as mere links in a chain of generations, we may have no choice in having the events and traumas experienced by our ancestors visited upon us in our own lifetime.

The book includes fascinating case studies and examples of 'genosociograms' (family trees) to illustrate how her clients have conquered seemingly irrational fears, psychological and even physical difficulties by discovering and understanding the parallels between their own life and the lives of their forebears. The theory of invisible loyalty owed to previous generations, which may make us unwittingly re-enact their life events, is discussed in the light of ongoing research into transgenerational therapy.

First published in France as *Aïe, mes aïeux!*, this fascinating insight into a unique style of clinical work is already a best seller and will appeal to anyone working in the psychotherapy profession as well as to mental health professionals.

Anne Ancelin Schützenberger is Professor Emeritus of Psychology at the University of Nice and co-founder of the International Association of Group Psychotherapy. She is also internationally renowned as a trainer in group psychotherapy and psychodrama.

The Ancestor Syndrome

Transgenerational psychotherapy and the hidden links in the family tree

Anne Ancelin Schützenberger

Translated by Anne Trager

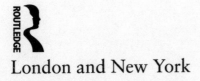

London and New York

First published in the UK in 1998
by Routledge
11 New Fetter Lane, London EC4P 4EE

Simultaneously published in the USA and Canada
by Routledge
29 West 35th Street, New York, NY 10001

©1998 Anne Ancelin Schützenberger;
translation © 1998 Anne Trager

Originally published in 1993 as *Aïe, mes aieux!: Liens transgénérationnels, secrets de famille, syndrome d'anniversaire et pratique du génosociogramme*

Typeset in Sabon by Routledge
Printed and bound in Great Britain by Clays Ltd, St Ives PLC

British Library Cataloguing in Publication Data
A catalogue record for this book is available from the British Library

Library of Congress Cataloging in Publication Data
A catalogue record for this book has been requested

ISBN 0–415–19186–6 (hbk)
        0–415–19187–4 (pbk)

To my daughter, Hélène, and my
grandchildren, Aude, Pierre and François.
To my trainees, clients and students, with
much gratitude for having taught me so much
about transmission and learning and
repetitions from generation to generation.

The dead are invisible, they are not absent.
Saint Augustine

Contents

PART II
Case studies with simplified genosociograms

Figures

Preface
The living past, or grandfather's parrot

It was summer – one beautiful morning. I was staying at a friend and colleague's house in the south of France for the weekend. Up early and not wanting to disturb the sleeping household, I quietly slipped into the garden and waited near the pool, under the pine trees, watching the sun rise over the mountains. Everything was so peaceful, orderly and calm, an example of Baudelaire's "grace and measure/Richness, quietness and pleasure."

Suddenly a commanding voice shouted, "Come and eat! Get a move on it...hurry, breakfast is ready!"

The dogs took to their feet, with me on their heels, and ran towards the voice, into the living room and...nobody was there. The male voice, self-assured, poised, used to giving orders and having them obeyed, repeated, "Hurry up, Monique, come on! Breakfast is on the table! And sit up straight!" Instinctively, I bristled and stood to attention.

Guided by the voice, the dogs came to a halt...in front of the parrot's cage, where they waited, begged, sat at attention and then lost interest, going back outside to lie down. As taken aback as they were, I returned to the garden to admire the morning sunlight.

Later, over a friendly and relaxed Sunday breakfast, my friend Michel explained that when his grandfather died, he inherited his hundred-year-old parrot who sometimes unexpectedly "spoke" like they used to speak in the family. It sounded so real as to sometimes even fool the family members themselves.

Sometimes it was the grandfather, an army officer, calling the family – particularly the grandchildren – to dinner. Sometimes it was another family member or friend. Nobody knew what triggered the parrot's memory nor whose voice it would take on, or when, or what it would disclose.

For Michel, his childhood family was there and alive. What presence! What emotions and feelings this parrot carried! What family reality and heritage, and what sense of roots and reassurance! But also, what secrets might it reveal, what family taboos or difficult moments might it disclose?

The parrot's voice embodied the past, the living past, a past still alive and interacting with the present.

This experience opened for me the pathway to the vividly present past, to the going-becoming (*allant-devenant*) that French child psychoanalyst Françoise Dolto described in the process of change and personal growth that occurs during therapy.

"The dead pass down to the living," according to Roman law.

We continue the chain of generations and, knowingly or not, willingly or unwillingly, we pay debts of the past: as long as we have not cleared the slate, an "invisible loyalty" impels us to repeat and repeat a moment of incredible joy or unbearable sorrow, an injustice or a tragic death. Or its echo.

Nice-Hyères, 1989

Acknowledgements

I would like to thank Franga Tomazi, without whom this book would not have seen the day, and Lolita Lopez, a doctoral student in psychology at the University of Nice, who kindly and patiently typed and retyped the dozens of corrected versions of this text (Argentière-Chamonix-Mont Blanc, 1993). And now, Anne Trager, for her patient work of translation (1997).

I would also like to thank Marcia Karp, without whose friendly persistence this English edition would not exist; and at Routledge, Edwina Welham and Kate Hawes, my Editors, and Kate Chenevix Trench, my thorough Desk Editor.

Part I

The transgenerational approach

1 A genealogy of transgenerational therapy
From the unconscious to the genosociogram

Every individual's life is a novel. You and I, we live as part of an invisible web, a web we also help to weave. Yet if we open up our perception and develop what Theodor Reik referred to as our third ear[1] and eastern philosophies refer to as our third eye[2] – that is, if we learn to hear what is difficult to hear and see what is difficult to see – then we can grasp, better understand, hear and see the repetitions and coincidences in our family history, and our individual lives can become clearer. We can become more aware of who we are, of who we could be. But how can we escape from the invisible threads of our family history, from the triangular alliances established in our family structure, from the frequent repetitions of difficult situations?

In a way, we are less free than we think we are. Yet we can regain our freedom and put an end to repetitions by understanding what happens, by grasping the threads in their context and in all their complexity. We can thus finally live "our own" lives, and no longer the lives of our parents or grandparents, or, for example, the life of a deceased brother or uncle whom we "replace," knowingly or not.

We can see, perceive or sense these complex links, although generally we do not speak about them: we experience them as part of the realm of the *unspeakable*, the *unthinkable*, the *unvoiced* or the *secret*. Yet there exists a way of modeling these bonds and our hopes so that our life measures up to what we desire it to be, to our true wishes, to what we want and need deep inside in order to be, rather than living a life someone else wants for us.

It is possible to seize the opportunity and take on your fate, improving your lot and avoiding the traps of unconscious transgenerational repetitions. You can go beyond what is transmitted consciously from generation to generation and bring to light what is transmitted *transgenerationally*, that is, what is transmitted without being "assimilated" because it was never verbalized and remains hidden among unspoken family secrets.

When you get right down to it, psychotherapy, training and personal development aim at making our life an expression of our profound being. After discovering and understanding him or herself, the psychotherapist is better able to hear, perceive, see and almost guess what the client[*] barely expresses, what the client may manifest in the form of pain, illness, silence, body language, failures, slip-ups, repetitions, "ill fortune," or existential difficulties. Then humbly, using all his or her "knowledge" – a knowledge that is more a knowledge of being, a knowledge of being with another, of hearing the other than it is a know-how or a theoretical knowledge – the therapist tries to become the go-between, to become the intermediary, a mentor who accompanies the client on the passageway between the client's "I" and "me," between the "knowing self" and the "self known," between the one who is looking for him or herself and his or her own truth and the "*accoucheur*" or "midwife," as Socrates referred to the therapeutic role.

Beginning with Freud...

From his own frame of mind and his own suffering, anxieties and questioning, Freud[3] discovered the "other scene," the "black hole" that every person carries inside, the "unspoken" or "unvoiced" (*das Unbewusste*, poorly translated at the time as "unconscious"); the gap, the "black hole connected to others," to family members, close relations, and society as a whole. He also uncovered the inter- and intra-psychic environment, the frame or context, which forges us and constructs who we are just as much as it drags us along blindly towards pleasant or tragic experiences, or sometimes even "deals us a bad hand."

Can we find profound meaning in the trivial and banal events of daily life, memory lapses, slip-ups, small accidents, dreams, nightmares or impulsive actions? What meaning can we give to our behavior and our reactions, or even to our illnesses, accidents, or

---

[*]   "Client" is a term introduced by Carl Rogers, who preferred it to "subject" or "patient," to designate a person seeking counseling or therapy in a relationship with no strings attached – a difficult relationship to achieve – with no transference, attachment, gratitude or need between the client and the therapist, nor social contacts outside sessions.

important and "normal" life events such as marriage (how many, at what age), choice of profession, number of children, "miscarriages," age at death? Can we give these events meaning without the help of a (good) psychotherapist?

Perhaps we can, or perhaps we cannot. Perhaps we cannot give them meaning, but by locating and recording them, we can approach this "thing" which works inside us. In doing so, perhaps like so many English novelists you will discover in yourself the talent to write, or to play the piano, or to garden, or perhaps you will allow yourself to return to school, or – finally – to make yourself happy.

It goes without saying that working on three or four generations sends us back to the unconscious as it manifests itself and therefore back to Freud and psychoanalysis. I would like to encourage the reader to read Freud, and particularly his *Introductory Lectures on Psychoanalysis*, *New Introductory Lectures on Psychoanalysis*, *Five Lectures on Psychoanalysis* and "The Uncanny," as well as Groddeck's *The Book of It*.

Let us trace the historical roots of the transgenerational approach by first taking a look at Freud's remarks concerning the choice of his children's first names: "I had insisted on their names being chosen, not according to the fashion of the moment, but in memory of people I had been fond of. *Their names made the children into revenants.*"[4] (The italics are mine.)

Elsewhere, Freud states the following:

> the archaic heritage of human beings comprises not only disposi-
> tions but also subject matter – memory-traces of the experience
> of earlier generations.[5]

> I have taken as the basis of my whole position the existence of a
> collective mind, in which mental processes occur just as they do
> in the mind of an individual. In particular, I have supposed that
> the sense of guilt for an action has persisted for many thousands
> of years and has remained operative in generations which can
> have no knowledge of that action. I have supposed that an
> emotional process, such as might have developed in generations

of sons who where ill-treated...has extended to new generations which are exempt from such treatment ...[6]

Jung, Moreno, Rogers, Dolto and a few others

The history of psychoanalysis is far from being a long, smooth road. As with all major discoveries and research there have been clashes, estrangement, alienation, reconciliation, alliances, trials and errors, interpretations, glosses, and flashes of inspiration.[7] And just as a book about transgenerational therapy cannot neglect mention of Freud's reference to a "collective mind" in *Totem and Taboo*, we cannot neglect Jung's[8] "collective unconscious."

Freud and his "heir," as Jung was referred to by the circle around Freud, split in extreme violence. To hate, one has to have loved intensely. Right before his retirement and death, Bruno Bettelheim of the Orthogenic School of the University of Chicago wrote that this estrangement could have been caused by Freud reproaching Jung for impropriety with patients – and particularly with the young Sabina Spielrein – which Jung seemed to have masked as a theoretical disagreement.[9]

Whatever the case, Jung's work complements Freud's by bringing to light the concept of "synchronicity," which refers to the coincidence in time of two or more causally unrelated events which have an important meaning for a person. Jung also elaborated the concept of the "collective unconscious," an inherited, transpersonal unconscious shared by all.

According to Jung, the collective unconscious shapes who we are. It is an unconscious transmitted from generation to generation in society, an unconscious that accumulates human experience. It is inborn and therefore exists outside of any personal experience. Obviously, this concept had a major impact on both psychoanalytical theory and clinical practice.

Although my choice was made by my Freudian training, I think that the time of quarrels between schools is passed. It is not my intention here to take a position for or against Jung, but to highlight the idea of transmission from generation to generation and of synchronicity or coincidences in time and space (serendipity).

I would also like to point out that if Freud was the one to discover the unconscious, the *unvoiced* and the "collective mind," and Jung the one to introduce the "collective unconscious," it was Jacob Levy Moreno, the founding father of psychodrama and group psychotherapy, who postulated the existence of the family and group "co-conscious" and "co-unconscious." He describes a conscious and an unconscious shared by several individuals joined by intimate bonds, as in a family, a surgical team, or a squadron on a dangerous mission.

At about the same time, during the 1960s and 1970s, French child psychoanalyst Françoise Dolto, Hungarian-French psychoanalyst Nicolas Abraham and their French followers, as well as Hungarian-American psychotherapist Ivan Boszormenyi-Nagy, all raised the complex question of *transgenerational transmission* of unresolved conflicts, of hatred, revenge, vendettas, of secrets, of what is "unspoken," as well as of premature deaths and choice of profession.

We build up knowledge through accumulation, and then all of a sudden a new hand emerges. In psychoanalysis, you work on your feelings and memories in the dark, not knowing where it will lead, and then all at once the meaning emerges. It is as if abruptly something like an "upholstery stud" – as Lacan would have said – joins several layers of unconscious memories and experience, shedding light on the meaning.

All therapists, whether psychoanalysts or some other form of therapist, are part of a lineage whose theory they have made their own. But often clinical practice goes against dogmatism, and in practice we make concessions, be they acknowledged or not.[10] What remains essential is the way a therapist receives, listens to, hears and observes his or her client. The therapist should hear and understand the client in the client's own frame of mind. The therapist should enter into communication with the client's mental and emotional world. John Grinder and Richard Bandler brought to light the importance of using the same modes of perception,[*] of being in empathy – which does not mean sympathy – and in this way, one unconscious can communicate with the other unconscious. The result is what Moreno called the "co-unconscious," an idea that Freud already hinted at when he spoke of the therapist's free-floating attention. The most brilliant and knowledgeable therapist will never be a real therapist if unable to really hear the other, if unable to hear the client in the client's own context and frame of mind.

According to Grinder and Bandler, we process our perceptions of the world in different ways and we tend to be either more visual, auditory or kinesthetic. So, for them, exceptional teachers or therapists by chance share the same modes of perception with their students or clients, or are able to pick up on these modes.

This is why in therapy, the most important things often happen and are expressed when the work and the words stop at the doorstep. Therapists are right when they say it is a trade unlike any other: you cannot learn it, it must be transmitted. It is as much an art as a science and a way of being in the world.

My professional lineage

In this perspective of transmission, I would like to mention my own professional lineage. I trained in Freudian psychoanalysis with two French psychoanalysts. The first, Robert Gessain, was also an anthropologist, at the time director of the *Musée de l'Homme* in Paris, who had accompanied Paul Emile Victor to the North Pole and for forty years lived with and sought to understand the Inuit. He taught me to understand different cultures. The second, Françoise Dolto, performed miracles with children, speaking their language from inside. At the time, many French psychoanalysts worked for short periods with Dolto in order to learn to open their eyes and ears to worlds different from their own.

I trained in psychodrama in the United States under J.L. Moreno in New York and with James Enneis, the head psychodramatist at St Elisabeth's Hospital in Washington, DC. I owe them my ability to sometimes turn a "frog into a princess".[11]

Later, other approaches enriched my practice and my listening. I owe much to the group dynamics specialist Leon Festinger, with whom I trained in observation at the University of Michigan's Research Center for Group Dynamics in Ann Arbor.

My practice was also influenced by the anthropologists Margaret Mead, Gregory Bateson and Erving Goffman, and the American psychotherapist Carl Rogers for his client-centered approach. I also owe some of my approach to the Palo Alto family therapy group; the specialists in non-verbal communication, linguist Ray Birdwhistell and anthropologist Jurgen Ruesch; and the family therapists Paul Watzlawick and Louis and Diana Everstine. But it is probably Moreno who transmitted to me and allowed me to develop the creative imagination, the sense of the encounter, the desire "to meet the other," and the stubbornness to help those who are suffering.

Moreno: a tribute

J.L. Moreno has never received adequate tribute for his contributions as founder of role theory,[12] of sociometry or the science of human relations, and as father of psychodrama and group therapy. His battle against psychoanalysis has something to do with it, be it the position he took with regards to Freud in 1932 during the First Congress of the American Association of Psychiatry – which was almost a psychodrama in itself – or the monograph he published in 1967: *The Psychodrama of Sigmund Freud.*[13] Basically, Freud and Moreno were two major creators whose works complement each other. In 1956, at the centenary of Freud's birth, Moreno wrote that if the psychology of the twentieth century belonged to Freud, the psychology of the twenty-first century would belong to Moreno. Isn't this a kind of murder of the father in order to be different from him and outdistance him?

Moreno also contributed to this "discovery" of unconscious minds that communicate in their own way on the couch or without it, or that communicate from "somewhere" in time – a circular time – and whose emergence we explore today through the genosociogram and the transgenerational approach. He can justly be named one of the founding fathers.

Among Moreno's key ideas contributing to transgenerational work, let us first mention the concept of "tele," which comes from the same Greek root as in telephone, meaning "at a distance." Tele is a "two-way empathy," a combination of empathy, transference and unconscious "real communication" – either positive or negative – between people, a communication at a distance.

Let us also mention Moreno's manner of representing the significant relations in an individual's life: the "social atom." This diagram includes people who make up the "subject's personal world": their family, friends, acquaintances, neighbors, work colleagues or sports companions; those present in the individual's life through love or through hate, be they alive or deceased. Generally, the subject – the protagonist – draws a visual representation on a piece of paper or a blackboard, situating these different people at a "social distance"* specific to each relation. So you can, for example, send a mother-in-law who annoys you far beyond the pale – that is, to the other end of the blackboard – and write in near to you a very present, loved and dear deceased grandmother. In the social

---

* Social psychology uses the concept of "social distance" to indicate the extent to which a person is psychologically close to or far from the subject, not considering geographic distance. For example, Brazil and its carnival are closer to inhabitants of southern France than Germany or Belgium, or my deceased grandfather more present then the neighbors downstairs.

atom, the subject generally starts by situating him or herself, "this is me, here"; although some subjects will complete the diagram before situating themselves in their family of origin.

The social atom represents an imprint, x-ray or snapshot of a life and its ramifications, its interests, dreams or anxieties. "Morenians" add to it the "sociometric network," the complex chains of inter-relations, and the "sociometric status," which is an individual's "love index" in a group based on the number of times a person is chosen or rejected by a group for participation in some activity. The social atom represents these emotional projections. In *Who Shall Survive?*, Moreno defines this representation of a person's personal world as "a nucleus of relations around every individual...the small social structure of the community..." and "a pattern of attractions, repulsions and indifferences...between individual and group." It represents the internal and external nucleus of relations around every individual.

One can say that the social atom is a "genosociogram" placed in the "here and now." The term "genosociogram" comes from "genealogy" and "sociogram," which is a representation of ties, links and relations. A genosociogram is a family tree that graphically represents and brings to light important life events and their connections. A "genogram" is a family tree annotated with a few landmark events and is used primarily by family systems therapists and by sociologists who, not being psychoanalysts, do not "dig" as deeply into life stories searching for hidden and unconscious links. This is what we do with the genosociogram, producing a more detailed and researched genogram. We also do not stop at three generations, but often go back five to six generations, tracing a family back two centuries, to the French Revolution (1789) or American Independence (1776).

Genogram and genosociogram

Based on Moreno's work, Professor Henri Collomb[14] started to develop the genosociogram technique we will explore in this book. He brought it back with him from Dakar to the University of Nice in 1978.

The genosociogram allows a visual sociometric representation of the family tree including surnames, given names, places, dates, landmark occurrences, bonds, and major life events such as births, marriages, deaths, important illnesses, accidents, moves, occupations, retirement. The genosociogram is an annotated representation of the family tree – a genogram – which highlights, through the use of sociometric arrows, the different types of relations the subject has with his or her environment and the bonds between the different people: co-presence, cohabitation, co-action, dyads, triangles, exclusions, etc. It pinpoints "who lives under the same roof," who "eats from the same dish," who raises whose children, who runs away and to where, who arrives – through birth or moving in – at the same time as another goes away – through death or departure, who replaces whom in the family, how things are shared – particularly through inheritance or donation after a death, who is favored and who is not, as well as repetitions and injustices in the "family bookkeeping".

Some therapists trace the origin of the genogram to a conference on family therapy given by Murray Bowen in 1967, but we could say that the genogram sprang from Moreno's first reflections on complex family systems and his social atom, although the diverse practitioners using family systems theory and the genogram have not retraced this "historical genealogy."

Those who use the genogram explore more or less deeply the different relationships, the bonds, the ins and outs of a family system. I work the genosociogram in great depth, in as complete a context as possible, and often reconstructing the past over two centuries, six to nine generations, and sometimes further.

We deepen and enrich the genogram, making it a genosociogram, with a psycho-social and psychoanalytical emphasis, using tools such as observation of non-verbal communication, giving feedback, or noticing changes in the client, in his or her breathing or skin coloring. We also bring to light what is spoken and unspoken, past and present social and emotional bonds and relationships in a *psycho-historic framework*, often working with a historic chronology of the nineteenth and twentieth centuries. We work with what is expressed through non-verbal communication, explore the "gaps" in what has been said, what has been "forgotten," the splits, the break-ups, the "broken hearts," the synchronous events and the coincidences in dates of birth and dates of death, marriage, separation, accidents, onset of illness, failure in exams, reconciliation. We note the important anniversary dates in the client's personal world, in his family universe, in his social atom, in his social and economic environment, in his personal psychological reality, with the goal of helping that person better understand his or her life and give it meaning.

Freud and the uncanny

Sometimes the things seen and heard in psychotherapy appear very strange, even to a seasoned therapist. But when you hear them over and over again from different clients, when you listen without preconceived ideas, when you lend an attentive, neutral and benevolent ear to everything a human being can recount, they can make sense, a subjective sense, for the suffering subject. And they can make sense to the therapist, particularly if that therapist does not "plaster" them with a theory which will probably unjustly simplify what could actually be new and unexpected. Then, and only then, can new paradigms be opened up and become clinical facts, paving the way for scientific fact, thus making sense in a new frame of reference.

Freud describes the following in "The Uncanny," which was written at the end of the First World War and published in 1919:

> all those properties of persons, things, sense-impressions, experiences and situations which arouse in us the feeling of uncanniness, and then infer the unknown nature of the uncanny from what all these examples have in common...the uncanny is that class of the frightening which leads back to what is known of old and long familiar...my investigation was actually begun by collecting a number of individual cases, and was only later confirmed...[15]

Freud defines "the uncanny" as the unexpected return of elements that should have been surmounted long ago – remains of primitive beliefs, a return of the archaic – or elements that should have been repressed and are "once more revived by some impression."[16] The uncanny is "what is frightening – what arouses dread and horror;...which, as may easily be guessed, lie in the times in which we live"[17] (an allusion to the First World War, only just concluded).

In the uncanny, we can perceive, as did Maria Torok, the lasting and haunting effect of a family secret, or the unexpected return of something repressed, such as war traumas. Freud himself treated victims of the First World War massacre at Verdun.

I think that in Freud, we can find the theoretical basis to support what I and other transgenerational therapists have observed – and which we will explore in more detail in later chapters – in the anxiety, the attacks of "deadly cold" similar to Raynaud's disease, and the terror and/or the repetitive nightmares suffered by descendants of those who survived tragedies, catastrophes, natural disasters, and the countless horrors of war. These symptoms often appear in periods of commemoration and/or anniversary periods ("time collapse"). And they can appear whether the facts, the war memories, the concentration camps, the bombings, the cataclysms were kept quiet or spoken about in the family, known or hidden, held secret and left unvoiced, or historically known, but not mentioned in the family.

2 Family therapy and the genogram/genosociogram

When the concept of the family and the use of films and videotapes entered the therapeutic scene, they brought to light the importance of family bonds and modes of communication in the health or dysfunction of a family. These developments allowed the genogram and the genosociogram to be conceptualized and perfected as tools for investigation and treatment.

What we call family therapy sprang from the research carried out by Frieda Fromm-Reichmann[1] (1889–1957) around 1948. She pondered the question of psychosis and especially schizophrenia. She worked with psychotic patients and their families and had them filmed by anthropologists and psychiatrists.

If dreams are, in Freud's words, "the royal road to knowledge of the unconscious," then the families of schizophrenic patients and their interactions – which were filmed and studied in slow motion – provided the road to unraveling the universe that exists inside families, with their modes of verbal communication and non-verbal expression.

Following Frieda Fromm-Reichmann and in relation to her work, other researchers gathered at the University of Stanford and in Palo Alto in 1956 around Gregory Bateson,[2] Jay Haley,[3] John Weakland, Don Jackson, and later Paul Watzlawick[4] and the famous family therapist Virginia Satir[5], and began studying these aspects of family interaction. Perhaps it was by some lucky chance or "serendipity" that so many high-level researchers from such different disciplines found themselves together in Palo Alto to exchange and confront different points of view. This is how the Palo Alto group was formed, most of the group being on sabbatical as fellows at the Institute for Advanced Study in Behavioral Science.

The Palo Alto group

The Palo Alto group elaborated the hypothesis of the "double bind," which refers to a serious disturbance in family communication: contradictory messages are sent out by a key family member, generally the mother, with no other adult to contradict them. These messages are structured in such a way as to verbally affirm one thing while at the same time expressing something entirely different through, for example, body language, so that the two affirmations cancel each other out. It is a "doubly binding double message." Therefore, if the message is an order, you have to disobey it in order to obey it. And, you are forbidden to talk about it, or even mention that the message is confusing, contradictory and "mandatory."

A person stuck in a double bind runs the risk of being punished or feeling guilty when he or she perceives things "correctly", and of being designated by the family as "mean" or "crazy" for pointing out the conflict between what he or she saw or perceived and what he or she "should have" seen or felt. This person is referred to as the "designated patient," rather than the sick patient, because the Palo Alto group considered that in many cases of schizophrenic children, the parents are sicker than the child and the family and family communication should be treated to restore health.

The classic family therapy approach that developed from the Palo Alto group's research is based on the idea that the family forms a "system" which develops a "homeostasis" or balance and functions with a set of family rules. The practitioners at the Palo Alto Mental Research Institute – Whitaker, Napier, Watzlawick – were already talking about "ghosts" which spring from a patient's past[6] during therapy. They were also referring to systemic family therapy and twenty to thirty years later would be using the genogram.

Strategic systemic therapy

Therapists of the theoretical school called "strategic systemic therapy" use this paradox, working on what generates it with the "designated patient" and his or her family. They consider that both patient and family know the reality of the problem at hand and found their approach on the basic principle that everyone can define his or her own reality. As a result, finding solutions to everyday difficulties – whether they concern physical or mental health – becomes the major problem to resolve. The therapy aims at redefining reality in a more operational way. We could say, in words that could have been those of the anthropologist Erving Goffman,[7] that you need to reach a point where you can see, perceive and replace an event in another perspective, in another framework, in another context. You need to "reframe" it.

Structural family therapy

"Structural family therapy," another branch of systemic therapy, seeks to modify family relational habits, to change relationships that have become stereotyped. This school formed around Salvador Minuchin[8] at the Child Guidance Clinic in Philadelphia, where many of their techniques were put into practice, particularly in child therapy. Their procedure centered on the here and now.

It was Murray Bowen who described a kind of family merging where an individual no longer distinguishes who he or she is, making it a long, painful and difficult process for a growing child or teenager to differentiate himself or herself from the family. Bowen drew up a scale measuring differentiation of the self from the fusional mass of the family ego. On the top of the scale, you find real adult persons with structured and differentiated selves, and on the bottom you find those living under the grip of the family ego, unable to distance themselves from their own family life experience. Bowen also pointed to the frequent triangular conflicts in families, where two gang up against one. He developed a technique for transforming a triangular relationship into a dyad, and in doing so raised the question of anxiety transmission from one generation to another if the triangular relationship is not broken.

In an interview with Ingmar Bergman published in 1991, concerning his production of Strindberg's *Miss Julie* for Sweden's Royal Dramatic Theater, he said: "This play recounts three mental wounds suffered by Miss Julie...there are people in this world who choose to carry the guilt of others, and she is one of them." Of course, this play, like all of Strindberg's work, was inspired by autobiographical experiences. It recounts the anxiety of a servant's son and the repetitive family dramas in the author's life. Yet, long before, the Greeks had already described this phenomenon in the story of Hercules who donned the tunic of the centurion Nessus whom he had killed. The tunic stuck to his skin and caused him so much pain that he put an end to his own life. So, like Nessus' tunic, family repetitions stick to the skin, storing up the anxiety of one's ancestors.

Analytical family therapy

The movement which interests us the most consists of the family therapists who, from a psychoanalytical basis, attempt to broaden analytical concepts and tools to the family, which they consider to be a series of dyads. This movement includes Nathan Ackerman, Ivan

Boszormenyi-Nagy and, in France, Nicolas Abraham and Maria Torok. More recently, French analysts such as René Kaës and André Ruffiot have been examining transgenerational links from an analytical perspective. Nathan Ackerman[9] bases his practice on dual interviews in order to help the family become aware of false ideas and particularly "relics" from the past.

In my own analytically based work, I sometimes make use of short psychodramas called vignettes, in which patients relive their past by acting it out, using classical psychodrama techniques including projection into the future or extended "surplus reality", in which it is possible to ask a dead grandfather to come and talk on the stage. I use these techniques to help people get rid of the "hot potato" passed onto them from previous generations.

3 Invisible loyalties

The therapist from the Philadelphia school who broadened the trans-generational approach was the Hungarian-born psychoanalyst Ivan Boszormenyi-Nagy[1]. Marking a clear separation from the Palo Alto school, Boszormenyi-Nagy considered that the relational bond holds much more significance than transgenerational communication models, and these relationships have to take into consideration *justice and fairness within the family*. Through them, our ancestors pass life – their life – on to us, and we then hand it down to our own descendants. In his practice, Boszormenyi-Nagy[2] had his clients speak at length about their lives, because for him, the goal and the force of a therapeutic intervention lies in reconstructing the ethics at work in transgenerational relations.

I find it most striking that although the concepts of the relation-ships with "parents of parents" and links to ancestors have run through all therapeutic thought and practice since Freud, the psychotherapists who founded the transgenerational approach all share an Eastern European or Central European origin. Could this stem from a legacy of emigration and a double culture? Perhaps this provides one more proof of an individual's implantation, whether conscious or more or less unconscious, in his or her "culture," in his or her "roots."

In Eastern and Central European countries such as in Russia, among Slavs just as among Mediterranean peoples, the family forms a very strong "social atom," a nest, a close-knit clan, a "womb" from which an individual builds his or her identity.

This connection is obvious to me; even more so with my own double culture: raised in Paris, educated from my tender years in French public school and French university, cradled by the Slavic tales told in Russian by my Russian great-grandmother Hélène, and trained in the United States at the University of Michigan in Ann

Arbor and then by Moreno, who inherited from his own European background an out-of-the-ordinary creative imagination and warm openness to others.

Somehow, I feel that I am who I am precisely because of my multiple roots which draw from several cultures, languages and traditions. It is the founding silence, which, like in analysis, is where everything happens. As I recall Margaret Mead saying to me in Holland in 1956, the basic things in any culture and family go without saying. The most important things are taken for granted, never clearly stated, leaving you to guess them through ways of life, hints, or non-verbal communication. But as the French poet and critic Boileau (1636–1711) said, the things that go without saying, go even better when said (*les choses qui vont sans dire vont encore mieux en les disant*). We experience unspoken things with more ease and comfort when they are named and spoken about, which is the whole point of this book.

I would go further to say that perhaps the French child psychoanalyst Françoise Dolto, one of my two analysts, was such a peerless therapist because her husband Boris shared with her the Slavic charisma which he received from his ancestors and which flowed from his entire being. She even attributed her intuition to a distant Asian ancestor (her "indian mark").

Ivan Boszormenyi-Nagy's concepts

After that brief personal digression, I would like to analyze the concept of "loyalty," one of the key ideas in Boszormenyi-Nagy's approach, a concept that offers two levels of understanding: a social, "systemic" level and an individual or psychological level. Loyalty is composed of a social unit which depends on and expects loyalty from its members and on the thinking, feeling and motivations of each member as an individual. Thus the concept of justice and "family justice." When justice is not accomplished, there is injustice, unfairness and exploitation among family members, which sometimes translates into fleeing, revenge or vengeance, or even illnesses or repetitive accidents.

Otherwise, there is affection and reciprocal consideration, balancing the family ledgers. So we can talk about "balancing family accounts" and the extended "family balance sheet" on which you can see if you have a credit or a debit, if you have debts, obligations or merits. If the ledgers are not balanced, problems can be passed on from generation to generation.

Parentification

Boszormenyi-Nagy's third fundamental concept is "parentification," which consists of an inversion, a wrong conception of merits and debts. The most important "debt" in terms of "family loyalty" is the one every child owes his or her parents for the love, affection, care, fatigue and consideration received from birth through to adulthood. We acquit these debts in a transgenerational manner, which means that what we received from our parents, we give to our children. This does not keep us from having debts and giving consideration towards our parents when they become old, including helping them live their final years and make the passage from life to death.

"Parentification" consists of the reversal of values, creating the situation in which children, even at a very young age, become the parents of their own parents, being obliged to take care of them. Let us take a classic example, a simple one. In a certain number of families, particularly low-income or rural families, the eldest daughter often takes the role of mother, the actual mother being weakened by fatigue or too many childbirths, being ill or sickly, and getting help, care and support from her daughter, who never marries. This is an unhealthy distortion of relations, of merits and debts. This is called parentification. A child who must become a parent at a very young age – even at the age of five, for example – and has to support her mother and take care of her parents and family lives in a significant relational imbalance, an imbalance which we discover through the analysis of the positions and roles held by the children in the family universe.

It is difficult to understand the transgenerational links and the "book of merits and debts" because nothing about it is clear-cut, each family has its own way of defining family loyalty and justice. It is in no way an objective concept.

To really understand, one has to make a transgenerational and horizontal study of the family over at least three generations, preferably five, in order to determine how the patterns in place operate. In order to do so, one has to rely on *retrospective information*, on *memories the living have about the dead*, on what the people currently living know about their families and what moves them – even if they do not consciously know what they know. One has to consider what was said and left unsaid, what is conscious and not conscious in the information transmitted, and this from the family's point of view.

The family myth or the family saga

Here, we touch upon the *family myth*, which only becomes clear when you understand the *system*, that sum of mutually interdependent units. For Boszormenyi-Nagy, an individual is a biological and psychological entity – to which I would add psycho-social – whose reactions are determined as much by his or her own psychology as by the rules of the family system. In a family system, one member's psychological position conditions the psychological positions of the other members: there exists perpetual reciprocal regulation. And the rules regulating the way the family system functions are both implicit and explicit, although, for the most part, they remain implicit, and family members are not consciously aware of them. The majority of the rules are taken for granted and considered obvious: "in our family we do this or that." The rules are therefore left unexplained.

The family myth manifests itself through an operational pattern: some families are organized according to patterns which I would consider "unhealthy," but I do not know how else to qualify treason, interfamily vendettas, assassinations, the healthy or unhealthy defense of the "family honor." These rites form a configuration, a sort of whole, an unconsciously structured relational *Gestalt** affecting all the members of a family. Each of these rites contributes to "balancing the family accounts," the "exploitative positions or attitude" being balanced or not by a "giving attitude." There are times when we use our family and the situation. Children "exploit" their families because they are taken care of, fed, housed, etc. and at the same time, they give the family love or something else; a balance exists between what is received and given, otherwise, more or less serious symptoms appear.

We consider ethical inheritance to be as important as professional and economic inheritance. The sociologist Vincent de Gaulejac even speaks of "family capital." Each family determines the various individuals' contributions to the family accounts. The family code determines the scale of merits, advantages, obligations and responsibilities, which are learned reactions, grounded in the family history, in the family's genetic and historic relatedness, and which we can uncover.

---

* "*Gestalt*": perception of a whole, a form with contrast on a background. Psychologists using Gestalt theory choose not to translate this term from German.

A personal example

I am going to provide a personal example. When I was a student in psychology just after the war, I was married, we had a child, and like so many young student couples, we had financial difficulties. One of my cousins spontaneously offered to lend me money. I accepted her offer, without feeling obliged or guilty. When I finished my studies and began to work, I reimbursed this money. However, my colleagues did not understand how my younger cousin could have so easily proposed to lend me money, and how I myself could have accepted it without difficulty. When I think about it now, I remember that my grandfather was orphaned at the age of fourteen and the eldest of six children. They were taken in by their grandfather (my great-great-grandfather) and raised with the children of a second marriage. My grandfather began to work very early on in order to help raise his brothers and sisters and offer them higher studies. So, somewhere in my family's unconscious, he "acquired merits" vis-à-vis his brothers and sisters.

Later, after finishing her doctoral studies in Switzerland, one of his sisters contributed to opening a laboratory of pharmaceutical products. At the turn of the century, she married a chemist and druggist; they earned a little money and settled in Paris. Then, my cousin, descendant of this sister of my grandfather, offered to lend me money. Somehow, it was "something for something," a balance. She said to me, "Pay me back if you can. If you can't, don't bother, or pay me back later, in five years, in fifty years, it's not important."

Taking into consideration the "family accounting system," I understand that it seemed like a normal thing to do for both of us, because she and I both knew that her grandmother and my grandfather shared mutual affection (what Boszormenyi-Nagy called a "giving attitude"). All the descendants of my grandfather's brothers and sisters find themselves in some way indebted to him (the eldest). They all loved him very much. And when my grandfather was old, and our family experienced a turn of fortune after the 1929 crisis, the descendants of one or another invited us over. We lived in Paris: my great-aunt Nathalie helped my grandfather and grandmother out, which "put some butter on the table" and "warmed the heart." We never signed any IOU. We never talked about money. We all spent most of our vacations on a big farm taking on "paying guests" – the brother and sister and their spouses, and us, the cousins: three generations together. The family links were maintained and strengthened.

A debt was reimbursed somewhere and it seemed normal to us all.

We never exchanged any paper, any signed "acknowledgment of debt." When my younger cousin lent me money, she refused to have me sign a paper. Of course, I repaid her.

Thirty years later, when I found myself in front of a jeweler's shop and spontaneously bought gold earrings for her daughter, I remembered that my cousin – who had since died in an airplane accident – had offered me costume jewelry...and lent me money. So, these gold earrings were also symbolic.

Family "accounting" and injustice

There exists *implicit family book-keeping*. We are not only talking about money. What I mean to say is that it was not so much money that my grandfather gave to his brothers and sisters: he gave money that came from his work. He had worked hard starting at a very young age in order to support them. Above all, he gave them love and affection along with support, joy, happiness and security. This is what has been transmitted among my grandfather's descendants and those of his brothers and sisters. We were four hundred people to gather in Paris to celebrate my grand-uncle and grand-aunt Nathalie's silver anniversary. It continues. We are now all very closely knit distantly related cousins, or as the French would say, "*cousins à la mode de Bretagne.*" We continue to mutually support each other. Aunt Nathalie's grandson Jacques and his wife continue to celebrate his grandmother's birthday (she died more than fifty years ago) and to invite us all over every 3 January, even if it means eating in turns. It's "the family" and it's a celebration. As the Russian proverb says, "overcrowded, but not disgruntled, not in a snit,"* or more commonly, "the more the merrier." It is a little bit in this line of thought that we find Boszormenyi-Nagy's accounting of merits and debts, as I understood it from his works.

In family accounting, there are *suffered injustices that hurt*. I see it often enough in the onset of cancer connected to stress and resentment, among other factors. Some people can't manage to forgive suffered injustices. It is connected to this very complex "book-keeping" of the " family ledger," to "what is due to you" and "what you owe" to others in order to "balance the accounts," to settle outstanding debts.

* "В ТЕСНОТЕ, НО НЕ ОδиΔи"

My thirty years of therapeutic experience have shown me that geographic distance or flight from the family ledger do not really free a person from what he would himself call his family "debts." Boszormenyi-Nagy points out that you cannot avoid the tyranny of your obligations by avoiding the creditor. Running away from family obligations – even very far away – can infuse all of an individual's human relations, for he or she becomes petrified by an unbearable, diffuse, objectless guilt. A person can become paralyzed by an "amorphous, undefinable, existential guilt."

Boszormenyi-Nagy also asks whether there exists an objective reality. Is there room for objective reality in close relationships? The word objective implies an absence of false or inexact information, an absence of emotionally distorted facts. For him, objectivity makes no sense in a relationship between two people unless it is accompanied by a simultaneous mutual awareness by each individual of his or her own needs and the needs of the other, both striving at the same time to make one another the object of their needs and wishes. This is a very complicated relational process. Boszormenyi-Nagy's thought is complex, but can be clarified by reference to J.L. Moreno and Carl Rogers: "seeing with the eyes of the other."

"Yet," Boszormeny-Nagy says, "we have to keep in mind that the individual's needs contain the *condensations of the unsettled relational accounts* of his family of origin, in addition to re-enactment of his own early psychic processes."[3] This is where we see to what extent family problems keep someone from living, as the French psychoanalyst Alain de Mijolla demonstrated in examining the life of the French poet Arthur Rimbaud: Rimbaud could not resolve his problems, so he ran away. One of his problems was his military father's departure when he was six years old. But, if we look back over the generations, we see the same phenomenon over and over again: one hundred years before, his great-grandfather had abandoned his six-year-old son, and the fathers of this lineage continued to abandon their sons at this same age by leaving or dying: these were the "unsettled accounts of the family of origin." It is this reaction at the same age that the psychologist and doctor Josephine Hilgard called the "anniversary syndrome" or the "double anniversary" (if the phenomenon is reproduced with each of the children) – a concept I discovered in my practice and developed during the 1980s in my work on health and the body.

In order to really understand a person or an individual, we must define him or her by the full scope of his or her needs, obligations, commitments and responsible attitudes in the family relational field

over several generations. Transgenerational therapy and the genosociogram (Boszormenyi-Nagy did not use genograms) provide the tools
that enable an individual to have "the courage to face the obligations and
the guilt before unpaid emotional debts." According to Boszormenyi-
Nagy, there is no family unit without an underlying solidarity and
original intrinsic loyalty prior to the birth of a child or children.

When people incessantly repeat the same attitudes and do not
change, being stuck in their roles, it means that "the fixity of their
roles serves the requirements of the total family obligation network,"
Boszormenyi-Nagy affirms.

In a family system where the roles are set and interdependent,
settling accounts can become stuck and therefore repetitive, or
forever put off until later: which is how neurosis or other symptoms
endure. An individual cannot feel better or resolve problems as long
as he or she cannot count on a just order, on loyal interpersonal relations – or on a change of perspective concerning *complementary*
positions and roles. Take for example the roles of nursed and nurse,
the helped and the helper, some always ill and others never ill (the
Lacanian *soignant* as *soi niant, soi nié*). We find an example in the
family of Charles Darwin, who was always sickly and always very
loved. His granddaughter, Gwen Raverat-Darwin, wrote about her
Victorian childhood and the love and pleasure of always being
nursed by one or another family member: "The trouble was that in
my grand-parents' house it was a distinction and a mournful pleasure
to be ill...This was partly because he was always ill, and his adoring
children were inclined to imitate him...nursed by my grand-mother,
and because it was so delightful to be pitied and nursed."[4] Another
example of helped and helper can be found in the New Testament
story of Martha and Mary.

Resentment

I am now going to digress to mention what we have observed in
serious illnesses and particularly in cancer patients concerning the
role of resentment. Many people when they fall ill often think of the
wrongs done to them. They turn these "injustices" over and over in
their minds. They hold it against those who have "done them
wrong": something was missing, or some event, some injustice – a
promotion they did not get, a theft, a "lack of emotional attention,"
a lack of recognition – "stings" the person and "eats him up inside."

It seems to me that resentment is connected to a concept similar to
Boszormenyi-Nagy's concept of suffered injustice. As children say,

"it's not fair." Somewhere, justice was not rendered; there was injustice, be it on a family level, a conjugal level, a professional level, or sometimes a national level (wars, massacres, oppressions, diverse genocides). People hold on to a resentment[5] that works away at them and undermines their health, sometimes leading to cancer or to death.

An unfair lot

The feeling of injustice is often complex. Injustice – inequality – is also experienced with regards to an unfair lot, due to health, physical endurance, or circumstances surrounding life or death ("it's not fair" to be handicapped, often sick, never sick, to die young, to be an orphan, etc.), as much as it is to economic injustice.

This feeling of an unfair lot often accompanies the survivor's guilt felt by a comrade who returned from the concentration camps where all his friends died, a brother who survives a drowning, or a sister who survived the terrible "Spanish flu" that killed 20 million people between July 1918 and July 1920. The same feeling can also accompany the guilt of the well-off.

Transgenerational terror, or trauma of the "wind of the cannonball"

During the retreat from Russia in 1812, leaving only 20,000 survivors of the original 500,000 sent on the Russian campaign, Napoleon's surgeons observed the traumatic shock experienced by soldiers who came within a hair's breadth of death and felt the "wind of the cannonball" which killed or massacred their buddy or brother in arms. Some, like Colonel Chabert in Balzac's novel of that name, lost all memory of the experience. Others were frozen to their souls with terror. It seems as if the shock wave that hit them was transmitted to certain descendants who are sometimes frozen to the bones (Raynaud's disease) or feel sick, experiencing anxiety, throat constriction or nightmares during certain anniversary periods, by a kind of telescoping of generations and time, a "time collapse." For some time now, particularly from 1992 to 1994, I have seen surge from the depths of memories the counter-effects of pathological or unfinished mourning in descendants of those dead without burial or missing and long awaited. These symptoms often appear in connection with the commemoration of important events that occurred during or at the end of the Second World War. Such vivid memories could be related to the "unfinished tasks" referred to by the social psychologists Kurt Lewin and Bluma Zeigarnick.

4 Psychosomatic/somatopsychic
The mind–body connection

The connections existing between the mind and the body have been known since ancient times, although they were later forgotten by scientific medicine. However, we are beginning – or rather beginning again – to pinpoint these links and explore them in more depth.

Influenced by psychoanalysis, the concept of the psychosomatic made its beginnings some forty years ago in reference to certain aspects of poor health or illness, although it was not until 1975–80 that real progress was made in this area. A new interdisciplinary science called "psychoneuroimmunology" developed around 1980, advancing the research done in the United States on what was called the mind–body connection.

The research inspired by psychoneuroimmunology stemmed from the discovery of more than 100 new neuroreceptors on white blood cells and in the immune system. The very way the immune system functions reveals that "states of mind" – happiness or sadness, guilt or resentment – may influence the number of T-cells and affect the immune system. The first research was published in a volume edited by Robert Ader in 1981[1] and I participated in the presentation of more recent research at the international psychoneurological colloquium held near Munich, Germany in June 1990. Norman Cousins provided the impetus for this colloquium, which was organized for thirty or so researchers by the German society for the study of cancer.

Transgenerational links and book-keeping of debts and merits

Felt injustice

From my practice of transgenerational therapy, I have concluded that the concepts introduced by Boszormenyi-Nagy – those of invisible loyalty, justice and book-keeping of debts and merits – shed new light on psychiatry, psychotherapy, psychoanalysis, holistic medicine and on the psychosomatic. If an individual truly becomes an adult, if a person manages to achieve a certain liberty, that person becomes equally free in his or her behavior, which implies a flexibility of roles and obligations in interpersonal relations. As a result, the family structures are no longer immutable: by settling old debts, one rediscovers the justice that should reign in that particular family, each member thus finding his or her place in a new balance of credit and debt.

All psychological relational events are motivated by the double structure upon which they are built: the "manifest behavioral structure" and the "hidden obligation structure." Consequently, we must understand relationships as being connected to two different accounting systems, one being the manifest motivations determined by questions of "power" and the other being the hierarchy of "obligations."

Take the case of a seventeen-year-old woman who loves the young man she is dating and wants to get married: should she – and has she the freedom to – marry him, have children and give these children what she received from her parents? Or for example, because she is the youngest and say her sister died leaving an infant, must she marry the widower and raise her sister's child because she and her sister were both orphans and she "owes it to her" – to her dead sister – and because "in our family, it's always been like that"?

So there are different kinds of accounting systems, different depending on each culture and each individual. But then, what makes one system prevail? What we often see happen is the creation of a "victim" or "scapegoat," or a sick person (the designated patient and/or one who chooses to be ill) who takes it upon himself to resolve the family problems in that way.

The therapeutic effort made with regard to a family, an individual or a group will aim at restoring justice and remedying the harm suffered by the scapegoat or the "victim." But this will not be enough, because the ex-scapegoat will find him or herself entangled in the systemic powers of the family system which perpetuates the scapegoating process. For Boszormenyi-Nagy, the therapeutic strategy should take into consideration the dimension of guilt connected to power; that is, it should work on the feeling of guilt experienced by those who benefit from the (unjust) situation.

Felt injustice in families often results from an apparently ordinary occurrence: for example, when one of the members receives the inheritance, or all the money, or "the big house," the factory, the jewels, the silver, the family portraits, the "beautiful carpet," "Aunt

Adele's buffet," or anything considered consequential and at the expense of others; and whether you are the beneficiary or the injured party, you remember it and remind your children of it, often over several generations.

Let us take a few larger-scale examples. Islam harks back almost a thousand years, even to the Crusades, to found certain claims; Armenia to 1915 when an estimated 1 million Christians were massacred by the Turkish government. After seventy years, the different people united under the Soviet regime separated into Russia, Estonia, Ukraine, etc., only to see struggles between ethnic groups, cultures and narrow-minded religious ideas arise. French political and historical writer Alain Minc describes the rise of these "tribal struggles" as a return to a kind of dark age where pockets of jungle-like violence and disorder – such as inner city violence – exist amidst civilization.*[2]

In families, a therapist cannot intervene without knowing that particular family's loyalty. According to Boszormenyi-Nagy, "The concept of a multipersonal loyalty fabric implies the existence of structured group expectations to which all members are committed.... Its frame of reference is trust, merit, commitment, and action, rather than the 'psychological' functions of 'feeling' and 'knowing.'"[3]

Family loyalty goes beyond the simple notions of a behavior that respects family laws, order and traditions. To use Moreno's vocabu-

---

* A recent example: Kosovo is important for understanding why the First World War started, as well as the recent troubles in ex-Yugoslavia, Bosnia and Albania – and for understanding the anniversary syndrome in politics (and genocides).

During the Middle Ages, Ottomans (Muslims, Turks) and Serbs (Christians, Orthodox) fought for leadership in the Balkans. The Battle of Kosovo Fields ("Kosovo Polje") ended with the defeat of the Serbs by the Ottomans on 28 June 1389 (cf. Volkan 1997). Serb leader Milos Kobolic assassinated the Sultan Murat; then, in turn, Milos's brother-in-law Prince Lazar (later canonized) – was decapitated by the Turks. With the fall of Constantinople (1453) to the Turks and the end of great Serbia (1459) the Kosovo Fields 28 June defeat became an historical trauma for the Serbs.

When, on the anniversary of the Kosovo defeat, 28 June 1914, Archduke Franz Ferdinand, heir to the Austro-Hungarian Empire, entered Sarajevo, he was assassinated by a Serb activist, Gavrilo Princip, for the humiliation of Serbia. This act sparked the First World War.

On 28 June 1989, Slobodan Milosevic, Serbian leader, made a speech at the newly erected monument to the recently returned remains of Saint (Prince) Lazar at Kosovo Fields (with its inscription "1389–1989"). He recalled Lazar's call to arms: "Never again will Islam subjugate the Serbs." 1998 is still marked by troubles in Kosovo and ex-Yugoslavia.

lary, there exists "role expectation." The individual is subjected to injunctions both of external expectations and internalized obligations, which could be the same or different. Remember that Boszormenyi-Nagy is a psychoanalyst and calls upon Freud's ideas and the function of the superego. Somewhere, obligations are the superego in us, or if we use Eric Berne's[4] terminology, they are the parent – mother or father – in us.

But not everybody has such a visible and clear sense of duty:

> The ethical obligation component in loyalty is first tied to the arousal in the loyalty-bound members of a sense of duty, fairness, and justice. Failure to comply with obligations leads to guilt feelings which then constitute secondary regulatory system forces. The homeostasis of the obligation or loyalty system depends thus on a regulatory input of guilt.[5]

We could relate this tug of rope and this double injunction to Leon Festinger's theory of cognitive dissonance:[6] when things are dissonant or discordant, we need to render them consonant for the sake of internal harmony. This need for consonance is individual. It is achieved by unconsciously shutting out information, perceptions and feelings concerning one of the elements in order to favor the other, to favor the decision made, meaning one no longer sees the "conflicting choice" and "reduces dissonance."

There are people who are more or less tolerant of dissonance. There are people who cheat and lie – or lie to themselves – more easily than others, and those who are not bothered when the left hand does not know what the right hand is doing. There are people who are sincere but not lucid about themselves and their feelings; there are those who cheat and lie without even knowing it, reducing dissonance by reducing their perception, and those who are so tolerant of dissonance that they are not even aware that things are dissonant, discordant or incompatible. Some psychotherapists even talk about a "false self," a non-awareness of one's self, one's deep, inner self. Different members of a family have variable guilt thresholds – and variable tolerance for dissonance.

The loyalty system is not solely regulated by guilt: according to Boszormenyi-Nagy, the structure of loyalty is determined by the group's history, by the internal justice of that particular family group, by the family myths, and each individual's range of obligation and position of merit in the system. We know that winners and losers

sometimes perceive merits and debts differently in relation to their
own system.

How can we determine "family loyalty" or "make it work"? The
members of a group can act under an external coercion, or by recog-
nizing the advantages of being a member of a family group, or by
feelings of obligation that are consciously acknowledged, just as they
can also act by an unconscious obligation stemming from belonging
to that particular family group. External coercion can be visible to an
observer, a sociologist or a psychotherapist, and the conscious advantages of the obligation can be recounted by the group members.
However, we can only infer the group's unconscious commitments
from complex, indirect indications, and then generally only after a
prolonged analysis of the family over a period of time.

Ultimately, loyalty in a family will depend upon each individual's
position within the justice of his world, which in turn constitutes a
part of the family accounting and also affects merits.

To understand how a group – a family or a professional group
– works, it is important to know who is bound by loyalty to whom
and in what manner, just as it is important to know the understanding each member has of this loyalty, which differs greatly from
individual to individual.

Everyone maintains subjective accounts of what he received or
gave in the past, what he receives or gives in the present and what he
will receive or give in the future:

> What has been "invested" into the system through availability
> and what has been withdrawn in the form of support received or
> one's exploitative use of others remains written into the invisible
> accounts of obligations.[7]

This means that it is sometimes very complex and difficult to make it
obvious and clear when we receive or give in a family between
parents and children, brothers and sisters, cousins, second cousins,
grandparents and others in an "extended family."

And some debts are too heavy to bear, such as vendettas, lost
honor, or memories of genocide and massacres. The case mentioned
by Claudine Vegh in *I Didn't Say Goodbye: Interviews with Children
of the Holocaust* (1985) of the young Robert, the son of a concentration camp prisoner who was saved by a priest on a farm in the south
of France during the Second World War – and whose daughter would
later bear the burden in Israel – is quite edifying in this respect.

"Gifts with teeth"

A large number of abusive mothers and fathers maintain a hold over their sons or daughters with such words as, "I sacrificed so much for you, it's the very least you owe me." In this way, a certain number of young people unfortunately enter a game and, as Murray Bowen would say, do not "differentiate" themselves and do not put a distance between themselves (their "me," their "self") and their family; they do not become adults because they feel bound by obligations which are, in fact, similar to what are known in Africa as "gifts with teeth."

These "gifts" can take the form of a ritualized exchange of presents, as in the potlatch.[8] There are people who give gifts to others, who offer feasts and banquets, all the while expecting reciprocity. In principle, you give a gift with "no strings attached," but the receiver is bound to return the courtesy. And what was intended as a heartfelt free act becomes an obligation.

Let us take a few examples. When someone invites you to dinner, generally speaking you return the invitation by inviting them for dinner. This is a tacit social obligation. If you do not want to invite them over, or cannot because you lack suitable lodgings, for instance, or find yourself in a less than well-off social situation, being say a student, an artist or uprooted, then you have several options: you can refuse the invitation, or you can accept it and offer your hosts either a gift whose value equals the meal, or a non-durable symbolic gift such as a bouquet of flowers or a box of chocolates. You thus discharge yourself of the social obligation. Yet, in a certain number of cultures, if someone frees him or herself of this obligation too quickly or too well, he or she would be considered "ungrateful." If you invite someone to dinner for pleasure or out of kindness towards them, and your guest arrives with a very expensive gift that you either do not want or do not need, you could feel embarrassed, because the nature or expense of the gift cancels out your gesture, or because your guest has spent beyond his means or gone beyond what could be considered the norm.

There are social and family systems which end up keeping the members in positions of servitude – for instance, by having "paid" for a gift such as an education – from which members can only be freed by an "eternal" gratitude for the services rendered, which must be expressed over a long period of time, or "forever."

Sometimes, this state of affairs gives rise to dramatic situations between parents and children. For example, a son of a poor widow "who bled herself dry to bring him up and pay for his studies" might feel obliged to keep his mother company continually and never dare marry or even go out with friends his own age as long as his mother remains alive. So, he either ruins or sacrifices his life, or makes a late life for himself after his mother dies.

Clearly, "family book-keeping" varies. Sometimes, families exploit gifts. Occasionally we see examples of this exploitation in the parents of young – even very young – and talented athletes or virtuosos, "wonderkids," or beauty prize winners.

Let us take a look at the observations made by the Palo Alto group during their twenty years of research on schizophrenia. "Mothers of schizophrenics" and "abusive mothers" often raise their children with great hardship to themselves. Nobody asked them to "sacrifice" themselves the way they have and, in fact, repaying them for all they have given would amount to an act of mandatory "parentification," becoming the parent of one's own parents, when in fact one should both provide the parents with affection and become a parent oneself in turn, "perpetuating the link," so that the child "pays his debts" and "returns" what had been given to him to his own children rather than directly to his mother – or father.

On this subject, Françoise Dolto writes:

> Every child is obliged to put up with not only the climate in which he is raised, but also with the scars left by the pathogenic effects of his mother or father's pathological past.
>
> He carries this debt contracted during his prenatal fusional period, and then carries the post-natal dependencies [debts] which structured him.[9]

Analytical therapy of psychotic patients pinpoints that these patients unconsciously express what happened in their mother's life before expressing what has happened in their own life:

> Analytical work must occur at an early age in order for the debt the parents have managed to endorse, but which has remained confined within them, not to become the burden another child has to express....And if it is not the parent, it will be the child, or it will be the great grandchild, but it has to be expressed in this lineage, because it is a symbolic test.[10]

The notion of "loyalty debt" is closely linked to the concept of "delegation" elaborated by the American therapist H. Strierlin.

Family book-keeping is a complex matter. It is not a direct "give and give" process. Similarly, in social and professional relations, one often feels bitterness, a feeling of having been exploited when there has not been reciprocity.

It is not my intention here to examine the problem of incest[11] in depth, despite the fact that we frequently encounter it between father and daughter, grandfather and granddaughter, uncle and niece, and sometimes between brother and sister, or more rarely between mother and son. (It is in psychiatric hospitals that we encounter the latter, the most serious in terms of personality destruction.) It is, for that matter, very often repetitive in families.

Some gifts are to such an extent implicating, and disagreeable at times, that Jacques Lacan ended up speaking about "the sacred duty of ingratitude."

What prevails is the idea of having to give something. Ancient Aztec culture functioned with this idea of always having to give something in return. One story recounts that some of the poorest mountain inhabitants had nothing to give in return for gifts received, so they offered lice, and the lice were accepted, for it was a return gift.

You do not always "give back" gifts to the very people who gave you the initial gifts: at times you give back to others. Someone was kind to you, so you are kind to others, to those weaker or less fortunate than you; you "return" the kindness shown to you, but not necessarily to the actual giver.

It is difficult to shed light on this system of exchange, and it is often totally unconscious and unnoticed. Sometimes it is voluntary or manipulative, but that is another story

Saint Nicholas's big book

In the Netherlands, Saint Nicholas traditionally "arrives" three weeks prior to the celebration of Saint Nicholas's Day (6 December), accompanied by dark-skinned Moor servants called "Black Peters" who carry switches to punish naughty children. Saint Nicholas carries with him a big red book which contains behavior reports on all the children and which he verifies, checking to see if the children were good or bad, and then rewards or punishes them. For three weeks, the children place a clog in the fireplace, with straw, a carrot and sometimes sugar and water for Saint Nick's horse or donkey, and generally during the weekend and the morning of the actual feast day, they find small presents or gingerbread. The feast day celebration revolves around the idea of Saint Nicholas "hearing everything" from the rooftops and rendering justice, which is often a somewhat frightening experience for the children.

Not so long ago, in the east of France, in Alsace and Lorraine, children would kneel on the stairs and wait for the Bogeyman and Saint Nicholas to arrive and reward goodness or punish evil, sometimes not totally without harmful consequences. Recently (in 1991), I treated people from this region who had been traumatized by Saint Nicholas's Day, who became ill every 6 December since their childhood without knowing why.

The month of December is often "marked" or traumatizing. There are many holidays, including Christmas and New Year. It is a time of celebration and conviviality or solitude. The winter solstice occurs around the Christian Advent (with the calendar the children uncover day by day), the Jewish Hanukah, and the feast of Santa Lucia (13 December)[12] celebrated in Scandinavian countries, all evoking (and perpetuating) the pagan "feast of light."

We are all descendants of "mixed couples"

To get back to the "extended family balance sheet" brought to light by Ivan Boszormenyi-Nagy, all family members also owe loyalty to the family group's principles and symbolic definitions. This kind of loyalty sometimes leads to a "can of worms," to entanglements and totally inextricable problems or difficulties in marriages – particularly when between people of different origins.

When we are married, we have obligations (which differ from loyalties) towards our family of origin, as well as towards the spouse's family of origin.

When marriages are inter-racial (also called "domino marriages"), or inter-religious, or between immigrant and native – or any such attempt at integration – we enter a complex system in which often people of the second and particularly the third generation no longer know where their family loyalty lies, nor what to do, nor where they belong.

A good example can be seen in three generations of mainly Muslim North African descendants in France: the first generation was nostalgic and discreet, their children became as French as they could, and their children returned to their roots, demanding the right to be different. Similar configurations can be seen among second and third generation Chinese or Italian immigrants, to name just a few, in the United States.*

If you come from an inter-religious, inter-racial, inter-ethnic, or intercultural family, where do your loyalties lie? In the culture of origin? In the culture of the host country or region? In the language of origin? In the religion of old? Fundamentalist? Modernized? Westernized? Which food? Which clothes? Who to marry?

The problem is hardly less complicated between different groups with strong cultural identities within a same country or in cases of internal migration. Take for example the Basque in France; or Scots or Irish in England; not to mention Louisiana Cajuns who still speak French after three centuries; and similarly, although this is perhaps slightly easier, someone from the American mid-west moving, say, to New York City.

And what about social and economic differences, about social classes and their different habits? Vincent de Gaulejac even observed that any attempt at "crossing the tracks" or climbing the social ladder could lead to failure (*social class neurosis*), often characterized by school failure of intelligent and gifted youngsters. In any case, the problem always arises – or almost always.

We all have both a maternal and a paternal lineage; we are all descendants of "mixed couples," because it is rare that our parents were second cousins born of second cousins. Therefore, we all have, in both our paternal and maternal lineage, family histories, family obligations, different family myths, ways of life or ways of cooking. It becomes even more complex when there are differences of religion, nation, culture, ethnic group, race, color, politics, or even culinary practices. We drink tea or coffee, beer or wine "in our house"; we cook with butter or oil; we invite guests home, or the men go to the bar with friends.

The members of the family therefore owe loyalty to the principles and symbolic definitions of their group of origin.

The individual and the family

By integrating certain of Boszormenyi-Nagy's conceptual tools into my practice, I realized that the potential for change inherent to intra-familial relations is far more decisive than the potential for individual

---

* In the United States, the history of Native Americans and African Americans is so heavily loaded with injustice that we will leave it aside here.

recovery; it is even more decisive than anything that could happen in a dyadic relationship, in individual psychotherapy – a doctor–patient or psychiatrist–patient or psychoanalyst–client relation. To effect change in behavior or in a patient's state of health, it is necessary to determine his or her *beliefs* and aim at mobilizing the lever inherent to the entire family relational network (their beliefs) if one wants to set into motion a process of change in the family.

François Tosquelles,[13] a French psychiatrist of Spanish origin who once headed the St Alban Psychiatric Hospital in Lozère, and a children's psychiatric clinic, discovered that when he treated and cured a psychotic child and sent the child back to his family, the following year or six months later, the family would bring for treatment another child who had become ill.

If we cure an individual without touching the whole of the family, if we have not understood the transgenerational repetitions, we have not accomplished much in therapy. We often only produce a temporary improvement. This perspective brings under question all existing forms of psychotherapy, classical and new, including the most famous, the most serious, the most respected – including individual psychoanalysis.

We have observed that in order for people to effect true and lasting change, it requires that the family, social and professional systems allow them to change, that *beliefs* change.

The eye of the family and the society, as well as family balance, have an impact on a person's development, health, illness and relapse.

The synchronous map of family events

Seeing and understanding the larger picture requires drawing up a synchronous map of family events which allows you to see what is happening at the same time with the various members of the family, rather than just with the individual. It means seeing what is happening in the here and now – synchronously – and also before and elsewhere in history and the family: it means making a synchronous and diachronic observation covering several generations. The simplest method consists of making a family tree showing all the important events and significant links: a "genogram" or a "genosociogram."

For instance, children who were abandoned and given up for adoption could somewhere along the line seek amends for the harm done to them because of a lack of affection, an "abandonment" and a "felt rejection."

The problem of adoption and/or rejection is further complicated by the experience in the foster or adoptive family. Michel Soulé and Pierre Verdier, who worked at length with problems of abandoned and adopted children, provide this clarification:

> Pathogenic unspoken events are not so very harmful because they keep the child in ignorance of various facts, but because they manifest the unbearable anguish the parents experience with regards to what they are hiding.[14]

Let us take a typical example. A nineteen-year-old maladjusted delinquent commits minor offenses and psychiatric assessment has been requested. Investigating the boy's history, his therapist discovers that his mother abandoned him a few months after his birth. He passed through a number of orphanages. He became, or so it was thought, epileptic and was placed in institutions for epileptics. Now, he harbors a bitter resentment against his unknown parents, given the fact that, in addition, he was born out of wedlock and the father disappeared abroad after his birth.

By some stroke of luck, he manages to find his mother, and when he finds her, he experiences intense turmoil and confusion. He does not know how to react because he feels a need to express a demonstrative social aggressiveness, and each time he directs his aggression towards his mother, the police call him to order. The therapist asks him to make an effort to understand what had happened to his mother and to question her about it. So, as a gesture of friendship, or affection, or positive transference with regards to the psychiatrist, he goes to see his mother and finds out what happened and why she abandoned him.

He learns that his mother had been very young and single when she had a passing affair with his father, who then left her. She had to work and because her son was ill, she had been obliged – given that he suffered from epilepsy and a serious liver ailment – to hospitalize him. Since this occurred in the United States, where she could not afford to pay for the very expensive hospital care, she had to "abandon him to save his life," so that others could take charge of him and treat him. The social services had become involved because this young girl could not take care of this seriously ill child.

When he learns these facts, the young man is completely turned upside down. He returns to see the psychotherapist and says, "My mother abandoned me, but it was the only way for both of us to survive, and especially for me to survive. I don't hold it against her any more, now she can give me what she had been forced to refuse me before."

From that moment on, his behavior changes, his protests and aggressiveness come to an end. He understood that it had not been an abandonment against him, but *for* him. Understanding the context transformed the meaning and healed his wounds.

A contextual and integrative approach

In therapy, it is important to understand at what level it is possible to intervene, at what level the exchanges can occur. Ivan Boszormenyi-Nagy describes three: a purely intra-psychic level including the id, the ego and the superego; an interpersonal level, covering, for example conscious or unconscious loyalties towards a relative, father, mother or spouse; and an existential interpersonal level where lie questions of having or not having parents, having or not having children, etc. To really understand these links, you need the whole context or frame of reference.

It seems to me that every school of thought is important, useful and enlightening. Yet in order to accomplish a comprehensive result, covering both the breadth of the family in the widest sense, including uncles, aunts, cousins, etc. and going back several generations through the line or lineage, one needs to work from multiple references. The systemic approach is sometimes a little reductive and insufficient, just as the individual or psychoanalytical approach can sometimes prove insufficient. Therefore, it is worthwhile complementing them with a contextual approach (such as Boszormenyi-Nagy's or Goffman's) which encompasses the two preceding approaches and also takes "everybody" into consideration: all the present and absent members of the family – even pets or household helpers; this is the concept of the "multi-person system," including lateral and vertical relations existing at the same time.

This approach calls on Moreno's ideas about roles, complementary roles, role expectations, dormant and reactivated roles and the social atom. We incorporate an anthropological approach, insisting on the vital importance of family rules and deciphering these rules, which more often than not are tacit rather than explicit.

Let us digress a little. Margaret Mead[15] related that when she began her field work as an anthropologist on the Pacific islands, her problem consisted of quickly understanding the civilization in which she found herself and adopting this civilization, or else she would have died of hunger or cold, or she might have been eaten or maimed by wild animals, or by the people themselves. Not without difficulty, she had to learn the language and guess, decipher and understand the society's spoken and tacit rules, all different one from another. From one island to the next, rules varied and, in every case, were far removed from those of the United States. She had to perceive, guess, decipher and learn these rules of interaction in order to be accepted and to survive.

In this perspective, it is important to understand what the *tacit rules* of a particular family or circle are when we begin to work with a family, or with an individual taking into consideration the family, whether we are treating psychological, psychiatric, health or existential problems.

Family rules

Let us mention a few rules[16] we often encounter in families. There are families governed by complementary roles such as the nursed and the nurse. There are people who nurse and care for others and people who are always sick. As we saw in the family of Charles Darwin, everybody took pleasure in this familial and convivial nurse–nursed relationship.

There are families where the rule is to do everything possible in order for the son to receive an education, and often the "eldest" is not the eldest child, but the first son. This means that if the son is the second or third child in a poor family, or a family bereaved by the death of the father, the eldest daughter goes to work at an early age so that her salary can enable her brother to pursue his studies. We see families in which the eldest daughter is a secretary (not having completed secondary school), the second is a social worker (two years of undergraduate studies), and the third child, the son, is a doctor (seven years of university studies). It makes you wonder why and how the daughters and the mother worked to "bring up the son" – and how they experience it afterwards. This male-dominant pattern is deeply rooted in western European history.

On the other hand, there are families where equality among the children is the rule. And there are families where the married son lives with his parents and takes over the family farm, while the second will leave (traditionally to take up the sword, go to sea or take vows); and other families where the children, even when married, continue to live under the same roof and still others where leaving the nest occurs at majority.

There are families where several generations live together under the same roof, others where the eldest keeps the house, the mansion or the farm while the others leave. There are families which "manufacture an eldest" who will take over the family affairs (farm, estate, factory, vineyard, study, etc.). This "created eldest" is often the second or third sibling.

In therapy, I once had a client who had just had a serious car accident; he was a "manufactured eldest" who couldn't understand why he, instead of his eldest brother, inherited the traditional name of the first-born. In this family from French Brittany, the eldest had been named Yves-Marie for the past three hundred years. But in this case, the actual eldest was named, say, Jacques, and the second Yves-Marie. The whole family relied on this second son. He had a lot of difficulty fulfilling this role of the eldest; in particular, he could not manage to marry, although he had children. He did not really understand why, nor what to do in order to fulfill this role of the "manufactured eldest." It was one of those family rules.

Yves-Marie took advantage of his almost fatal car accident to (re)think the entire situation and finally discuss it with his family. He discovered secrets and unspoken truths and was finally able to start over again, to start a new life – his life, rather than the life of a role-carrying false-eldest.

When examining a genosociogram and considering family rules, it is important to look for what the rules are and who elaborates them. It could be a grandfather, a grandmother, or a grand-aunt who established or proclaimed the law and then transmits it. Sometimes, we see families where the people only manage to get married after the death of their mother or father.

When you begin to really perceive the rules of such a family, as a therapist you try to help the family achieve a lesser dysfunction in relationships and a better balance of debts and merits for each member. That is, we try to restore things so that nobody feels wronged in the distribution of tasks, the distribution of property, the distribution of memories (and mementos), the distribution of income, the education received or to be received, and thus the distribution of future possibilities.

Everything is not easy to understand when we decipher a family. To better understand what follows, I invite the reader to construct his or her own genosociogram, his or her family tree (made from memory), to which you add major life events. This will allow you a glimpse of how your family operates, and, implicitly, how you operate.

Being a loyal member of a group

By exploring your psychogenealogy, you will become aware of what it means for you to be a "loyal member of a given group," in particular of your family. Everyone is led to internalize the spirit, aspirations, demands and uncertainties of his group and to use a combination of specific attitudes in order to be able to conform to internal or internalized injunctions. If you do not fulfill this kind of obligation, you feel guilty. This guilt constitutes a secondary system of regulatory forces, a negative feedback to disloyal behavior.

Boszormenyi-Nagy states it very clearly, and I have verified it myself: the elaboration of loyalty is determined by family history, by the type of justice practiced by the family, and by the family myths. This loyalty finds a resonance in each of the family members and incumbent on each member are, on one hand, the obligations connected to their position and role and on the other hand, the obligations connected to their feelings with regard to debts and merits and their personal style and manner of conforming to them.

We should recall that every culture, nation, religious group, and professional group has – like families – its own myths, to which people are loyal or disloyal.

Not so long ago in France, for a period of about forty years, loyalty to the Communist Party and to the Soviet Union was the acceptable thing among a large number of left-wing intellectuals. For the French, this loyalty was often linked to the Second World War and to the bonds created clandestinely in the Resistance Movement (after 1942) and with the Russians who died in Leningrad and Stalingrad. However, after Soviet troops marched into Hungary in 1956, imposing martial law and making mass arrests, and later invaded Czechoslovakia in 1968, things began to change, and many intellectuals and activists found it difficult to clearly distinguish, accept and integrate the new information and to rid themselves of this attachment and loyalty. It was not that they were forced to do so. It was something internal, that touched upon a fundamental loyalty: respect for the dead, "gratitude for services rendered in stopping the enemy," an ideal and the difficulty of reducing "cognitive dissonance" in the face of contradictory information and behavior.

This fundamental loyalty consists of an internal commitment to safeguard the group itself, the family itself – blood family, adoptive family, chosen family, political family – or the history of the family.

I have already mentioned "parentification." I would now like to provide an example which illustrates a societal phenomenon: you are certainly all acquainted with some charming, single young woman who dedicated her life to her aging, sick mother and never made a nest of her own until the elderly mother died, until she was liberated by the mother's death and then encouraged by some outside intervention. The habit being so ingrained, women like this require a nearly miraculous encounter, such as the one in the delightful French children's book, *Ces dames aux chapeaux verts* by Germaine Acremant, in order to make a life of their own.

This is an example of what I consider severe psychopathological effects of family loyalty; we see them as I already explained in "parentification," when a child is forced to become "parent of his parent" at a very young age.

Context and social class neurosis; school failures

Our approach is at once contextual, psychoanalytical, transgenerational and ethological. Each one of these sciences is important and their contributions are complementary in three – body–space–time – dimensions. They provide a personal and familial perspective, with Lacan's "upholstery stud" connecting conscious, unconscious and co-conscious effects of some traumatic events, which we always frame in a personal, family and socio-economic context or frame of reference.

Intra-psychic relations (the id, ego and superego according to classical psychoanalytical theory) are fundamental, but in transgenerational work we should not omit the internal aspect of the interpersonal level (invisible loyalties towards a relative or a spouse). We must work on the anniversary syndrome as well as cultural and ethnic links. At the same time, we must not forget the consequences on real life, that is, the existential aspect of the interpersonal level.

And to all that, we have to add the social and economic aspect of these family loyalties (social class neurosis) which have been so brilliantly analyzed by the sociologist Vincent de Gaulejac.[17] He demonstrates to what extent it is difficult for a good son or a good daughter to surpass his or her parent's level of education. He or she will, for example, become sick or have an accident the day before an important examination, or will suffer a momentary "blackout," or will turn in a blank paper even, and especially, if he or she is brilliant and at "the head of the class." This occurs because in effect, and unconsciously, social and intellectual promotion runs the risk of creating a distance or a division between the son or daughter and the family: they would no longer have the same habits, the same tastes, the same table manners, the same type of furnishings, nor the same

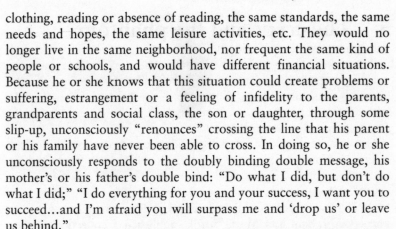

clothing, reading or absence of reading, the same standards, the same needs and hopes, the same leisure activities, etc. They would no longer live in the same neighborhood, nor frequent the same kind of people or schools, and would have different financial situations. Because he or she knows that this situation could create problems or suffering, estrangement or a feeling of infidelity to the parents, grandparents and social class, the son or daughter, through some slip-up, unconsciously "renounces" crossing the line that his parent or his family have never been able to cross. In doing so, he or she unconsciously responds to the doubly binding double message, his mother's or his father's double bind: "Do what I did, but don't do what I did;" "I do everything for you and your success, I want you to succeed...and I'm afraid you will surpass me and 'drop us' or leave us behind."

The son or the daughter will forget to set the alarm the night before the examination, or will forget to bring identification papers, will arrive late, will have an accident on the way, will fall ill or need an operation...just like a father could take his son out of school the day before the final examination and put him to work – just that day, not the following day.

We often encounter this kind of slip-up at decisive stages of studies (secondary education examination, university entrance exam, under-graduate finals, Master's degree, postgraduate degree), or at entry into an active professional life – the day before or the morning of an important job interview, for example.

To bring this chapter to a close, I would like to recall that fidelity to ancestors, which has become unconscious and invisible (invisible loyalty), governs us. It is important to make it visible, to become aware of it, to understand what impels us and possibly see if we may not have to reframe this loyalty in order to become free again to live our own lives.

"The parents ate unripe grapes and the children's teeth are set on edge," says the Bible (Jer. 31:29).

5   The crypt and the phantom

In 1978, two Hungarian-French classical Freudian psychoanalysts, Nicolas Abraham and Maria Torok, published a collection of their articles in a book called *L'Ecorce et le noyau*, partially translated into English under the title *The Shell and the Kernel*.[1] This book introduces the concepts of the "crypt" and the "phantom," drawn from their clinical research. They worked with patients who said they had done this or that without understanding why. The patients' families explained that they really "acted as if they were somebody else." Abraham and Torok postulate that these experiences occur as if there were an "acting ghost" which speaks like a ventriloquist and even acts in the person's place.

This ghost would be like someone who returned from the poorly shut tomb of an ancestor, after a death that was difficult to accept, or an event "which shamed us," or a "difficult situation" for the family, something looked down upon, something "ugly," shady, or "bad" in view of the mentality of that period in history. It could be an assassination, a dubious death, tuberculosis, syphilis, psychiatric internment, imprisonment, bankruptcy, a "shameful" illness, adultery, incest. What happens is that the family does not speak about and then forgets something or someone who had been disgraced or had disgraced the family, something or someone shameful, something or someone "we don't talk about."

The ghost-like experiences occur as if a member of the family had become the sole guardian of this now-secret unspoken event, which that person keeps locked up in his heart, in his body, as if in a coffin or "crypt" inside. And from time to time, this ghost seems to leave the crypt and manifest itself after one or two generations. Of course, if after unfinished grieving the "ghost comes out of" a family member's crypt, it is because this son or granddaughter has not assimilated the unfinished mourning of someone or something: he neither assimilated it nor introjected it, and thus has created a sort of special link between the generations.

Abraham and Torok base their explanation on the idea of "incorporation," which is the process by which a subject, in a more or less fantasy-related mode, absorbs, incorporates and keeps an object inside. So, based on this idea, Abraham and Torok suppose that the prohibited object – the unspoken family secret – settles inside in compensation for a failed introjection, that is, a failed attempt, to identify with or embody an object and the object's inherent qualities. The end result is the creation of something similar to an "imaginal link," "imaginal" being a term coined by Henri Corbin referring to something that is neither imaginary, nor real, but imaginal, of the *mundus imaginalis*, a kind of intuition of the Other's world.[2]

But let us look more closely at Abraham and Torok's definitions:

The phantom is a formation of the unconscious that has never been conscious – for good reason. It passes – in a way yet to be determined – from the parent's unconscious to the child's.[3]

The phantom is what works in the unconscious from an unspeakably shameful secret belonging to another – incest, crime, illegitimacy, etc.[4]

What haunts are not the dead, but the gaps left within us by the secrets of others.[5]

Its manifestation, the haunting, is the phantom's return in the form of bizarre words and actions, in the symptoms...[6]

[the phantom] is manifest in symptoms and gives rise to 'gratuitous' or uncalled for acts and words, creating eerie effects: hallucinations and delirium, showing and hiding that which, in the depths of the unconscious, dwells as the living-dead knowledge of someone else's secret.[7]

The unspeakable shameful secret

It is a *secret* that cannot be told, often a parent's shameful secret, a loss, an injustice. By hiding this unspeakable grieving, it settles inside, in a "secret tomb," in a "crypt." It becomes a "ghost," concealing somebody else's secret, a secret too shameful to be mentioned, a secret that can be transmitted from a parent's unconscious to a child's unconscious, from one generation to another. It is as if some half-buried dead person has a hard time remaining in the tomb, removes the tombstone, roams about and returns to hide in this crypt carried inside some family member – in his or her heart or body – and from which the ghost emerges to be acknowledged, to not be forgotten.

Many traditions incorporate reminders of important past events in order that they not be forgotten. The Christian Church provides an example with the annual reminder of Christ's passion; Jews and Muslims recall important moments in their history, just as different countries celebrate national lay holidays in commemoration of heroes, those who died for the country and important events. The American celebration of Halloween consists of dressing up like ghosts and begging for candy, but in fact at its origin was an annual reminder of the dead.

So honoring and acknowledging the memory of the dead forms part of the background of our civilization, although it seems we play with this notion rather than taking it seriously, except in transgenerational therapy. There are no reminders of the "martyrs" of recent genocides, assassinations or unjust deaths in individual families.

The therapist working with a transgenerational approach will help the client identify the crypt, name the "ghost" and free its carrier, who can then "unidentify" and "differentiate" himself from the ancestor's "ghost"...and allow the phantom to leave in peace.

The life of French poet Arthur Rimbaud offers a striking example. In *Les Visiteurs du moi*, Alain de Mijolla considers that Arthur Rimbaud's "abnormal" behavior – when he stopped writing poetry, left for Africa, roaming "everywhere" and returning to France to die of knee cancer – was due to the fact that he was haunted by his father's ghost. You could say that Arthur Rimbaud mistook his own identity: he confused the city of his birth with the city in which his grandfather was born (Dole). He said he was fleeing the military police, considering himself to be a deserter of the forty-seventh infantry regiment; but he had never been in the military and it was his father who belonged to the forty-seventh regiment.

If we look at the history of Rimbaud's family, Arthur's father abandoned him at the age of six, and the grandfather – who was born in Dole, the city our poet considered his birthplace – had abandoned Rimbaud's father at the same age of six. We can thus speak of a family repetition of the father leaving the family with a son at the same age, and of a "double anniversary," a form of "anniversary syndrome," resulting from "unsettled accounts."

The "ghost" seems to carry out its work in silence and secretly. It manifests itself by eclipsed words, by something unsaid, by a silence, by gaps in reality, by blanks left inside by somebody else's secret.

Let us take a fictional example. Suppose that I am Joe Smith and I know that my mother was born out of wedlock. I know she was born out of wedlock and raised in a very small mountain town. If I do not want to mention it to my children, I will end up never talking about my mother, never talking about the small mountain town, never talking about the mountains. I will say that I hate mountain sports, and that I only like swimming and the seaside, and then drag everyone to the beach.

An unspoken secret, like an oil spot, contains dark zones, spreading ever larger.

Eclipsed words, according to Abraham and Torok, behave like invisible goblins, which, from the unconscious, work towards breaking down consistency in the psyche.

Repetitions occur without awareness or rationalization of what is happening. On the other hand, family secrets invest the libido and determine choice of professions, leisure activities or hobbies.

The butterfly chaser

Nicolas Abraham recounts the story of a man who knew nothing about his grandfather. This patient was a geology lover. Every Sunday he went out looking for stones, collecting them and breaking them. He also chased butterflies, caught them and stuffed them in a jar of cyanide before pinning them up. Nothing more normal than that! This man felt very uncomfortable and sought counseling. He tried several therapies, including a psychoanalysis, without much success. He did not feel good about his life. He went to see Abraham, who had the idea of exploring the man's family, researching information going back several generations. He learned that this man had a grandfather (father of the mother) who nobody mentions. It was a secret. Abraham recommended that his patient go and see this grandfather's family, where he discovered that his grandfather had done shameful things. He had been suspected of bank robbery and probably committed worse crimes. He had been sentenced to forced labor, to "break rocks" (*casser les cailloux* in French, which means to do forced labor) and then he had been executed in the gas chamber, none of which his grandson had known. "What does our man do on weekends? A lover of geology, he 'breaks rocks,' catches butterflies and proceeds to kill them in a can of cyanide."[8] A symbolic circle had been closed and the grandson expressed the secret (of "his mother's inner object"), a secret he had not known.

In a certain number of cases, pastimes, hobbies or leisure activities, which can derive from family secrets, are surprisingly full of meaning. Used as a single tool, individual psychoanalysis or psychotherapy, which only attaches importance to a symbolic past and its traumas in individual life, is not enough to unravel these secrets. Transgenerational work sends clients out hunting down their family secrets, their complete genealogy, their history in its true context. When we find secrets and providential revelations, a certain number of affects connected to a difficult experience, harmful repetitions and traumas disappear.

From a transgenerational perspective, a person who suffers from a ghost leaving the crypt suffers from a "family genealogical illness," from an unconscious loyalty, from the consequences of something unsaid that became secret. From a psychoanalytical perspective, Abraham and Torok perceive in this kind of manifestation "a formation of the dynamic unconscious that is found there not because of the subject's own repression but on account of a direct empathy with the unconscious or the rejected psychic matter of a parental object."[9]

It is evident that some of us carry "crypts" inside like tombs in which were tucked away the half-buried, the half-dead – those buried with secrets unmentionable by their ancestors, or the unjustly dead (premature deaths, assassination, genocide). Strange behavior, illness or delirium often embody this ghost, which acts out in verbal agitation or actions a secret buried alive in the parental or grandparental unconscious.

A question remains unanswered concerning the way in which family secrets are transcribed and transmitted in daily life when things are left unsaid. It is the question of *transgenerational transmission*. How is a secret passed on? Nothing we know about psychology, physiology or neurology allows us to understand how something can hound several generations of a same family.

Nicolas Abraham and Maria Torok postulate that a "phantom," as a witness of a dead person or event buried inside another, takes root in the dual mother–child unity which is transformed into "an internal dualist union between the conscious and the ego." The descendants of a crypt-carrier could be haunted by these "gaps left within us by the secrets of others," and according to Abraham and Torok, it is the unspoken, pinpointed by silence and denial, that is speaking and acting.

6 Origin and death

Hergé and Tintin

What hidden quests do your favorite comic strips recount? Comics fans have all heard of the marvelous and fascinating stories of Tintin, his dog Milou and Captain Haddock. Using these characters, the French psychoanalyst Serge Tisseron reconstructed the life of the French author, George Rémi (thus the initials in his pen name, RG) Hergé.[1]

The colorful character Captain Haddock always has a bottle in his hand. Searching for information on one of his ancestors, he finally finds out who he is by using hints discovered in a mysterious castle where equally mysterious papers had been burned. This ancestor, the knight Haddock, appears to have been a hidden illegitimate child of Louis XIV. A parrot keeps repeating things and pointing out what was hidden, revealing this secret. And when Captain Haddock reconstructs the story found in the castle, thanks to the parrot, and the hidden secrets reveal that Captain Haddock is descended from the Sun King, he finds himself cured of his drinking problem and becomes a normal, dynamic man.

Serge Tisseron reconstructed Hergé's biography from the Tintin series and guessed that Hergé himself had lineage problems and that probably his mother had been an illegitimate child of a nobleman. In Hergé's notebooks, published after his death, we discover that he wrote in a cryptic manner and that he felt tormented about being an illegitimate child, probably of a Belgian baron. In fact, in 1990, the story was verified one generation up: Hergé's father, a twin, was probably the illegitimate child of a nobleman – or perhaps even a king. (Read the *Tintin* stories on Dupont and Dupond, who "don't understand a thing.")

In certain novels and stories, you can, treading lightly, discover the shadows of the writer and also understand your own shadows.

Unconscious family repetitions on anniversary dates: the widow's accident

Let us examine the true story of a widow's accident. The husband of the secretary of an association for which I worked in Paris was a serious businessman who loved his family and very much loved his father. His father was a very active man of 89 who, for some unknown reason, fell on an escalator, injured his head, and since the accident had not been well at all, begging to be left to die. In a way, his active life had ended. An informed look into the history of this family uncovered some astonishing facts. The grandfather went out alone on 26 October, took the subway and went to a department store where he took the escalator and fell on his head, tumbling down a whole flight. When we looked for key moments in the family history and at what happened to this man's wife, we found she died on 26 October, ten years prior to the accident. So, the elderly grandfather fell on his head on the anniversary of his wife's death. Pure chance? Coincidence?

I have seen so many coincidences of this nature that I now consider them unconscious family repetitions and manifestations of the *anniversary syndrome*.

The illness of the adopted child

A young woman had cyanosis, or "blue disease" – a cardiac condition which could be genetically transmitted. She was operated on and recovered, just like her grandmother who had been operated on for the same ailment. The woman decided to get married, but not to have children, since she did not want to pass the illness on to her children. She and her husband decided to adopt a child.

They received a child born in India, about whom nothing was known except that he was an orphan. He was a very beautiful baby. After the child's arrival in France, they discovered he was ill: he had cyanosis, the same illness the young woman had, the same one she had not wanted to risk genetically passing on to her own children. The child was operated on, by pure chance by the same surgeon, in the same hospital, and on the same date that the woman had been operated on several years earlier. The hospital administration had proposed the date.

Coincidences, of course, but strange coincidences nevertheless, this "nearly family" repetition of an illness and a date of surgery, for an adopted child who was "loved like our own" and who "had always been part of the family."

A colleague, Dr Ghislaine Devroede, professor of surgery at Sherbrooke University Hospital in Quebec, now always asks for anniversary dates in order to avoid surgery on those dates in an attempt at improving the patient's recovery.

Secrets about parents' deaths and about origins: children of concentration camp prisoners

A very revealing field of research concerns children of concentration camp prisoners from whom people concealed the truth about the departure, the deportation, the camps and the deaths of their parents. Among those working in this field, Claudine Vegh[2] wrote her dissertation on descendants of people who had died in concentration camps during the Second World War, and whose children had not known at the time what had become of their parents, had not been able to say goodbye and, in addition, had been obliged as children to go into hiding during the war. The majority of these children were taken in by families and often carried false names. Other children were taken in by convents or communities.

These children had been told that their mother and father had left on a trip and they had been forbidden to talk about them. They did not know what happened. In fact, often the adults did not know what became of the people rounded up, nor where the trains on which they had been loaded went.

It is hard for children not to betray a secret and to be cut off from their loved ones and their habits, no matter how kind the host family. And this experience often makes for poignant memories accompanied by a heavy *debt*, sometimes too heavy a debt to bear, which may take the form of memories or even a thirst for vengeance: the vendetta.

In addition, often the sad truth was kept from the children "for their own good." A few years later, at the Liberation, these children waited in vain for their parents, only to learn that their parents had probably died in concentration camps.

Research has shown that somehow, over three generations, these children and their families carry with them nightmares and traumas they cannot overcome.

Robert – brutal separation and secrets

Let us take one of the examples provided by Claudine Vegh: Robert, a fourteen-year-old Jewish child, whose father was taken away (deported) and cried out to Robert as he left:

" 'Robert, don't forget you're Jewish and must remain Jewish!'...These were his last words, I can hear them as if it were yesterday. He didn't say, 'I love you, don't be afraid, take care of yourself,' but just that one sentence...after all, am I living?...I hold it against them, don't you understand? Yes, I hold it against the dead who paid for my life with their own! It's unbearable! They didn't do anything to survive....And they left me, alone, the only one of the family; and I had to survive at all costs.... I have gone back to Dordogne twice with my wife and daughters. You know, 'a criminal always goes back to the scene of the crime,' isn't that right? Yes, I did say criminal, it's strange...but after all, they died and I'm alive.... My eldest daughter, who is a student, is moving to live in Israel for good! She said she has to do what I haven't done....The circle is closed.... My father would have been proud of her."

Robert's debt to his father ("Don't ever forget you're Jewish!") is paid back by his daughter. But Robert knows he has not settled his debts and balanced his accounts, because "it's unbearable!"[3]

And this will haunt him and "ruin his life." It may be linked to "survivor's guilt."

For Claudine Vegh, the secret, the unspoken truth about death is such that it impedes normal mental functions: it is better to know a truth, even if it is difficult, shameful or tragic, rather to hide it, because what we hide, others pick up on or guess (because we are not all professional actors) and this secret, this unspoken truth, becomes a more serious trauma in the long run.

Secrets always create problems. Remember Greek mythology: King Midas hid his cumbersome ears and only his barber knew the secret. The barber was forbidden on pain of death to tell anyone about the king's ears. But the poor man, weighed down by the secret, could no longer contain himself; he dug a hole in the ground and confided to the earth that Midas had monstrous ears. The reeds which grew on that spot repeated the king's secret when the wind ruffled them: "King Midas has ass's ears!"

Freud already reminded us that "he who has eyes to see and ears to hear observes that mortals can keep no secrets." "He who silences his lips speaks with the tip of his fingers, he betrays himself with all his pores."

This leads us to understand and keep from underestimating the importance of non-verbal communication and the impact of expressing feelings through body language and revealing moments of silence.

Often writers – authentic writers – are the ones who decipher the black holes of our psyche better than anyone else. I am talking about writers for whom writing is like a catharsis, writers like Proust, decoder of memory; Musil on the state of twinhood; Virginia Woolf on the ups and downs of the conscience; or contemporary authors like Marguerite Duras and Patrick Modiano, just to name a few.

Childhood traumas have been recounted marvelously by Marie Cardinal in *The Words to Say It* and in the book *Enfances* by Françoise Dolto, who discovered, through her psychoanalysis when she was an adult, the traumatic suffering she had experienced at the brutal separation from a "nanny" – a separation from which she almost died at the age of six months.

Genocide and suffered injustice: slavery, deportation, exodus – the psychological engram of suffered harm

The problems raised by genocide – all genocide – are vast, and even long-past genocide continues to have major counter-effects and consequences, whether we consider the Holocaust suffered by the Jews, the Armenian genocide (two million people) or the Africans decimated by slavery and the slave trade. Residues of slavery and the resentment between blacks and whites in the United States are far from over, despite the official policy of equal rights. We have witnessed riots in the 1990s. The fact that slavery (of blacks by blacks) existed in Africa at the time of the slave trade changes nothing.

We are still seeing the counter-effects of the Crusades as experienced by the Arabs at that time – considered by modern Muslims to have been a massacre of innocent people and a genocide. With the awakening of Islam towards the end of the twentieth century, Amin Maalouf explains in *The Crusades through Arab Eyes*:

> It is tempting to confound past and present when we read of a struggle between Damascus and Jerusalem. In a Muslim world under constant attack, it is impossible to prevent the emergence of a sense of persecution, which among certain fanatics takes the form of a dangerous obsession. The Turk Ali Agca, who tried to shoot the Pope on 13 May 1981, had expressed himself in a letter in these terms: "I have decided to kill Jean-Paul II, supreme commander of the Crusades." Beyond this individual act, it seems clear that the Arab East still sees the West as a natural enemy. And there can be no doubt that the schism

between these two worlds dates from the Crusades, deeply felt by the Arabs, even today, as an act of rape. [4]

Memories endure

We have seen many upheavals in the last decade: the tumbling of the Berlin wall on 10 November 1989, glasnost, the fall of the Soviet communist regime on 8 December 1991, the subsequent rebirth of Russia, the Baltic countries, Ukraine, Georgia, Azerbaijan, Tadzhikistan, and the various other republics that had lived in relative peace under the Soviet regime, under a sort of *Pax Sovietica* perhaps corresponding to Augustus' *Pax Romana*. Along with these changes came a rise in nationalism, racial hatred and religious tensions. In post-communist ex-Yugoslavia warring Christians (Catholics and Orthodox) and Muslims sought "ethnic purification" by extermination and deportation: exactly what we thought we would never again see in Europe after the Inquisition and Nazi barbarism.

In 1992, as we commemorated Christopher Columbus's discovery of the New World, the King of Spain, Juan Carlos, requested pardon from the Jewish community for the forced deportation of Jews five hundred years earlier, a deportation requested by the Inquisition and ordered by the Catholic King Ferdinand and Queen Isabelle. According to Jacques Attali in his book *1492* (1992), everyone was left to themselves in an exodus/exile/emigration that often turned out for the worst, similar to the current plight of the "boat people." The choice was difficult: abandon everything or be forced to convert to Catholicism and remain in a climate of constant suspicion, watched over by the Inquisition. Flight by sea offered just as many dangers: pirates, slavery, murder, storms. Some Jews left with Christopher Columbus.

In 1992, the Mayor of Salem, Massachusetts organized an expiatory ceremony to "repair" the damages and condemn the Salem Witch Trials, whose judgments were revised in 1993 by the Supreme Court. In 1997, similar proposals of reparation for black Americans were under debate in the United States.

In 1992, the European Community was preparing for unification under the Treaty of Maastricht, while in ex-Yugoslavia Serbs and Croats were killing each other, and a powerless Europe watched the attempted genocide of Bosnian Muslims by Serbs and Catholic Croats by Orthodox Serbs: a reawakening of ancient antagonisms, dating back to the Kosovo defeat of 1389 and to 1896 and the boomerang return of exactions by pro-German partisans in 1941–1942 during the Second World War.

In 1992, following the acquittal of two white police officers accused of brutalizing a black man in California, racial riots broke out in Los Angeles, once more revealing the hatred and claims of black Americans following this judgment, which was considered to be "unjust" – a heritage of slavery, non-integration and non-reparation.

Can we forget without forgiving, without pardon being asked for and accepted? The assassinations of President Kennedy (22 November 1963) and of his brother Robert (6 June 1968), of the black American leader Malcolm X (21 February 1965), of Martin Luther King (4 April 1968), demonstrate how difficult it is to forgive and that we cannot limit the solution to economics or politics. If you allow me this extrapolation, perhaps we could envision a solution linked to invisible family and cultural loyalties and to the large family, racial and cultural "balance sheet," a solution starting with *being able to speak the unspeakable and unthinkable*, making oneself heard, *having the facts and the wrongs done acknowledged*, in an effort to "repair death," suffered injustice, eviction and rejection.

Civil wars, wars of internal fratricide, are also traumatic experiences. Families and countries experience difficulty repairing them. For example, those banished – "removed from their land" – during the Spanish war (1936–9) never returned. Nor did Russian emigrants – neither those who emigrated in 1906, nor those who emigrated in 1917 – return in 1992. Nor did the Protestants who fled after the revocation of the Edict of Nantes in 1685 return to France from Germany or Switzerland. And when the Algerian-born French returned to France, they did so because, after the Algerian War, they were only given one choice: returning "with their luggage or in a coffin."

Old secular hatred is often kept alive through the teaching of national history, through regional tales and stories, through the history of religion taught to children, through family stories and even through the holy books of old. And on the smallest pretext, they reawaken, be it between Christians, Jews, Muslims, or Hindus in India, Muslims in Pakistan. And each reawakening produces hundreds or thousands of deaths and innocent victims, perpetuating the memory of martyrs and feeding, with a certain idea of honor, a kind of vendetta marked by a desire for vengeance of a "blood debt" and a yearning for "repairs." The circle is vicious and reveals how powerless the United Nations remains in its efforts to seek resolution of these conflicts because politicians remain ignorant of the historical ins and outs of accumulated "debts." They combine utopian ideas with a lack of knowledge about the problems connected to belonging to a land, a religion, a culture, a tribe, which leads to other problems.

Right by birth, by blood, by victory, by seniority, by inheritance – so many "just claims" that bring more deaths. The legacy of the various versions of biblical history, of genocide, invasions, wars, exterminations, crusades, forced conversions, "ethnic purification" and similar injustices are heavy loads to bear.

The second half of the twentieth century has seen the return of mass deportations and "concentration camps," for the "reception" or "regrouping" of refugees who left their homes through fear or force, creating thousands, or millions, of displaced persons.

For black Africans, studies have evaluated at 38 million the Africans brought into slavery between 1490 and 1899: 11.7 million exported with a mortality of 13 million, but also as many as 13.8 million passing through the Sahara trade (from the eighteenth to the nineteenth century).

Families of those gassed during the First World War store memories of Ypres on 22 April 1915 – the first use of gas in the trenches by the Germans. And families of Armenians remember the week of 24 April 1915 for the genocide perpetrated by the Turks, and denied, although 2.5 million people were massacred in a matter of days. It took terrorist actions and other violent demands more than fifty years after the fact in order for this genocide to be mentioned, acknowledged and recognized throughout the world, or, at least, by the International Court of Justice at the Hague.

Armenians still have no country, nor do the Kurds. Neither African-Americans nor Native Americans are satisfied with the "little bit of space" they are accorded by whites. Africa has resolved none of its problems of minority, tribal and racial conflicts which could lead to its destruction. A split in Ireland is only now moving towards reconciliation; the problem of Tibet remains unsolved; Basques continue to claim their specific cultural identity, and I could go on and on.

We seemed to have been working towards a resolution of so-called "minority" problems, until this bloody and brutal reawakening at the end of the second millennium. Now, no solution appears on the horizon.

Perhaps ethnologists, psychosociologists, transgenerational therapists or genosociogram specialists could add their small contribution to an attempted solution. Because one must first of all remember – "Remember," said Charles I as he mounted the scaffold – and then, either forgive or "turn the page" before finally forgetting, in order to put an end to an otherwise endless vendetta of deaths and violence, in order to put an end to the suffering. And also, in order for descendants not to be burdened with the bothersome "ghosts" and/or mental troubles that mark these events left unspoken.

I have worked using the genosociogram with people from several countries and ethnic groups (Armenian, Kurdish, Jewish, Irish, Arab, etc.) who suffered health problems related to genocide, and we managed to sponge up the physical and psychological traces by "cleaning the family or the group genealogical tree." (See the clinical examples with Jacqueline's story of the Armenian Genocide on page 102, and the sections on the trauma of the "wind of the cannonball" and the comments on the terrible nightmares occurring in descendants of those killed or injured in wars, some 50, 100, 125 or 600 years later.) But, of course, these were all individual solutions, which in no way foretell other possible applications of these techniques which remain to be found.*

* The American-Turkish psychoanalyst Vamik Volkan is currently (1998) working to help some countries overcome their hatred, which he discusses in *Bloodlines: From Ethnic Pride to Ethnic Terrorism* (1997). The hatred is related to time collapse and transgenerational transmission of war traumas, as discussed at the 1998 conference of the International Association of Group Psychotherapy.

7 The genosociogram and the anniversary syndrome: my research

I became interested in transgenerational psychogenealogy twelve years ago when my daughter said to me, "Mum, do you realize that you're the eldest and only survivor of two siblings, that dad is the eldest and only survivor of two siblings, and I am the eldest and only survivor of two siblings....You know, even before my brother died, I kind of worried about him after Uncle John passed away."

I was dumbfounded. It was true, and all the more disturbing because each and every one of them died in accidents – car accidents.

I then set my memory to work recalling my family history and found deaths and repetitions of deaths. My goddaughter was one of a lineage of orphans: her mother was orphaned young, as was she and her own daughter. I also remembered my much-loved grandfather, orphaned young – and the eldest sibling.

I went on to research my husband's family. I searched the records in Alsace for information concerning my father-in-law's family, and in the south of France for my mother-in-law's family. She was also the eldest, and the second sibling had died at a young age. With the help of research their "cousin the priest" had carried out in Marseille for his dissertation, and then using the archives established by a real genealogist in Provence and in Paris, I was able to clarify the genealogy of her grandparents for the sake of my own grandchildren. Imagine my surprise when I found the family had roots in Normandy, right near the area where, "by chance," my son-in-law's parents just happened to buy a house. What is more, the two families' surnames were very similar: one hundred years ago, they went by the same name with only one letter variation in the spelling. A coincidence, of course.

Another incident encouraged me to pursue transgenerational work. One day, "by chance," I received a letter that had not been intended for me. My mother-in-law had written it to her best friend but "by mistake" – or Freudian slip – had slipped it into an envelope addressed to me. Since the letter began with "My dear," I read it before understanding that it was "not for me." My dear mother-in-law had written that her son's marriage to "an outsider" had surprised her and she felt like she was "face-to-face with someone straight out of Africa" because we come from such different upbringings and milieus. Her comment surprised me, coming from one Parisian talking about another Parisian, both from white, academic and medical families. It made me understand what it means to be "like a patch" on a traditional family, a family that can trace its history back to participation in the Crusades.

A daughter-in-law never belongs, she will always be an outsider. This understanding enabled me to perceive the existence of oral tradition and "unwritten rules" in families.

I nevertheless ended up becoming my father-in-law's "son." In his family, women did not work, while in my family they did: two of my grandfather's sisters had even received their doctorates from the Zurich Polytechnic in 1864 and 1868. I ended up following my father-in-law's path and inheriting his legacy by becoming a psychotherapist and loving his native Alsace. But from my Provençal mother-in-law, I only ever claimed her olive oil salad dressing, without ever really feeling accepted by her.

Subsequently, my daughter, although born in Paris, returned to her grandfather's ancestral land of Alsace to pursue her university studies, one hundred years after the German annexation of Alsace-Lorraine. Her great-great-grandfather had left Alsace for Paris just prior to the Franco-Prussian war and the Sedan defeat in 1870 which led to this annexation. Historical wounds remain open wounds, and for many years the words of a common French song were on everyone's lips: "We'll get Alsace-Lorraine back." It was not returned to France until the end of the First World War.

Discovery of the anniversary syndrome

There exists yet another reason behind this personal and family-oriented research on what I somewhat by chance called "psychogenealogy"[1] and which particularly influenced my research into the anniversary syndrome.[2] In 1975, I began working with terminal cancer patients using the "Simonton Method"* as I understood it at the time, prior to the publication of Simonton and Simonton's first book. I was surprised when I observed a newly-wed and happy bride without undue stress in her life who was diagnosed with a terminal cancer at the age of 35, the same age at which her mother had died of cancer.

From that point on, every time I worked with a new patient, I sought "repetitions," "invisible and unconscious family loyalties" and unconscious identifications with a key person in the family history, loved or unloved. And I found the links to key people: cancers occurring at the same age that a mother, grandfather, motherly aunt or godmother had died from a cancer or in an accident.

This intuition, which led to numerous clinical observations, was confirmed by Josephine Hilgard's statistical research on the anniversary syndrome (see Appendix 2). By studying admissions to a California hospital over several years (1954–7), Hilgard demonstrated that psychotic episodes in adults could be linked to the family repetition of a traumatic event experienced during childhood, such as loss of a mother or father to death, psychiatric confinement or an accident. In a statistically significant number of cases, when the context repeated itself, the incident repeated itself. So in the case of adult psychosis, there was a repetition of the same symptoms by the daughter when that daughter reached the age her mother had been when she "disappeared" (either through death or psychiatric internment), and when the daughter's own daughter reached the same age the daughter herself had been at the time of the tragic loss (a double anniversary).

As a result, I added the use of both family genealogy and sociometric links to the genosociogram. I vaguely remember an interview many years ago with Jacob L. Moreno in which he might have used the term "genosociogram," although his wife, Zerka Moreno, found no trace of this term in his writings. A medical student at the time did remember the use of this term and spoke of it to my friend and colleague, Professor Henri Collomb, and some of us at the University of Nice inherited this tool in 1980. I do not really know if Henri Collomb spoke about the "genogram" or "genosociogram," and therefore I do not know whether or not, in the long run, "genosociogram" is in fact my denomination and the mark of my school of thought and my students. The

---

*   Cancer specialist Carl Simonton and psychologist Stephanie Matthews-Simonton developed a form of complementary care for patients with terminal illnesses that approaches the illness by considering the patient's psychology and stress due to traumatic incidents in his or her life.

tool is also used by Nathan Ackerman – who formerly worked with Moreno – in his family therapy practice in the United States.

"Children and house dogs know everything..."

The fourth reason behind my interest in psychogenealogy dates from my first encounter with the French psychoanalyst Françoise Dolto, when in 1955, after my return from studying in the United States in 1952, I asked her to supervise my first psychodrama groups in Paris.

"And were your grandmother and great-grandmother happy and fulfilled women, or 'respectable and frigid'?" she asked.

When I protested, saying I did not know and had no way of knowing, she responded, "In a family, children and house dogs know everything, always, and particularly when it's left unsaid."

This comment was my first introduction to transgenerational work and to unconscious and involuntary family transmission.

"Children and house dogs know everything...".

Exchanges

I should also mention the many encounters and exchanges that have inspired my work. Before I went to teach at the University of Nice in 1967, every Thursday night at my home in Paris, a group of psycho-analysts and psychotherapists met to discuss their approaches, their questions, their research. François Tosquelles, Yves Racine, George Lapassade, Nicolas Abraham and others occasionally attended, and we discussed transmission and inheritance even before *L'Ecorce et le noyau* was first published in 1978.

Several fascinating discussions with Margaret Mead in 1956 and Gregory Bateson in 1972 opened my eyes to the anthropological approach and its observation of natural behavior, ideas further developed in France in formal and informal "human ethology" meetings with Hubert Montagner, Jacques Cosnier and particularly Boris Cyrulnik. During the several lunches Jurgen Ruesch and I shared in Europe and in San Francisco between 1957 and 1975, he introduced me to non-verbal communication, to body language, to interaction and the way very careful observation allows one to practically guess what people are thinking and feeling through the study of non-verbal expression, body movements (kinesics), the use of space (proxemics), the harmony and synchrony of movement, and through the imitation of gestures and facial expressions (mimetics or "pacing").

This study of non-verbal communication allowed me to deepen

the psychodrama work I had undertaken in 1950 with J. L. Moreno and particularly with Jim Enneis: observing and using body language through careful imitation of gestures and micro-movements, particularly in the "double of the protagonist" technique (alter ego). This technique was developed after ten years' work, research and the repeated observation of video recordings. It became the subject of the dissertation I wrote on non-verbal communication for my PhD at the Sorbonne.

My approach

For me, the genosociogram, or "contextual transgenerational psychogenealogy", consists of clinical observation and synthesis based on a joint effort made by a client and a therapist (psychotherapist, psychoanalyst, psychiatrist, etc.). The therapist should be a trained practicing clinician who respects his client's personal experience and has a very fine sense of "hearing and seeing." He or she must be able to remain centered on the client, on the client's experience, on what he or she *says* and on what he or she *expresses* in other ways, for example, through non-verbal communication. The therapist listens to what is said and observes the emotions and sentiments the client reveals indirectly. At the same time, the therapist must focus on his or her own associations and own train of thought, on the "helper," on the therapist and the therapist's counter-transference and own experience. He or she must be able to focus on the other, the client, and at the same time remain aware of his or her own "personal radar." In addition, the therapist must be able to think quickly to catch his or her own associations, his or her own psychological, sociological, economic, historical and artistic knowledge, in order to make suggestions and ask "open" and "meaningful" questions when necessary. The therapist does this in order to seize hold of and then pursue the leading strand, the structure, the configuration or pattern in the client's family and personal life while remaining in the context and using language that belongs and is specific to the client's family experience, to his or her family myths, in the broad sense of the word.

In order to do this, I use my own classical Freudian psychoanalytical, group analytical and psychodramatic clinical practice. I call on my experience as a clinical psychosociologist and field anthropologist who has worked on four continents. I make use of my experience listening and observing, my knowledge of verbal and non-verbal communication and indirect expression of emotion through body language. I observe posture, gestures, muscular microtension, use of space and territory, and breathing rhythm, retention and liberation. I notice choice of colors, clothing, jewelry, haircut, tailoring and ornaments. I scrutinize gesture synchrony, as well as how the client opens or closes up his or her body, for example by crossed arms, or where he or she places a briefcase.

This careful observation allows me to perceive the signals that, with reason or not, seem to me to be significant. From these significant signals, I try to get the working client to speak and to make associations.

During this first stage, I listen to the client talk about him or herself and their family while they draw their annotated family tree – their genosociogram – either on the blackboard when in groups or on a piece of paper in one-to-one situations.

I base my method on the family tree annotated with important life events, keeping in mind Holmes and Rahe's questionnaire of major life events such as marriage, widowhood, divorce, birth, departure of children, displacement, death, separation and uprooting through moving or loss of a loved person (parent through divorce, loss of grandparent, dismissal of a helper/nurse/nanny). I have been using this questionnaire for more than fifteen years now and have added to it, pinpointing "loss of loved objects" (a person, pet, house, job) and coincidences in dates and ages, either synchronically and diachronically (anniversary and double anniversary syndrome). For example, we may uncover the age of the mother coinciding with the daughter's age at a time of grieving or separation.

I bring to light the repetition of these configurations in successive generations, working back three to five generations looking for coincidences with an illness or accident. I pay particular attention to repetitions when the client faces a surgical intervention. I use this psychogenealogy – or genosociogram – method to help the patient prepare for surgery, or in order to help fight a serious illness, or avert or overcome undue failure in school or further studies.

I add to this listening process my own interest in history and historical fact. We pay attention to the artistic, social and economic environment, pinpointing political, cultural, military and even sporting events that are important to the working client, and which will color the context and often give it meaning.

I find it important to listen and see with what Freud called "free-floating attention" and what Carl Rogers referred to as "client-centered" attention in such a way as to enter the other's "personal world," to "see with his eyes" as Moreno said, and to listen with the "third ear."

In this way, the therapist can hear what the client really says and expresses, in the client's own context. We can then help him or her structure it. We can shed light on his or her goals, itinerary, difficulties, identity, or rather, his or her unconscious identifications and counter-identifications, choices and rejections, view of his or her world.

I like to work with groups of five to seven people. The client maps out his or her family and structures it on the blackboard, or on a piece of paper, and the group helps, sometimes by asking questions at the right moment, and/or by having him or her make free associations, or "follow the red thread of his associations," of his or her/our connections. This is one way of using the group co-conscious and co-unconscious, in a kind of Winnicott's "swingle."

A genosociogram is more complex than a genogram. It sheds light on sociometric relations, context, and important facts and events. In addition, it makes use of the experience and unconscious of both the therapist and the client (his or her dreams, slip-ups or errors, free associations).

My thought-process is integrative, and I use several conceptual models at once, which I will now list.

First, I use the psychoanalytical concept of "invisible family loyalty" elaborated by Ivan Boszormenyi-Nagy, especially in an effort to uncover this kind of loyalty to or unconscious identification with a member of the family who, in many cases, died tragically or disappeared. I also call on Boszormenyi-Nagy's work on "debts and merits," the "family ledger" and the concepts of justice and injustice.

As a result, unsettled grudges and resentment often come to the surface, connected to the feeling of having been robbed of something valuable by family members. Possible reparations or attempts at reparation also become clear, and particularly any attempts at recuperating a lost status – an aspect of "class neurosis" – by a parent or grandparent or great-grandparent concerning the right to education, a house, a farm, a lost factory. One even finds the unconscious return to certain regions, towns or villages. Reparation could be important years or even centuries later, as we can see in the case of the Armenian genocide, the apologies made for the Salem witchcraft trials, or the desire to recuperate the large Arab-Muslim territory: it is nearly eight centuries later, and we are still talking about it.

Second, I make use of the concepts developed by Nicolas Abraham and Maria Torok concerning "the crypt and the phantom" which can in a way "inhabit" a descendant following a traumatic experience. They are often connected to unjust events, such as the death of a parent at a young age during a war, or even a person having been buried in a communal grave or at sea, without an actual burial site. Crypts and phantoms are often linked to family secrets that are considered shameful, secrets such as murder, assassination, incest, imprisonment, psychiatric confinement, bankruptcy, illegitimate children, gambling losses, loss of family fortune, tuberculosis, cancer and now AIDS.

Third, I look for family alliances and the exclusion of certain family members (Murray Bowen's "triangulings") and pay attention to who lives in the same house with whom, and who raises the children.

Fourth, I work with the idea of "replacement children": children conceived to replace a dead person – generally a child who died young, but sometimes a close relative. I establish the links and draw the age and date connections on the genosociogram. I look for births connected to grieving – generally of the father or mother. Sometimes the grieving has not been accomplished (cf. the "dead mother" referred to by the French psychoanalyst André Green, as illustrated by a mother in depression or grieving at the time of a child's birth, and therefore not "living" or not receptive to the newborn child).

Replacement children resulting from unfinished grieving differ from *repairing children* who receive a warm welcome and hold a good position in the family.

Fifth, I work with school failure among intelligent children, which can be linked to social class neurosis, including fear of or ambivalence about doing better than the parents and/or subsequently cutting oneself off from them socially and professionally. These failures are often connected to the difficulty these children have in reaching a school, university or cultural level beyond the one reached by their parents, who, for example, did not finish secondary school. They are also often linked to the parents' unconscious ambivalence to social advancement, connected in some way to betrayal of class or milieu of origin.

Sixth, I pay particular attention to the *anniversary syndrome*. A birth, marriage, illness or death could come at a time – age or date – that marks the anniversary of an event that had an impact on the family or the person: loss by death, psychiatric confinement or distancing of a cherished person, parent, loved one or any other "loved object." The event could also occur on the anniversary of a happy occasion – a celebration, marriage, birth, awards ceremony, or received honor or decoration.

I intervene using a four-step process:

- I observe, watch and listen attentively while the client talks and constructs his or her family tree, and genosociogram, from memory.

- I perceive important clues, which are often subliminal and can be verbal or non-verbal, such as change of breathing rhythm.
- I attribute meaning to a clue which I consider significant based on several different criteria – the work calls on multiple references. I then ask a series of questions to guide the working client.
- I establish a dynamic link between the meaning and the signal, and use this link to get the subject to evolve towards his goals, hopes and world view. In order to do so, the therapist moves from *attentive listening* to *active dialogue* and needs to be able to set into motion what seems to be operative for the client and in his world. For this, I use several interpretive grids, including both an integrative psychotherapy and a transgenerational psycho-analysis approach.

Details concerning the construction of a genosociogram

It takes time to construct a genosociogram from the family tree with life events *drawn from memory*. We spend two or three hours per person to do the ground work, take stock of the situation, map it out graphically on the genosociogram, and find the vital lead, the leading strand to follow.

In one-to-one situations with individuals who have a problem to resolve or a serious illness, we see them for the first interview at the end of the morning or a day's work, in order to be able to go over time if necessary. The doctors we have worked with schedule an hour to an hour and a half for the first interview with, for example, a cancer patient – providing the possibility of working over into lunch hour.

The anniversary syndrome

It seems that the unconscious has a good memory, likes family bonds and marks important life events by repetition of date or age. This is the anniversary syndrome.

We have often observed that frequently a birth occurs as if to remind us of an important family event, be it happy or sad. Coincidence accompanies many births, as if to mark an anniversary of the birth or death of the mother of the mother,* as if to remind us of the link between the mother and her own mother (or father), in

---

* I purposefully write "mother of the mother" as opposed to grandmother, because it has a different meaning for the unconscious, which hears what is pronounced.

the bond itself of birth – as if there were some complicity between the mother's unconscious and the preconscious of the child to be born, so that these dates become significant. Coinciding dates can often uncover the meaning behind a premature or late birth, through a connection with an important family member, dead or alive.

Numerous "replacement children" are born on the very anniversary date of the birth, death or burial of a previous young child whose mother did not complete the mourning process. The psychoanalyst André Green discovered many cases of schizophrenia among replacement children, children born to a "dead mother," that is, a mother who was sad, depressed or grieving at the time of birth.[3] In many cases, people at the end of their lives "wait before letting go" for their birthday – say their sixtieth, eightieth or ninety-fifth – and the foreseen family celebration, or for the marriage of their granddaughter or for their son to return home from abroad.

After a critical, sad, difficult or dramatic event, such as the accidental death of young parents or psychiatric confinement, one often sees an accident occur a few years later, or the onset of a serious illness such as cancer, or a psychotic episode. A daughter or son falls ill, has an accident, is put into a psychiatric institution when he or she reaches the age at which the parent died. It can happen on an anniversary of age – at the same age – or ten or fifty years later. This is often the case of the "double anniversary": the child has become a parent, reached the age of his lost parent and at the same time has a child of the age he was at the time of the initial loss.

Josephine Hilgard used the term "anniversary syndrome or reaction" for specific cases of psychotic episodes marking the age of a lost parent, at both the same parent and child age.

I use the term "anniversary syndrome" in a broader sense, because I have seen numerous different cases with repetitions of accidents, marriages, miscarriages, deaths, illness, pregnancy, etc. at the same age, over two, three, five and even eight generations, going back through two hundred years of family history.

It is easy to trace back two centuries when a child knows one of his or her great-grandmothers who tells stories about her childhood and her own great-grandmother. The child can then hear actual living stories about, for example, Nelson at Trafalgar, Moscow on fire, the deadly cold during Napoleon's retreat from Russia, or Benjamin Franklin, either through stories, a portrait, a medallion, a painting, a piece of furniture, a Bible or a box of letters found in the attic. I have included several examples in the case studies found in the second part of the book.

American historians have noted that the second and third presidents of the United States, Thomas Jefferson (1743–1826) and John Adams (1735–1826) both died on the same day: 4 July 1826, the fiftieth anniversary of the signing of the Declaration of Independence (4 July 1776). It is as if they waited for this date to participate in the event, to take part in the celebration of the fiftieth anniversary before "going off" to die.

The actress Marlene Dietrich died on 6 May 1992, the day before the opening of the Cannes Film Festival that was dedicated to her, her image on all the posters. Of course this was pure chance, but one could say it was a coincidence. Her death made "the headlines" and although not previously scheduled, her films ran everywhere, including on all the television channels in France.

Participating in an event even with one's death can be played out unconsciously in many ways. Certain fathers and mothers wait for a son to return home or a daughter to get married before allowing themselves to "let go" and die.

Some of these historical or family coincidences could be better understood as reactions to anniversaries, which, like an anniversary syndrome, we could explain as an expression of the family and social transgenerational unconscious.

Certain people get anxious or depressed every year at the same period, without knowing why, nor do they remember that it is the period marking the anniversary of the death of somebody close – a parent, a relative or a friend – and they remain unable to establish a conscious link between these repetitive facts.

As if by chance, numerous people have surgery on the anniversary date of the death or accident of a father, brother or relative, a "coincidence" they discover only following post-operative complications, for example.

It seems important to present the concept of the anniversary syndrome to family doctors, surgeons, cancer specialists, psychotherapists, social workers and other health-care professionals in order to help them help their patients, because *physical and mental vulnerability is so frequent during anniversary periods* and the symptoms difficult to discern as long as this link to the anniversary is not brought to the foreground.

An American doctor, George Engel, studied the phenomena in his own life (1975). He describes that he had heart attacks on the anniversary dates of his brother's tragic death at the age of 49 by heart attack. The first of these attacks, on the first anniversary of this death, was very serious. Perhaps we could suggest that an unconscious identification with his brother was making him react in the same way to anniversary stress, to anxiety about death. Yes, in the same way, but to a lesser degree, since Dr Engel survived and spoke about it. He wrote an article on the subject, describing his anxiety at the age of 49. He suffered another bout of anxiety connected to the anniversary syndrome: his anxiety about dying at the age of 58, the age his father died. Unconsciously, he "decided to forget" this age in order to survive.

It is this difficult passage at the same age as the death of a father, brother, mother or other close relation that I call the period of vulnerability linked to anniversary stress. (See the example on page 110 of the two brothers, Bernard and Lucien, the survivor and the deceased.)

One often sees a tragic death signaled down through the generations of the family's history by a repeated accident that becomes less and less serious after one hundred to a hundred and fifty years. The story of the accident at the battle of Sebastopol in the nineteenth century (page 135) provides a good example, as does the story of the young Roger and the beginning of the school year (page 106). Or the tragic incident could be signaled by a birth on the same day of the year in the following generations. Another example consists of grandchildren of French soldiers wounded in the bloodshed at Verdun during the First World War (starting on 21 February 1916) who were born on 21 February or on 11 November, the date commemorating the signing of the armistice that ended the First World War in 1918.

8 How to build your genosociogram

As we have mentioned, the genosociogram is a kind of family tree drawn from memory, without researching information or documents, and annotated with important life events, including dates, links and emotional context or framework (sociometric links, marked with arrows or colored lines). The genosociogram is more than a simple family tree situating relationships. What is important is the way in which the author of that particular "phantasmal" tree perceives the different characters, their roles and the links connecting him or her to ascendants and collaterals. Often even the blanks, the family memory gaps, say much about what has been "erased from family memory," quite like the silences on a therapist's couch.

The most revealing, interesting and new aspect of this kind of work consists of establishing the probable links between events, dates, ages and situations. It is postulating the possible interaction between, for example, a death and a birth, suggesting links in the coincidences in dates or ages (synchronicity, anniversary syndrome), in the repetitions, in the reactivation of feelings and the *stress of anticipation*, or anniversary stress, at certain periods in a person's and a family's life.

Conventional symbols

The conventional symbols and graphic representation used are very simple: a circle for women, a triangle for men (most medical professionals use a square). One or the other indicate the children when linked by a line to a capital U connecting the parents, a dashed line being used to represent an abortion or a miscarriage.

A double line between two people signals marriage, a single line an unmarried couple, a dashed line an important intimate relationship. For marriages, a slash signals a separation and a double slash, divorce.

A husband is generally placed to the left of the wife; the siblings are numbered; the age is placed inside the circle or the triangle. We note the deaths with a cross † followed by the date and the cause of death (see abbreviations below: for example, † 1915 Verdun).

People living under the same roof are enclosed in a coloured circle. The person building his genosociogram (subject) places him or herself in the center of the blackboard using a circle or a triangle, framed by a square in order to be easily noticed. An arrow indicates positive bonds when pointing outward, negative when inward. The major graphic representations used are shown in Figure 8.1.

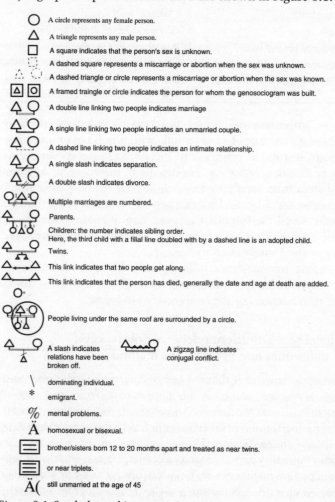

Figure 8.1 Symbols used in genosociograms

We also add abbreviations to allow for a simple notation of events and illnesses:

m = marriage	d = divorce
s = suicide	A = accident
W = war	C = cancer
HD = heart disease	AA = alcoholism
Ab = abortion	Dp = depression
ad = adoption	Tb = tuberculosis
Mc = miscarriage	Sb = stillborn
SD = sudden death	F = father
M = mother	MGM = maternal grandmother
MGF = maternal grandfather	PGF = paternal grandfather
MGGF = maternal great-grandfather	MGGM = maternal great-grandmother
PGGP = paternal great-grandfather	MGGGM= maternal great great-grandmother

Dates are important milestones and keys to unlocking memory, often along with the day of birth, a link with a holiday or an important religious, historic or other event. Precise dates sometimes unlock memories of illnesses, accidents, estrangement, marriages or anything that could stem from family myths. And if your memory fails you, it is important to ask why, and particularly to remember "the parrot" which could unveil the forgotten areas of family history, like the old spinster of a great aunt who acts as a kind of "family secretary," depository of the "family memory".

This graphic representation allows both therapist and client to grasp the repetitions, the wanderings of a ghost, synchronicity or significant coincidences, or the anniversary syndrome.

Biographical reconstitution: reference points, keys, memory milestones and limits of the method

It is important to remember that the genosociogram's family tree annotated with reference points is built primarily from memory. A genosociogram is *what the family remembers*: dates, important events, key moments, distribution of inheritance or links, true or false injustices, and emotionally charged events. The genosociogram built from memory also includes "memory gaps," forgotten events, blanks: what we do not know about certain members who have left, are far away or who we no longer see. Neither the genogram nor the genosociogram consist of objective genealogical research; it is more than a simple family tree.

On the genosociogram are found both objectively important "significant life events" such as level of studies, profession, dates of births, marriages, deaths; and subjectively important events such as reunions, promotions, failures, separations, moves, qualities; as well as the links. It includes given names, places where the family lived or went on holiday, houses – certain objects can serve as keys such as a ring, a piece of furniture, etc. – dates of wars, moves, retirement, family celebrations. In addition to the biographical reconstruction of the family, it is important to recall the historical, political, sociological and economic context, which will say a lot about the evolution of mentalities and (probable) family experience during that time period.

This reconstitution is not very difficult to accomplish. Count twenty-five to thirty years per generation. If your father married your mother in 1930, you can deduce that probably his father married around 1900. When your grandfather married your grandmother in 1898, he was probably 25–30 years old, so he was born around 1870. Then you try to see the context in which he was born and raised. If he was born, say, in Europe around 1870–2, the Franco-Prussian War was going on. If they lived in Paris, they would have lived through the siege and the famine that followed. You can therefore note events such as the Commune, the Sedan massacre which brought the end of Napoleon III. Use a good encyclopedia to complement your historical knowledge. Afterwards, you know there were a series of economic scandals such as Panama, and then the First World War from 1914 to 1918 and the Second World War from 1939 to 1945. You can develop a few sociological, historical and economic theories concerning your grandfather's childhood based on these historical events.

I often work with groups, because I find it is more interesting for everyone, both because often the same problem, drama or family configuration can be found in several participants, and also because the political, sociological, economic and historical memory of each participant adds to and awakens the memories of other participants.

You notice that often when the client remembers nothing, just when you start to suggest historical, economic or sociological possibilities, some door unlocks in his or her head, "Oh, that's right, I remember now, it wasn't during the Panama crisis that the family became really poor, but during Suez; they changed my grandmother's school, something had happened."

Suddenly, whole stretches of memory open up, simply because we unlocked the door – how can I say – to zones of memorization: free associations can begin and people can then remember very important events they knew without knowing they knew. Afterwards, they will remember that they know a grand-aunt, a neighbor of a godmother or grandmother, grandfather's buddy from the same regiment who the grand-aunt continues to see, and so forth. This means they will be able to ask questions and find more information.

When solicited in this manner, memories suddenly come back. And in this context, we should mention other people or places likely to provide information: friends or neighbors, distant family, local archives, church records, tombstones, works on regional history, the local press, diverse archives, etc.

Every country and culture has key dates in its history. For Protestants, it could be the revocation of the Edict of Nantes in 1685, which led thousands into exile; for Jews, the flight from Spain (1492), the Holocaust (1942) or the "Six Day War" (1967); for others, it could be the Armenian genocide (24 April 1915), the famines in Ireland (1846–8), migrations, the First or Second World War, the Crusades, the Algerian War, the Korean War, the Vietnam War, or, in the United States, the Declaration of Independence in 1776 or the conquest of the west.

Although this method can prove very enlightening, it does not provide a universal panacea and cannot, in a single session, replace psychotherapy, although it does complement therapy or could be used to begin one. Nor does it provide a real genealogical reconstitution which would require more comprehensive research and actual complementary genealogical work.

The foundations of identity: family name and given name

What is your name? Where are you from?

When you state your identity – your given name and your family name – you situate yourself socially, geographically and culturally, often adding an ethnic or religious designation. It places you as being "from here" or from elsewhere, as being part of some group or a "same world" ("one of us"), or as being a foreigner, or even a potential enemy or descendant of an enemy, thus provoking aversion, fear or even aggression.

The question "What is your name?" implies that soon we will know when you were born, where you were born and to whom you were born. Even the Bible recounts history in this fashion: Jacob, son of..., etc. In Jerusalem, a convent established a family tree for Jesus tracing through Joseph's line back to Adam and Eve, neglecting the fact that if he were the Son of God, he could not have been the son of Joseph, so important is the patrilineal line.[1]

A person's name places him or her in time, space and history. Where are you from? Who are your parents? Or the typical class question, what does your father do? What culture do you come from? What tradition? What rank? What sex? What race? What religion? What age group? One's identity, one's self, one's profound being, the self-for-self is connected at the same time to the self-for-others (the image that you give of yourself to others, the image others project on to you, perceived status, roles and role expectations), the self-in-self (the so-called "objective" self) and the feeling of self and of one's identity.

Identity comes through the body and through social labeling. According to a study carried out by the French scientist Aimée Pierson in 1980, children begin establishing their filial link at the age of four-and-a-half and by the age of seven-and-a-half are able to articulate the "parental atom," which means they are able to recognize the filial link to their parents. Only later on will the child become aware of the notion of generations and relations.

The filial relationship is at once a biological reality, a social reality and a psychological reality. But in the long run, the biological reality is actually fictive: the parents' marriage is what founds the filial relationship, even if a child is born from adultery, or voluntarily recognized, either truthfully or to create a social fiction.

The French psychiatrist and psychoanalyst Jean Guyotat divides the filial structure into two main lines: the "instituted filial relationship" and the "imaginary or narcissistic filial relationship". The instituted filial relationship consists of how a person identifies himself, being say the son of, daughter of, father, mother, or other position, and includes the group to which he or she belongs.

In Russian civilization, men always present themselves as being "son of...," so, for example, Nicholas Vassilievitch Gogol means Nicholas, son of Vassili. It is impossible to address someone without using his given name and his father's given name ("Attitchistovo"), even if you have to mumble it under your breath in case of hesitation. Similarly, in a large number of African tribes, people mention lineage in their names. The instituted filial relationship is therefore a meaningful link provided by the social group, using language, legal or customary structures, and stemming from rules of inheritance and belonging.

The imaginary or narcissistic filial relationship is a psychological reality written in a past or future history. This psychological filial connection can often be perceived through the importance given to physical resemblance between generations: "it is a link of resemblance through the body." This is where we might find the chains of repetitive events in a family: a dead child, a dead parent, a suicide, a hereditary illness, or an illness experienced as hereditary.

Guyotat notes that when difficulties occur on the level of instituted filial relationship – an illegitimate child, uncertainties about the father, problems of heritage or eviction, changes of family name – it weakens the instituted axis and tends to exalt the imaginary axis in a kind of dialectic relationship between the two.

We can recognize difficulties as being linked to the singularities of an instituted filial relationship: absence or premature death of the father, marriage beneath one's station as a breach of social convention, illegitimate children, children by adultery or abandoned children, some particularity in the attribution of a given name, name changes or placement outside the lineage through disinheritance or malediction. Many people keep their *nom de guerre* particularly when it is famous – like the well known French General Leclerc – or when a new identity and sense of belonging becomes interiorized. Some people keep their pen names or their stage names. This phenomenon can also be seen in cases of passing over the "racial or religious line," and sometimes in legal name changes authorized for names with negative connotations.

The consequences of situations related to a difficult instituted filial relationship can take the form of marginal behavior, for example. Guyotat, in *Psychanalyse à l'Université*,[2] proposes a grid for pinpointing the singularity of a filial relationship with a few examples of expressions through delirium, repetitive somatic attacks, etc.

The family name, the patronymic, marks the relationship to one's ancestors. It is a name that is transmitted, not a name that is given, which remains the exclusive privilege of given names. In our patriarchal civilizations, a man gives his surname to the woman he marries, and also to the children he recognizes as his own, by legitimate birth, recognition or adoption. In a radio interview, the French psychoanalyst Bernard This recalled that in the past, the land belonging to women was registered on documents, and that it was only after the French Revolution that passage through the husband's surname was established in France.

In many cultures, the importance of the surname is bound to the son. For example, in Upper Egypt, a man needed a son to ensure his funerary cult and to have "his name live on," just as many Asian cultures require sons to continue the cult of the ancestors. Although we no longer live in an era when a bishop, as at the Council of Macon in 538, supposedly said, "Evil to him who thinks that women have no souls, they have a kind of soul like those of animals and flowers," and our modern laws stipulate equality between men and women, the unconscious continues to wish for sons and the continuation of the family name.

Importance of a given name: Ariadne's clew

The given name forms one of the foundations of identity. Given names are often traditional and familial, grandparents' names that remind us of those passed away, names of godparents, biblical names, names connected to politics, sports, cinema, theater, or sometimes fashionable names or names of the saint celebrated on the day of birth. In certain regions, a name like Mary is common or even required, or the first son will always receive the same name. Many names come from the Bible, such as John, Peter, Luke, Anne or Mary.

A lot of first names come from a personal choice connected to some tender memory held by the couple say about their honeymoon, such as Florence or France. Sometimes it could hold a secret, like the given name of a former lover...or even the actual father. It could be a disguised name, slightly transformed. Sometimes a fashionable name is given, the name of a star.

Sometimes, people wonder where their given name comes from. For example, I once worked with a young woman who had a series of car accidents and who wondered why she was named Ariane, hardly a common first name. She wondered about her father's relationship to her, which she did not know about since he died at her birth. The only thing she knew about her father was that he chose her first name, and so this name Ariane held a link to him. She had learned Greek mythology in high school, and so she looked into Ariadne [Ariane in French – Trans.], Ariadne's clew, the labyrinth of Theseus, but this did not lead anywhere. She did not feel there was a possible relationship between her name, Ariadne's clew and the image her father could have had of a soon-to-be-born child, whether desired or not. So we began to work together on her father and the context of his life.

The importance of historical, cultural and economic context

I already mentioned the importance context can play in a person's life, be it political, historical, social or economic context, or even literary, musical and theatrical context. With Ariane, we thought about the years when her father had been young, and suddenly, I remembered that I had seen a film with Maurice Chevalier and Audrey Hepburn called *Love in the Afternoon* whose main character was named Ariane. It had been based on a novel by Claude Anet called *Ariane, Russian Maid*. It reminded me of another film based on the same novel which appeared in 1931 called *The Loves of Ariane*. I also think there was a play. I suggested to my client that she ask the people around her, her relatives, cousins and her father's friends if the name of this play or book meant anything to them. One of her aunts said, "Oh yes, of course, I remember now, your father acted in a play called *Ariane, Russian Maid*." From there, my client was able to really begin answering the question, "What was going on in my father's head about me?" It was obvious that if her father acted in a play called *Ariane, Russian Maid*, and he wanted his child to be named Ariane, then he had been attracted by the character of that name. In the book, Ariane was a modern woman with an education (prior to the war of 1914), who was independent, courageous, a little marginal, who chose her own destiny, lived alone and who, in addition, fell in love with an original and brilliant man who traveled a lot and who loved her. My young client was able to identify with the heroine of this novel. She took up traveling around the world. She had been able to pinpoint and resolve her identification and identity problems.

Searching for one's identity can often be very complicated. The context in which people are born is important and therefore so are the customs and habits of the time, the moral standards, the crises, the fashions, the period: these form the ethological niche, the ecosystem. Context also influences the choice of given names, which as we have seen can come from any number of influences: family, tradition, religion, fashion, politics, theater, movie stars, performing artists, athletes, etc.[3]

One needs to be careful when following the thread of a given name: a little girl, born say in Paris in 1897, could have been named Victoire because of her parents' desire for victory and revenge after the loss of the Franco-Prussian war in 1871, just as it could have been related to a social victory over the misery of the period, a political victory due to the father's stance, or given in homage to Queen Victoria for her jubilee, or in honor of a great-grandmother or a "close friend."

As a rule, it is important to only suggest hypotheses or "working theories" which may or may not unlock something in the client, just as they may or may not prove correct (which is important to verify).

Life context – studies, travel, living abroad and coded, disguised or encrypted given names

Although I normally work in France, I have worked and continue to work on four of the five inhabited continents, with many different cultures, and can say that I have a certain idea of the universal nature of transgenerational family problems.

Here is an example: an illegitimate child, whose only clue to her father lay in her given name. She was an American named Ellen. She wondered who in the world her father could have been and why she had been named Ellen. We reconstituted the context in which her mother lived when she had been young and pregnant with Ellen. Ellen remembered that at the time, her mother had been studying at a college far from her family.

I helped her look for the meaning of her first name. Ellen could also be LN, considering that some Americans like to use initials. I was thinking about a kind of secret evocation, a disguised name with a secret meaning that could be deciphered through initials. I therefore suggested that she look up the list of professors who could have taught at that college at that time. She looked for an LN and she found a Louis Nicholas. She then went to find this Louis Nicholas and asked him if, by chance, he had known her mother. This man was in fact her father, had never known that he "had got a girl pregnant," and he was very happy to find out he had a daughter and to meet her.

There are threads we can follow and weave together when we begin to reconstitute situations and events in their context. It is like a Sherlock Holmes story or a puzzle. And as with puzzles, the more you do, the quicker you are able to do them with habit, a little bit of experience, and even more so with a real experience of transgenerational therapy, with cases to call upon, to which you can add a few social and historical milestones. This work of reconstitution allows you to put forth hypotheses which often prove to be true and which all require being verified in fact.

Each and every one of us has a "family novel", and every family has stories to tell, which are told and retold; every family has a mythical history, a saga...and secrets. We all inherit this tradition, or part of this tradition, this history.

Are we all mixed-breeds? We all inherit two cultures

We are all of mixed blood. Each of us comes from a blend of two different families, our father's and our mother's. Even if these families live down the street from each other, or if our parents are distant cousins, or colleagues, or from the same race or religion, the same skin color, the same circle, the same social status, the same social class, the same nationality, the same culture, they do not necessarily have the same taste in food, in literature, in music, the same reactions to heat or cold, the same lifestyles.

In general, one of the two families ends up imposing itself, while the other becomes the "patch." Often we only inherit one culture, rather than two: there is a dominant culture and an excluded or rubbed out culture. It is not simple, nor is it foreseeable. And often the problems of culture shock in mixed marriages complicate matters.

Once again, think about the gathering of many cultures in the major countries during the nineteenth century; and compare the fratricidal struggles, religious and racial wars, and the awakening of regionalisms at the end of the twentieth century, with the rise of nationalism and "tribal wars." The after-effects of this clashing cross of cultures can be seen in therapy and transgenerational research.

Illegitimate children: examples of family social shame

Some problems people face stem from belonging to an excluded or ignored family – although they appear to be so-called normal families. There are many fine literary examples of things that happened to excluded descendants, often causing problems.

The famous play *The Lady of the Camellias*, by Alexandre Dumas Fils, plays out the drama of a young man from a well-to-do family who falls in love with a woman from another social circle, who is being "kept." Through her love for Armand Duval, Marguerite Gautier rediscovers a second virginity and the experience totally transforms her. But the family intervenes, he does not marry her and she dies of sorrow. One could ask why Alexandre Dumas fils wrote this story. He was a "fine" man, son of the famous author of *The Three Musketeers*, with a good position in Parisian society at the beginning of the century. If you look at photos of his father, you notice he had curly black hair, inherited from a black grandmother and a mother of mixed blood: he suffered at times from not being "like everyone else," even though he was a famous writer.

We could say that the play witnesses the pain Alexandre Dumas père experienced due to this completely hidden aspect of his ancestors which included an ancestor of color, despite the fact that this ancestor had been brought to Paris by a nobleman, his real father. And it was his son who wrote out this pain and its echo.

We have examined this same literary phenomenon in the comic strip *Tintin* written by Hergé. Through studying the character of Captain Haddock, Serge Tisseron demonstrated that the author's ambiguous genealogy caused him pain and that he could have healed his wounds through writing.

The goals of the genosociogram

Below is a list of goals for the use of the genosociogram:

- To "speak of one's life" and clearly show and understand the history of the nuclear family and the family of origin by clarifying the relationships between the different members.
- To discover that the world did not begin with our own parents, but that they too are the fruit of a world that began to exist long before them, which means to situate oneself in a transgenerational perspective and to start researching one's roots and identity.
- To bring out transgenerational transmission processes and phenomena of transgenerational repetition, for example, through "invisible family loyalties," family secrets, family myths, synchronicity, and anniversary syndromes.
- To understand the effects of unfinished grieving, the effects of the unspoken, to understand situations like "replacement children," to pinpoint a "dead mother," or the work of a ghost in the family unconscious.
- To bring to light the different family roles and the rules behind them, in order to understand the transactional modes at play in a family; to pinpoint the manner through which a life scenario could have been transmitted within a family, or who raises the children, or who takes over whose profession, whose flight or whose illness.

Applicable primarily in psychotherapy, the genosociogram can also be used in training health care professionals and other care-providers. Finally, the genosociogram can be used as an institutional tool, for example in industries or hospitals, or even in schools. From understanding the interactional modes used between a subject and his group of origin, we can gather much useful information about a subject's behavior in an institutional group: position and role in a group, demands, reactions to others' problems, interaction with a subgroup in a care-taking position, meaning of verbal and non-verbal behavior, etc. But to use this tool, it is important to have a good basic training in professionally listening to others and to have started work on oneself in this direction.

Above all, the genosociogram is a tool for knowing oneself, one's own family, one's invisible family repetitions. By constructing his or her own genosociogram, a therapist, trainer or any individual will better understand the history of his or her own family and better understand what could have been passed on from one generation to the next. Understanding these facts, individuals will be better able to understand their own way of functioning, and can therefore clarify certain aspects of their behavior. They will better understand from where they listen, and what is impossible to hear (for example, suicide, divorce, illegitimate children, death from a serious accident or illness, or to hear talk of Germans, Japanese, Arabs, "foreigners," etc.). They can beware of what is prone to projection, while continuing to listen to their associations. They can therefore listen better, hear better and be more receptive.

9 My transgenerational clinical practice

I rarely work with individuals, except in cases of serious illness, and then primarily with cancer and sometimes AIDS patients. I mostly work with very small groups.

Personally, I find that the energy circulating in a group and the group dynamics help people specify and get their problem out in the open and sometimes even enunciate it. I have noticed in working with small groups that one person's experience awakens another's memories. We support each other, warm up to each other and memories start coming back; one remembers, revisits, sees and speaks – finally. After two or three intensive sessions of two to five days each, the members of these genosociogram groups manage to better understand their family, family myths, family system and family history, as well as their own identity and what keeps them from being who they really are.

Robert Musil wrote about family in *The Man Without Qualities*: "Without a doubt, individuals have to be already an architecture in themselves if the whole they compose is not to be an absurd caricature." Such a remark makes one think.

The groups I lead often consist primarily of women, as if the members of this "oppressed majority" were more and more concerned about their identity. The group work lasts about twenty hours, over two and a half days in the "semi-marathon" formula, or over a week.

The people who participate come from different milieus, including people from the middle and upper classes, civil servants, business owners, social workers, lawyers, judges, doctors, nurses, psychologists, professors, sometimes priests or pastors, psychotherapists, "housewives," and also trainers and sometimes business executives. It is difficult to explain in a few words how people who come from such different circles with such different problems manage, in such a short time, to shed the ban against expressing their pain – a pain we could not have guessed at – and to speak about things they never mentioned to those close to them, not even in therapy or psychoanalysis.

The most striking aspect of my clinical experience is the discovery of a kind of link or similitude between the participants' different family histories, which sometimes even have just about the same theme or revolve around the similar problems or traumas. Another astonishing aspect is the group's capacity for listening, with conviviality and empathy coming very quickly.

The group's echoes allow the person constructing the genosociogram to continue to delve deeper and deeper into his or her discoveries, and at the same time, each member of the group finds himself or herself helped in the comprehension of his or her own genosociogram by the person who is retracing her family transgenerational history.

Similar stories often have occurred in several of the group members' families, even though prior to coming to the group, the participants do not know each other and "randomly" register for the groups, only to find themselves in a group of people reflecting their own family events. For example, in one group, there may be a number of war orphans; in another, many young women having been victims of incest and/or rape by the father, brother, grandfather, the father's friend, a day worker, a "big kid" in the same building; in one group, there were many sons or daughters of men who died at sea, which meant we were able to find the names of sunk ships, of naval battles and other historical events. In another group, there were many violent deaths: the sister of a participant had been murdered in a parking lot, the uncle of another had killed his wife out of jealousy, a secretary had been the victim of a terrorist bombing in Paris, the uncle of another participant had committed suicide, as had the husband of the godmother of yet another.

In another group, we had many "welfare children" who had had a difficult experience being children "without fathers," illegitimate or abandoned and "rejected by the mother," which is how they experienced their adoptions. Several other participants had been in boarding school, for whatever reason, or had been raised by a grandmother or an aunt, because their parents traveled a lot for their work or had been on assignment abroad. This was generally experienced as a rejection by the mother or the parents, and carried a certain shame – aggravated by a difficult separation when the parents took back their children from the grandmother, the aunt or the nanny. The worst case was when one single child of several siblings had been raised by someone other than his mother, something which is often repetitive in families.

In another group, there were migrants, emigrants, displaced people, exiled people, who, despite their different races, cultures or political opinions, recognized themselves as "brothers and sisters."

An example of a group

One day I led a group of seven people in a European capital. The group included a woman from a wealthy family who had serious problems with her children, and particularly with her son; a nurse having relapsed after breast cancer; a beautiful and dynamic divorced woman; a yoga teacher; a genealogist; a relaxation therapist and a psychotherapist.

It was not their family or social situation or their professions that mattered: all of them had problems they could not face, problems too heavy to bear. All of them seemed like peaceful, responsible, socially integrated women around the age of forty – an important age in the life cycle, a time of questioning, thresholds to cross and a time when children leave the house – and for each of them, we found "gaps" or "holes" in their genosociograms, traumas and occasionally "ghosts."

For one, we discovered that she was part of a lineage of three generations of brilliant ophthalmologists, and she had vision troubles, as did her daughter. On her husband's side, the sons had always worked for their fathers, a prospect her son, unconsciously probably, did not accept, which would explain the hard time he was having and the drugs and alcohol, etc. This is typical of families where personal identity, the feeling of "being," of having a separated self, grows from the moment father, mother or key person provides recognition, a role, an identity – a self. It is this recognition that allows an individual to exist. And all accept with a smile – their good education makes sure of that – the lead weight of this introjected obligation to submit to family rules. But sometimes they cannot submit and the body takes over, creating in this particular family strabismus and drug addiction.

Claude, the nurse who relapsed after breast cancer, carried the name of her grandmother, who had also been a nurse and who had died of a medicinal cirrhosis. Her grandmother had fallen into a coma when, in 1944, she learned that her father had died in a concentration camp. He had been a member of the underground during the Second World War, resisting German occupation of France. Many members of the underground were captured, tortured, deported and killed. They were considered to be heroes. Her father had no burial site. In a dream, she traveled to the concentration camp to find his tomb.

She was the daughter of a hero on her father's side, but one of her maternal uncles, whom "we never mention," collaborated with the German occupants during the war, after the armistice requested by Pétain and the Vichy government. When the war was over, many of these collaborators were sought out and tried. And of course, in October 1946, the Nuremberg trials judged leading Nazis and sentenced them for crimes against humanity. Fifty years later, in the 1990s, problems still arise and are brought before the courts. Some families cloaked certain acts of collaboration in secret, because socially these acts were considered a shameful "tare." In France, this divided families as much as the Dreyfus Affair between 1894 and 1906.

Claude felt that something had been left unsaid which caused her pain. When she was a child, she always felt like she was a child too many and thought she was adopted. She developed her first cancer not long after she learned that her daughter had become the girl-friend of her own boyfriend. Supported by all of us in the group, she had been able "to say it." Clearly relieved, she said, "When you see things, it hurts; when you can talk about it, the pain goes away and it feels better."

Marie had been a very loved and happy child. Then, at the age of seven, her maternal grandfather died. After watching her grandfa-ther's body being put in the casket, she began to have headaches generally on Thursdays (a day off in the French school system), Sundays and holidays. Her headaches never went away, even after seeing numerous doctors and specialists, and they ruined her life. At the age of twenty-two, she married an oil specialist and they moved at least ten times. Seven years prior to this group, she had witnessed her two brothers have a very serious car accident . From that day on, she continued to see her eldest brother's hand in the second's brain. All these experiences created problems and anxieties which she managed as best she could. Divorced at the age of thirty-three, she began to earn money easily, "I had my own money for the very first time."

Her two children lived with her ex-husband, with whom she remained on friendly terms, but her son was taking drugs. Fulfilled on the outside, she never talked about "living her own life," but rather about surviving. She always had this childlike vivid expression on her face, her social mask, even though the headaches, on their special days, set the rhythm of her life.

We worked with Marie on her family and her childhood traumas and we built her genosociogram. When she spoke about her grandfa-ther and his death, we played it out in a psychodrama, and she felt and expressed a surge of strong emotion, a catharsis in the true psychoanalytical or psychodramatic sense of the word: in a "surplus reality," she "spoke" with her "grandfather" (an alter ego) of the pain and fear she experienced at his burial – he explaining himself and what happened and she reiterating her feelings of affection, letting out a large sigh…of relief. Since then, her headaches have disappeared, and she lives, finally.

Margaret had a very "successful" career and had practiced yoga for several years, which she undertook for the love of her daughter who had spent a long time in India. Then she studied astrology,[1] perhaps to try to understand why in her family, for the past three generations, someone had always gone very far away: first it was her grandmother, nobody knows where she went; then her brother left France for the United States; and then finally, her daughter spent five years traveling here and there in Asia, to finally settle in New Zealand. As the memories came back, we discovered on her father's side of the family tree that a great-aunt had successively married three brothers, the first two having committed suicide one after the other. Another married great-aunt committed suicide by throwing herself into a well, and the husband of this well-suicide married someone whose father had committed suicide…by throwing himself into a well. One could wonder if these "well-suicides" who let themselves be pulled by the mirage of water were not, in this family, the pioneers of this line of distant travelers. Of course, this is nothing but a hypothesis.

Veronica was a teacher whose job provided living quarters. She was respected by all her colleagues. And yet, she felt an almost irrepressible desire to change everything: her job, her living quarters, her companion. She left her boyfriend because she wanted to live with someone she had not yet met. Her genosociogram illustrated what transgenerational therapists refer to as the "inconceivable," genealogically speaking.

Traditionally, we distinguish the conscious from the unconscious and the preconscious. Now, we are beginning to differentiate what is said and thought from what is thought and known, unsaid, kept quiet and transmitted in the form of a secret and is so difficult to express and to admit (the unspeakable, unmentionable), and further distinguish what is so terrible that you do not even dare to think about it (the unthinkable, the inconceivable). We speak of a secret or an unspoken event being transmitted and becoming a taboo, a foreclosure, an avoidance, or even something unmentionable or unthinkable. Normally, feelings and emotions have a representation, and therefore a mental elaboration. This is not always the case when

an event is considered to be serious and so traumatizing or so premature that no mental representation was possible: this is an
unthinkable, inconceivable event, and therefore not elaborated,
leaving only sensorial or motor traces that are corporeal or psychosomatic. For many modern therapists, this would correspond to a
trauma that occurred at such an early age that mental integration
was impossible. Remember, Françoise Dolto thought that babies,
little children and dogs perceived and integrated everything.

To simplify the process, we could say that when a traumatic experience occurs, the grandparents keep it quiet and transmit something
unsaid, their children then pick up the scent of this unsaid event and
transform it into a secret (unspeakable, unmentionable), and for their
children (the grandchildren of those who experienced the trauma) it
will be unthinkable, inconceivable.

Alberta "felt" a *family trap* being set up for her; she had the clear
impression that she had to "carry" the secrets for the others. Her
genosociogram was a novel with many ins and outs, with secrets
hidden in each branch.

For the past five generations on her mother's side, the women did
not raise their own children, or at least one of their children. This
pattern seemed to date back to a young woman at the beginning of the
nineteenth century. She had been adopted and raised by a chatelaine
who could have been the child's real mother. It was also said that
Alberta's own grandmother had had a hidden, illegitimate child.
Apparently, this grandmother and her husband were an "ideal
couple," although tensions would lead to dialogues like the following:
"I'll keep you from leaving." "Then you'll have to kill me." "I had to
stay, I didn't have a choice, otherwise he would have killed me."

On the father's side, three generations back, a man was said to
have died of yellow fever, although family rumor held that he died in
a psychiatric hospital. This is a good illustration of the kind of
shameful secret kept in a family that could be painful to descendants.
Just as the midwife had predicted, the great-grandfather's brother
was born with his fingers stuck together and died at the age of eighteen months. Alberta was raised along with one of her sisters by the
grandfather who taught them to read, write and count. So here
again, we see the family tradition of having some of the children
raised by someone else, and generally by the grandparents, a tradition going back to the adoption by the unknown chatelaine.

Alberta's sister had been three months pregnant when the grandfather who raised them died, so she gave birth while full of the sorrow
of mourning. This is an example of what André Green called the

"dead mother":[2] a living mother who is like a dead person, lost in sad thoughts. This sister's daughter was psychotic. Another sister, raised in a boarding school from the age of four on, had attacks of delirium: she claimed she was the daughter of a German soldier, conceived during the war.

Alberta felt all these "secrets," and she patiently uncovered them in order to finally speak the unspeakable and the unthinkable. She felt relieved, but she couldn't seem to get rid of the threads this "trap" set for her. She had more work to do on her story.

Obviously, bringing to light a past family trauma, secret or unjust death is not enough to effect a radical life or health change, but "getting the problem out in the open," speaking the unsaid, expressing it at last, can bring relief, which is a first step to change.

We could continue to dig and uncover secrets, unsaid or "difficult" events, and emotionally charged situations which to a greater or lesser degree influence the following generations and, in particular, certain descendants.

Many researchers and schools are working on the question of transmission: how are things passed on? To whom? Why?

I began by saying that everyone's life is a novel. When the "gaps" and "blanks" in the family tree are many, it hurts in one way or another: we no longer know "who we really are." Everyone feels a strong need to situate themself, like the characters in a Gauguin painting: "Where do we come from? Where are we? Where are we going?" Otherwise we cannot help but be that "absurd caricature" described by Musil.

Rediscovering one's identity: transmission

Clinical work and research on abandoned children taken in by orphanages, cared for by a succession of nurses or by the social services, reveals a tendency towards a series of psychological problems – sometimes psychotic problems – such as difficulties at school, or the impossibility of pursuing studies or professional integration. Martine Lani describes these phenomena, and much of the research done under my direction has revealed the same phenomena.

We also see these problems among "street children" and children of single mothers who had successive "fathers" or "uncles" in reconstituted extended families, in which they "could not find their place."

How to find out where you come from

The first step could consist of a transgenerational therapy in order to discover where you come from and who you are and what you inherited – your identity – with the support of a therapist and a group.

You can expose and express real or fantasized memories and then, at last free of them, in a second phase, you find your place in this lineage, and you can broaden your horizons, think of yourself in the future and formulate your own hopes, needs and life project. You rediscover your identity, your "I" and your "me." Stripped to the essentials, we always face the same problem from birth on, the problem of cutting the umbilical cord, differentiating one's Self from the Other – the mother or the family, as Murray Bowen demonstrated. We have to pursue this "unmerging," often with difficulty, in order to acquire our own identity among the long line transmitted to us. It is a question of maturity, of becoming adult following personal development work or psychotherapy. Since Carl Rogers, American therapists have referred to this process as "growth" – growing up, blossoming and becoming adult.

How does transmission work?

Transgenerational work is only beginning to be understood and studied. Statistical research is rare, almost non-existent, with the exception of Josephine Hilgard's studies done in 1953 for her dissertation in psychology.

As for questions of transmission, although here and there some light is shed on the subject, we are far from explaining this memory, these memory traces. How does it work? Is it a genetic memory?

Man is a being of language, probably the only one of its kind. Could the transmitter be the word, the said or the unsaid, language itself (meaningful, verbal or non-verbal body language)? Or is there another transmitter to be discovered?

In 1909, Freud described "family romances" as being an expression of a subject's fantasies concerning his links with his parents, imagining, for example, that he was a found child or the child of a prestigious father given to be raised in another family, or a child of a nobleman, or a child stolen by the gypsies (this is similar to Otto Rank's theory about the myth of the birth of a hero, 1909).

Currently, we sometimes use the term "family romances" to indicate a "family saga," that is, the story a family tells about its own history, a mixture of memories, omissions, additions, fantasies and reality, which has a mental reality for the children raised in that family.

Most people raise the question of their origins in relation to the primal fantasy, classically connected to the primal scene, concerning the conception of the individual and also the vision of sexual relations between the parents, often seen through the keyhole...fantasy or reality?

In his first writings, Freud already specified that in the unconscious and the memory, factual reality does not exist:

> There are no indications of reality in the unconscious, so that one cannot distinguish between truth and fiction that is cathected with affect.[3]

> They [phantasies] are made up from things that are *heard*, and made use of *subsequently*; thus they combine things that have been experienced and things that have been heard, past events (from the history of parents and ancestors) and things that have been seen oneself. They are related to things heard, as dreams are related to things seen.[4]

> Phantasies arise from an unconscious combination, in accordance with certain trends, of things experienced and heard.[5]

In the past few years, a certain number of psychoanalysts have been exploring the questions of origins and the primal fantasy in connection to the transmission of the something important from one generation to another. It seems to me, from re-reading Freud and his commentators (particularly Laplanche and Pontalis), and the papers from the November 1983 psychoanalysis colloquium held in Montpellier, that these questions are resurfacing. In re-reading the various drafts of Freud's work, particularly Draft L and M, and his references to family "revenants," it seems that in a way, Freud was interested in the possibility of mental transmission (mentalization) from one generation to another, although he did not explore this point further, nor discuss it in published works.

We could define the primal fantasy using André Green's words, as the "subject's relationship to his progenitors in the double difference of sex and generations, of which we know the fundamental effects it has on the structuring of the personality as a whole and its operational modes."[6]

Freud's intuitions are nothing but intuitions and clinical observations; in-depth research on transmission remains to be done, both for animals and for humans.[7]

Transgenerational and intergenerational memory revisited: living memory and ingrained memory gaps

We differentiate between two kinds of family transmission, conscious/unconscious, "assimilated" or not. "Intergenerational transmissions" are transmissions thought and spoken about between grandparents, parents and children. They include family habits, skills, ways of being: one is a doctor, a teacher, a farmer, a notary, a sailor, or an army officer from father to son; one "works for the government" or "has a green thumb," "a good ear," is a "good cook," or "eats a lot." Either we follow suit or decide to do the contrary.

"Transgenerational transmissions" are not spoken about; they are secrets, unspoken, kept quiet – hidden events which are sometimes banned even from thought, sometimes they are unthinkable – and they are passed down from generation to generation without being thought about or assimilated. And then we see traumas, illnesses, somatic manifestations, or psychosomatic manifestations which often disappear when you talk about them, cry, scream or work them out. We even see terrifying nightmares in the grandchildren of concentration camp prisoners, members of the French underground or the Nazis, those dead at sea or without a burial site, and even in descendants of survivors traumatized by a very difficult past experience, like the trauma of the "wind of the cannonball."

Part II

Case studies
with simplified
genosociograms

10 Anniversary syndrome and invisible family loyalty

The following case studies will demonstrate what I have discovered and verified in my practice. For nearly twenty years now, I have accompanied seriously ill patients through the terminal phases of cancer and helped them have a more positive experience of their illness, discover a better quality of life and often survive longer. I discovered, to my great surprise, family repetitions in the lineage of these people suffering from non-genetically hereditary terminal illnesses.[1]

It is as though something checks in and is transmitted from grandparent to grandchild. In any case, one could say it is as though something which cannot be forgotten is passed on down the generations, as if a life event could not be forgotten or mentioned, but is transmitted without being spoken about. The following case studies will explain these apparent contradictions.

Charles: anniversary syndrome and invisible family loyalty

I will begin with the case study of a patient I wrote about in my book about cancer patients, *Vouloir guérir*. Let me describe the case of this man whose name is, say, Charles, and who had cancer of the testicles. He was thirty-nine years old. He had a job. He was operated on and recovered. All was normal. Six months later, he relapsed, with metastases in the lungs. This happens. But Charles refused chemotherapy; he refused all treatment, his case worsened to the point where he could have died in a few months' time if the doctors did not intervene. They tried, but Charles continued to refuse treatment. We tried to review the situation with him: he was married, had a nine-year-old daughter, he loved his wife and his job, he came from a family with a long lineage settled in the French Alps; he was seriously ill. One might wonder why he accepted the operation, and why he then refused chemotherapy and all other treatment.

We talked with him and based on what he said, we transcribed in his presence his annotated family tree, his genosociogram. We began with himself, his wife and their daughter, and then we went back "up" his family tree: his father was seventy years old, his mother sixty-nine. His father was a butcher and in good health. Here, noting that his father was a butcher and considering that Charles accepted an operation, we could put forth the theory that because his father knows how to use a knife – and very well at that – then he believes in the use of a knife, it being a familiar instrument to him. He accepted being operated on, with a knife, a scalpel. But then why did he refuse further treatment? We still did not understand why he refused chemotherapy.

So we went back further on the family tree: his grandfather died at the age of thirty-nine – when a camel kicked him in the testicles! This is a true story. And camel kicks are not inherited. This is why I chose this case as an illustration.

So we can notice that he was preparing to die at the same age at which his grandfather died and that he was wounded in the same part of his body. We could say that "by chance" the cancer struck his testicles, the very same spot where his paternal grandfather had been mortally wounded. A coincidence? An invisible loyalty?

We continued the genealogy on his mother's side: his mother had also been orphaned at a young age. His mother's father – his maternal grandfather – died at the age of thirty-nine and a half, gassed during the First World War – that is, he was wounded in the lungs.

We can observe – and we can observe it at length in many other cases among the three to four hundred genosociograms I have in my files – that when people get married, it is not by chance: they often marry someone with the same family constellation as their own family of origin, or with the same illnesses, the same given names, or the same childhood traumas. The two families of the couple appear to mirror each other.

Let us look closer at the personal history of Charles's parents. His mother was orphaned at a young age. His father was orphaned at a young age – at the age of nine. The two grandfathers died at the age of thirty-nine. The maternal grandfather was gassed during the war. It no longer seems so astonishing that Charles, with his lungs struck by cancer, refused chemotherapy, which, as we know, was apparently derived from mustard gas that the Germans used during the First World War in the trenches at Ypres and Verdun in 1915 and 1916.

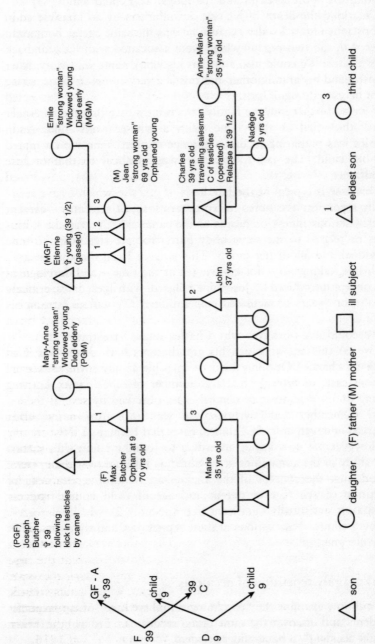

Figure 10.1 Charles's simplified genosociogram: double anniversary syndrome – repetition at father's same age (39) and child's same age (9)

Charles was afflicted in the same two parts of his body as his two grandfathers – the testicles and the lungs. You could almost say he was marking the death of his two grandfathers by an invisible and unconscious family loyalty because he was the same age as both and suffered in the two organs which were associated with his grandfathers' deaths. We could also add that his wife's name was Mary, like his sister and his grandmother, but this is a very common name, so it is not necessarily significant.

If we go further into the family structure, we see that the paternal grandfather died at thirty-nine, with a nine-year-old child. And Charles was preparing to die at the age of thirty-nine with a nine-year-old child. The family structure was identical to that of his grandfather.

This case is typical of the hundreds of cases in which I have seen family repetition over three to ten generations, of accidents – car or other – serious illness or deaths at the same age, or even the same dates or related to the same body parts that are significant to the individual and his or her family. This is what I call the anniversary syndrome, taking up – not knowing it at the time – and developing the concept introduced by Josephine Hilgard, with ages, dates, critical periods, or "years of increased vulnerability." We will go into more detail later.

We could ask ourselves why Charles refused treatment after his relapse, at this age at which his grandfathers both died? Was it a death by chance? Or some kind of invisible family loyalty? Is it a random case, or typical of a large number of other cases? Are we talking about a number of clinical cases observed by several therapists? Remember that psychoanalysis was born from a few well observed and well described clinical cases that became models.

However, we now know, according to Josephine Hilgard's statistical study of the admissions at a California hospital over a four-year period, that the concept of the anniversary syndrome, this double repetition of age (age of parent and age of child at the time of trauma), is statistically significant (see Appendix 2), which reinforces my own clinical observations of these repetitions, and those made by my colleagues.

Mark: family repetition of accidents

We will now examine the "psychological inheritance" of car or plane accidents and discover the same thing: repetitions. Let us begin with a flight accident – a hang-glider accident.

A charming young man arrived at one of my psychodrama groups with everything to please – he was dynamic, relaxed, open, smiling – and he was skillfully handling a wheelchair. Mark had come alone by car over 350 miles to attend the group. He returned to his car alone, bringing the wheelchair alongside the car where he opened the door, jumped into the front seat, folded up the wheelchair and threw it in the back: this was more than an athletic exploit, it was truly astonishing.

I "stupidly" made the following comment: "You seem really happy and full of life. You must be well, and I bet the wheelchair is only temporary."

He answered, "You're quite mistaken, the wheelchair is for life: I'm paraplegic. I had a hang-glider accident and can only move my head and my arms."

"How did it happen?" I asked

"It was so stupid! I love the sport. Normally, I always went out with a group of friends, but that one time, they couldn't come. I went to the take-off area anyway, and someone I didn't know said, 'If you want, I'll pull you.' And he pulled me. Every time, when my friends pulled me, they always asked if I was properly attached, and I verified and answered yes. This guy didn't ask me anything. I forgot to hook myself in, the hang-glider took off, I fell on my back. I hurt my back and now I'm paraplegic. I did a psychoanalysis, Gestalt, bioenergy. I still haven't understood why or how I did something so stupid!"

So I suggested we try the genosociogram.

I asked his age and he answered, "Thirty-two."

"Do you have children?"

"No!"

"Are you married?"

"No, but it's just like I was: I live with my girlfriend."

"Was anyone else in your family in a wheelchair?"

"I've looked, there's nobody!"

"That really surprises me," I responded, "Think hard, try to remember."

"Oh, yes, that's right, my father." (And he had forgotten!)

I asked, "Why was you father in a wheelchair?"

"My father was one of the people deported to work camps in Germany during the war. He worked in a foundry with a group of French. One day, the team he worked with couldn't come and he went to the factory alone. Someone else was working with him and that other person forgot to attach a vat of boiling iron which

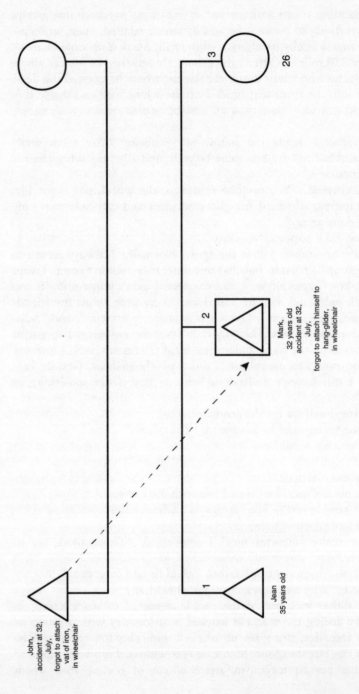

Figure 10.2 Mark's simplified genosociogram: a case of a repeated serious accident

John,
accident at 32,
July,
forgot to attach
a vat of iron,
in wheelchair

Mark,
32 years old
accident at 32,
July,
forgot to attach himself to
hang-glider,
in wheelchair

Jean
35 years old

1

2

3

26

overturned on to my father's feet. It was terrible...he couldn't walk anymore."

Together we compared dates: both he and his father were the same age – thirty-two – when the accidents occurred. And the accidents occurred the same month: July. He couldn't remember what day.

This kind of accident cannot be hereditary! But it is nevertheless part of the family history over two generations (we could not go back any further): someone in a risky situation, used to doing a dangerous activity, taking proper safety measures with "buddies." One day the friends are not there, the security measures are not taken, and a "stupid" accident occurs, injuring the legs. For both the father and the son, the accident occurred at the same age, during the same month and under the same psychological conditions.

A working prisoner in Germany during the war forgetting to attach a vat of iron is plausible: it can happen. But forgetting to attach oneself properly when hang-gliding is far more rare.

This is an example of a simple repetition, a simple unconscious invisible family loyalty, an anniversary syndrome (repetition at the same age).

I worked a lot with Mark. He was both very surprised by the coincidence and relieved to find a reason for what had happened, even if it was unreasonable and illogical. He worked, earned a living, was able to get around alone, he "lives with a girlfriend," still goes hang-gliding. He has an almost normal emotional, family and professional life. He even just had a child – two years after this group in which we worked on his family.

So we could suggest that there had been an invisible family loyalty: something serious had occurred, nobody talked about it, "it was not fair." It is as though one could not forget and was forbidden to remember.

Do not forget to forget – do remember to forget

When I asked Mark if someone in his family had been in a wheelchair, his first response was no. He had "forgotten" that the same thing, or almost the same thing, had happened to his father. Yet, at the same time, he had not forgotten, because he had not forgotten to forget to attach himself properly to the hang-glider at the age and anniversary month of his father being injured in the feet because of something someone forgot to attach, causing an accident which kept him from ever walking again.

Kant said: "Let us remember to forget." It is therefore important to not forget to forget, without forgetting, all the while being forbidden to mention it. It is almost a paradoxical injunction, a doubly binding double message, the "double bind" described by the Palo Alto group.

What happens and how it works is not at all clear. Why the repetition? And why did this accident happen to Mark and not to his brother? Why does it happen to one sibling and not another, or all of them?

We could say we see a family repetition. We can almost foresee that if "we do not heal the family tree," then a "bad event" could repeat itself, but we cannot predict which of the siblings or cousins will take on the invisible family loyalty. As things stand now, the repetition is observed after the fact.

Jacqueline: the Armenian genocide

A charming young woman attended a group I led in France. She agreed to have me use her case, so I can mention her name: Jacqueline. At the time, she wore a neck-brace. I asked her why and she said she had had a car accident. When? A little while after she buried her child. I asked her about the circumstances: she had been married (she later divorced), and she had a little girl who had died at the age of thirteen. Her little girl was born with the umbilical cord wrapped around her neck, stayed in a coma a long time in intensive care, became physically and mentally disabled, was placed in an institution for ten years, where she died in 1986.

I asked Jacqueline what she did for a living: she was a hairdresser. I asked her if she had other children and she responded, "No. When I saw my niece, I didn't want to have any more."

"Your niece?"

"My sister's daughter."

Her sister had a daughter who was born with a herniated cervical disk, or as she said, with "her brains dripping from her head." Each of the sisters had been present when the other gave birth. Both experienced difficult deliveries. Jacqueline did not want to try again.

I asked her for more details. They were the only two siblings and both had children with "serious head problems." When? At birth. And the marriages? Both sisters married on the same day. I started to construct the genosociogram. The father was a hairdresser. The mother was a hairdresser. We went back further: the grandmother was a hairdresser. So, this family has taken care of heads for three generations.

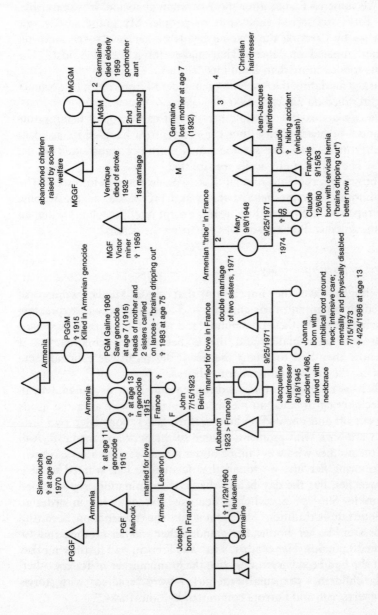

Figure 10.3 Jacqueline's simplified genosociogram: children of the Armenian genocide

I asked where they were born. They were born in France, in the mountains. And her father? Born in Beirut. And the grandparents? Her grandmother was born in Turkey.

"In Turkey?" I ask. "But why did you come to France?"

"We came to France after the Armenian genocide. It was terrible. The Turks massacred thousands of people. My grandmother saw them go by carrying the severed heads of her two sisters and her mother impaled on lances. That makes for a lot of heads!" The deaths totaled more than 2 million.

I asked the date of the Armenian genocide: 24 April 1915. Jacqueline's daughter died on 24 April 1986.

We can discuss the possible heredity of cancer, or of being prone to cancer or heart disease, but car accidents, a hang-glider accident or other incidents – like severed heads – are not transmitted by the genes! They are not physically transmitted.

And what a shock to find all these women being hairdressers. The grandmother saw the heads cut off and ever since, all the women have repaired and prettied-up heads, except one, Jaqueline's sister, an anesthesiologist. Perhaps she was repairing the deaths?

Expressing with the body

One might have the impression that these French women of Armenian origin and their children had a strange way of expressing what happened in their community and their family: they expressed it through their bodies and the bodies of their children. As if somehow they had to repair the genocide, recall the genocide, the injustice, the unjust and premature deaths.

There is no explanation, medical, paramedical, psychoanalytical, no deciphering dreams, no means of explaining why after the heads were cut off and impaled on lances, three generations later, two little girls were born with problems related to the neck and the head. And why the mother who was talking about it was wearing a neck-brace.

Exploring her life, we found that Jacqueline had wanted to be a gym teacher, but the day before the final examination, she sprained her ankle. Slip-up? Social-class neurosis? Need to fail in order to continue family tradition? She did not take the examination, became a hairdresser like her mother, her grandmother and her brother, and she put on 20 pounds. Her mother, who was French, had lost her mother when she had been very young, like the grandmother in Turkey.

The children – particularly the girls – were "cradled" with stories of the terrorism and horrors committed by "the Turks."

I do not understand why these repetitions occur, but I observe them and the more I construct genosociograms, the more I see "invisible family loyalties" and repetitions and "unbelievable" repetitions. Can we say that it is pure chance? Pure coincidence? The story of this Armenian family is striking and perhaps the most mysterious because we have no understanding of how such a thing is possible.

My colleague and friend, Pierre Weil, professor of psychology at the University of Belo Horizonte in Brazil, who spent three years, three months, and three days in meditation in a Tibetan ashram in France, thinks you could suggest possible reincarnation. But that is not my path nor my way of reasoning. I take note, I collect clinical cases and I hope that the current interdisciplinary research in psychoneuroimmunology and transgenerational psychoanalysis will provide some answers.

Valerie and Roger: can you "inherit" car accidents?

I will now present the "possible psychological inheritance" of car accidents, by way of an unconscious family loyalty and a kind of anniversary syndrome.

From time to time, I lead training seminars in hospitals to prepare nurses and other carers to work with terminal illnesses, especially cancer, and to prepare patients for surgical interventions. I have the hospital staff do practical exercises and in order for them to really understand what stress is, I ask them to speak about the most recent stress they experienced and we analyze it together.

A charming nurse told the following story.

"It was nothing serious, just a little car accident which wasn't really a stress."

"How did this accident happen?" I asked.

"I was driving with my little girl in the car, and a reckless driver ran into us. He was at fault."

"How old are you?"

"I'm twenty-eight and my daughter is four."

"Have you already had other car accidents?"

"Never."

"Think hard."

"Oh! When I was a little girl, I was in an accident with my father. I was…four years old. What do you know… it's true, I had the accident with my daughter at exactly the same spot, on the same road, when my daughter was the age I had been at the time of the accident with my father. That's strange. I'd never thought of that before. I'd forgotten."

It was a coincidence in age and a coincidence in circumstances, a double anniversary repetition, and she had forgotten.

Let us take another example of the psychological heredity of a car accident. A twenty-seven-year-old psychologist named Roger recounted the story of a small, very ordinary car accident he had one day when he was bringing his child to school for the first time. He was married, his child was six years old; and in September he had had the car accident. It was nothing, just a small dent.

I asked, "Have you or anyone in your family already had a car accident?"

"Never."

"Think hard."

"Oh, yes, when I was a kid."

So I asked him to question his father and grandparents about the accident, which he did.

When he was six years old, he had been in a car accident on 1 October on his way to school for his first day. His father had also had an accident when he was a child, going to school for the first time with his own father (Roger's grandfather). The grandfather had not had an accident going to school because he had not gone to school. His (the grandfather's) father had just been killed in the First World War, and his family had been very poor. At the time, young war widows in France did not get paid a war pension, or at least not right away, so the grandfather herded cows, eyeing the school from afar.

Since then, every first day of school in each generation has been marked by a car accident on the way to school, the child going with his father by car, the father choosing to take the child to school for this special day. We could note that often it is the mother who takes the children to school for their first day, not the father.

Why a car accident? And why only one? Why on the way to school? Why on the first day? Is it pure chance? But is that statistically plausible? Is it truly coincidence, over four or five generations? Or is it due to "something" stemming from an internal necessity?

How? Why? What is working in the memory? What must we not forget, because it is marked by something: the premature death, considered unjust, during the war? The lack of a war pension for "a long time"? The poverty of the son of a hero who died on the field of honor? Deprived of school? The indifference of the neighbors, the society or the family concerning their hardship? The date of the first day of school varied over the five generations (October or September), but the timing remained the same (on the way to school the first day), as did the configuration (double anniversary) and the

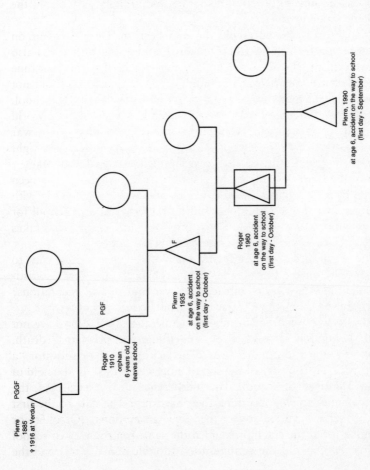

Figure 10.4 Roger's simplified genosociogram: repetition of a car accident from generation to generation

PGGF
Pierre
1885
✟ 1916 at Verdun

PGF
Roger
1910
orphan
6 years old
leaves school

F
Pierre
1935
at age 6, accident
on the way to school
(first day - October)

Roger
1960
at age 6, accident
on the way to school
(first day - October)

Pierre, 1990
at age 6, accident on the way to school
(first day - September)

context, with the same family situation (father taking son for this entry into the world through school).

So once again, we have an example of a double anniversary repetition, in the same circumstances, or rather, in the same configuration.

11 Family configuration and the double anniversary syndrome

By family configuration, I mean a parent (father or mother of such and such an age, say, thirty-one years old) with a child of such and such an age (say six) and a "life event" (for example, an accident on the way to school for the first day, as in Chapter 10).

With my many years of experience using the genosociogram and numerous cases on file, I have seen very many configuration repetitions, double anniversary repetitions, over two or three generations, and sometimes of five or more generations. This leads me to believe that perhaps people undergo a period of increased vulnerability when they near the age at which one of their family members had "troubles" or a traumatic experience, be it a serious illness, an accident, a death, an injustice. This period becomes an anniversary period.

Vulnerability and anniversary stress

Simone de Beauvoir died on the night of 16 April 1986, the anniversary date of the death of Jean-Paul Sartre (15 April 1980): the same date, within a few hours of each other, on the night between the fifteenth and sixteenth.

Sometimes, there are bad periods marked by a series of troubles and "hitches." People do not understand why they are anxious, why they "don't feel right," do not sleep well, do not feel well, why they "catch anything that's in the air," why "things happen" to them one after another: a cold, a small car accident, a sprained ankle, or even something serious, maybe even fatal. They often feel ill at ease, suffering from something that "doesn't show on the x-ray," nor in a blood test. They experience this "rough passage" without knowing why. They see doctor after doctor who finds nothing, or sometimes they have cancer and need an operation, or have an unexplained accident during the operation, or post-operative complications, or a car accident.

When we draw up a genosociogram, we note the important life events on the family tree with dates and ages which often enables us to visualize that period, that age – and as if by chance, it is just at that moment that someone died, or a separation occurred, or an estrangement, a hospitalization or some other traumatic event.

Here is an example: Jan was very frightened by a small car accident when her car stopped in a tunnel and she had to push it out. She had feared she would be killed. Then she accused herself of negligence: her dashboard indicated a need for repairs and she had ignored this mechanical "warning." In her work with the group, she suddenly remembered that she was the exact same age as her father had been when he also had a car accident, which had been fatal, and her accident occurred on the same date: 6 December. We could suggest that maybe Jan unconsciously took risks – which could have been fatal – for this anniversary of the death, whose date she had forgotten.

On 22 November 1963, J.F. Kennedy chose to drive through Dallas with the bullet-proof roof of his car down, having "forgotten" both the death threats and that the father of his grandfather, Patrick, had died on 22 November 1858. He had forgotten the event, without forgetting to take risks.

Two brothers, one survivor

Every year for the past decade, I have taught a course at the University of Nice on "the unspoken" in family emotions examining student genosociograms drawn on the blackboard. One year, a student who was feeling a little "empty" volunteered. He was thirty-three years old. Let us call him Bernard.

When we drew up Bernard's genosociogram, his family tree, it showed that his elder brother died – I would not say he committed suicide – from an involuntary overdose of medication at the age of thirty-three. When Bernard reached the age of thirty-three, the age at which his brother Lucien died, Bernard had a whole series of illnesses and incidents: the flu, bronchitis, pneumonia, car accident, etc.

When he was able to talk about it and bring to light the connections with his brother's death, his symptoms disappeared, without a formal psychotherapy, but with the probable therapeutic effects of the demonstration and the few interviews that followed.

Bernard realized that he had, in fact, "taken over his brother's life as it had been." His brother Lucien had two children, three years apart. Bernard had two children, three years apart. His brother had lived in a large house. Bernard had just bought a large house that resembled his brother's house. Bernard was almost entirely identified with Lucien and waited, with great anxiety, for his thirty-third birthday and – the end of his life.

He no longer had any future plans. He slept poorly. Nobody around him understood what was happening to him – not his family, not his doctor, nor the psychotherapist he was seeing.

We began to work together, trying to discern the internal programming (unconscious) he had given himself, the "life script." We touched upon his well-behaved and studious childhood in a Catholic middle school and the importance his brother had given to Christ's passion – at the age of thirty-three, and lectures on the imitation of Jesus Christ. We tried "deprogramming" and "reprogramming." With my help, he decided that he was not obliged to die like his brother, at the same age. Once he had understood the repetition and decided not to fall into it through an *invisible family loyalty*, he regained his strength, blossomed and affirmed himself. He then completely changed his life. He had a third child and was very happy. He and his wife were thinking about having a fourth. He changed careers. He sold his large house and took an apartment elsewhere. When I saw him ten years later, he was doing very well.

This unconscious identification with his brother was relatively easy to understand, but when we look back over his family history we find totally inexplicable facts. Perhaps we could say that these inexplicable incidents that are repeated in the family occurred by chance. Maybe it was coincidence or maybe it was internal necessity. Let us take a closer look at his family history.

Lucien: genealogical incest

Bernard's genosociogram revealed that he had twenty-six second cousins born from second cousins. Out of these twenty-six, fourteen were named Luke, Lucien, Lucy or Lucienne. Nine died at young ages in tragic or accidental circumstances.

Going back further through the family tree, we see that more than a century ago, his great-great-grandfather, who was of Italian origin, had been found on the steps of a church by a doctor who had him adopted by a family of farmers. This family was poor. The following year, they took on another baby who had been found in the same village. The little boy and the little girl were raised together and

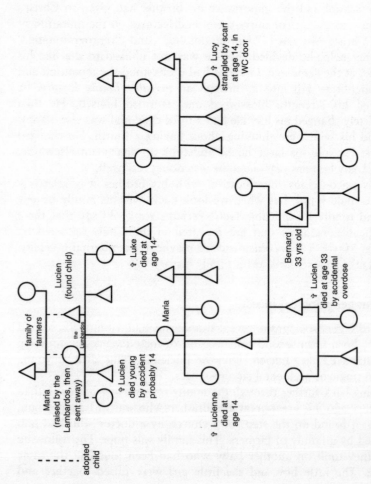

Figure 11.1 Lucien and Bernard's simplified genosociogram: identification with deceased elder brother

loved each other, like brother and sister, of course. The farmers did not have the means to keep both children, so they did not adopt the little girl and sent her to a convent to be taken care of by others.

The little boy, who loved this little girl, made tremendous efforts to find her. When he did, he paid for her studies and married her. They were not really brother and sister. They had not even been officially adopted by the family, but had only shared the same wet nurse who raised them together for a short while, who adopted one and sent the other away. So there was no "incest," for they had only been raised together. We call this situation a "genealogical incest."

The boy's name was Lucien. The majority of descendants who bore this name died under tragic circumstances – according to the family history. Why? We do not know. There is no explanation, only individual reasons specific to each one. How? We do not know. Is it only by coincidence?

It is as though in this family there was a desire to punish this "genealogical" – rather than real – incest by giving this name over and over again and then "punishing" through a repetitive accidental death. This raises the question of the unsaid and repetition.

Can it result from a "prophecy stress"? In this story we have a little girl and a little boy who are not brother and sister, since they were found and raised by a mother/wet nurse. They get married and have several children; among the descendants, many who were named Lucien like the first died in accidents. Lucien, Bernard's brother, died accidentally and the remaining sibling almost died, until we "broke the chain" through a transgenerational exploration. Whether this had been due to an unconscious "self-fulfilling prediction" and "invisible loyalty," a "prophecy stress" occurring through the stories told by the family, a "repetition," or "a psychological engram," it happened more in the head than in the genes.

"Mrs Andrew"

"Genealogical incest" is frequent. Take the case of a young woman whom we will call Monica, Monica Andrew, daughter of Henry Andrew. She married "Andrew Smith." In her home town, she was called "Mrs Andrew," in order to distinguish her from her mother-in-law and sister-in-law, but also using the same name given to her own mother, "Mrs Andrew," as if she had been married to her father. This is not incest – not even an attraction for the same name. It is not forbidden by law. But it can cause a series of problems, which can become very serious: cancers, suicides, depressions. In *L'Ange et le*

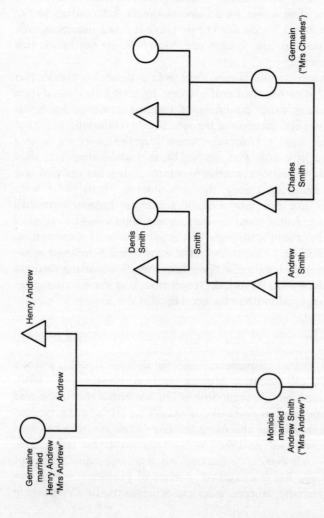

Figure 11.2 "Mrs Andrew's" simplified genosociogram: a "genealogical incest"

fantôme,[1] French psychoanalyst Didier Dumas describes this kind of family, the Martin-Leroux family: two sisters marry men with the same family names and one sister has what we call a "genealogical incest," which ends with a series of dead husbands and children, suicides and so on.

The Martin-Leroux family: triple genealogical incest

Let us examine this case of genealogical incest cited by Didier Dumas through the genogram and analysis made by one of my students, Catherine Mesnard, at the University of Nice. Towards the middle of the twentieth century, Alphonse Martin married Victorine Rosier, who gave him three daughters: Mary, Augustine and Josephine. The two younger children had feminized masculine given names, because Alphonse Martin expected sons.

Josephine Martin married a man whose first name was Martin. Her name became Mrs Martin-Leroux. First genealogical incest. Mary Martin, the eldest sister, also married a man whose surname was Leroux, although his first name was Emile. Second genealogical incest.[2]

These men not being related, we see how Josephine and Mary, by renouncing their father's name, end up being married to each other – although Josephine retaking the name Martin introduces a confusion of genealogical position. The imaginary marriage between the two sisters, in denying the function played by the father's name, above all denies the role of femininity.[3]

After giving Josephine seven children, Martin Leroux hanged himself. The widowed Josephine lived with another man for a while, but when she got pregnant, she left this man and he disappeared from the family novel.

Mary's husband also died, from tuberculosis. She then married Auguste. Knowing that Mary's sister's name is Augustine, we could suggest a doubling of her genealogical incest. Her second husband committed suicide after giving her two children.

Lucy Leroux, the only child of the Mary/Emile couple, was six months old when her father died. She went on to marry her cousin, Edmond Leroux, himself widowed from his first marriage. Third genealogical incest. Their grandson, Jean-Michel, was autistic and stopped talking at the age of three, cutting himself off from the world.

Two Mrs Browns: unresolved genealogical incest

To better understand "genealogical incest" and "double connection

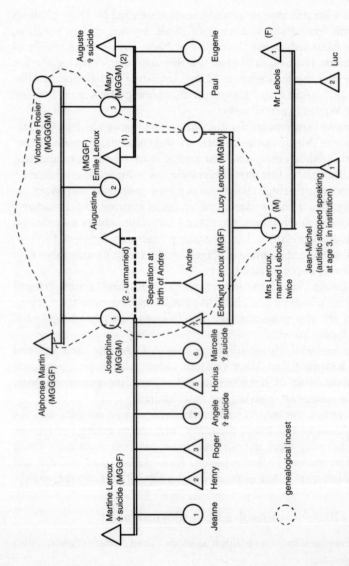

Figure 11.3 Simplified genosociogram of the maternal line of the Martin-Leroux family (case cited by Didier Dumas, genosociogram established by Catherine Mesnard)

marriages," let us examine another case study. A charming forty-year-old woman named Josie had breast cancer. We explored her life circumstances at the onset of the cancer to see what was happening at that time. She told me that nothing happened in her life, and she did not understand why she got cancer. Her life was simple, easy. She was a medical secretary in a center that was doing well, living in a medium-sized city. No stressful event had occurred that could explain the onset of this cancer in 1986.

I asked, "What happened one year earlier in 1985?"

"Nothing."

"And then? Think."

"My sister got married."

"To whom?"

"To my brother-in-law [her husband's brother]."

So, we have two sisters who married two brothers. Josie was the youngest, who throughout her childhood had always had a difficult time in this position of the "little sister." She never had a room of her own. She had been a little bit of an accident, so a third bed had been added to her two sisters' room. She wore her older sisters' clothes and had "nothing of her own" until she got married and became "the young Mrs Brown." She blossomed and became very beautiful. She was "so nice," she invited her brothers, sisters, brothers-in-law and sisters-in-law over. And then, one of her sisters, Jacqueline, married her brother-in-law, Jack, and also became "the young Mrs Brown." Josie found herself both "dispossessed" of her new family name and of her new-found position. There was another, new "young Mrs Brown," and perhaps one too many.

And worse yet: her mother-in-law liked her sister very much, just as her own mother had preferred her sister. Without even daring to feel any resentment over this intrusion of her territory and this dispossession, she fretted and, she said spontaneously, "got cancer." Her sister had "stolen" what belonged to her: being "the young Mrs Brown." And now there were two, and "it didn't work for her." She felt once again dispossessed of her identity and her territory by her sister. It became intolerable. In addition, she felt defenseless, "powerless" in this situation, and without hope. Hopeless and helpless, specialists would say. It was a major loss of identity and situation, a *second loss of loved object*, which awakened the trauma and wound of a major loss of loved object during childhood, a loss which could not be talked about or cried over, for which grieving could not be accomplished.

We often encounter this kind of situation in the onset of cancer, as

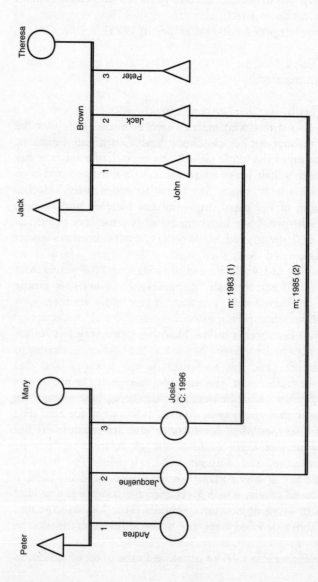

Figure 11.4 Josie's simplified genosociogram: the two young Mrs Browns – two sisters marrying two brothers

the psychologist Laurence LeShan has already noted.[4] He speaks about the loss of a loved object in the life of patients, and how a second loss reawakens the trauma and wound of a major childhood loss of loved object, for which there could be no grieving, and how this often has occurred often in cancer patients, particularly when they are reserved people.

After Josie got all of that out in the open and worked on it, she recovered and was then able to be cured of her cancer, through, of course, medical care, sports, daily relaxation, positive visualization, yoga and psychotherapy as well.

This case could also illustrate genealogical incest. Josie remained very attached to her family of birth, having married, "by chance," someone whose first name happened to be her father's surname, although her husband's surname differed. We should also note the many encounters occur and bonds are created that lead to marriage during family encounters and celebrations such as baptisms, marriages, burials and so on.

The incest taboo does not cover relations by marriage and their families. There does not even exist a word to describe the relations between two families united by the marriage of their children – nor between the children of two divorced people who remarry together – and who live under the same roof in an extended reconstituted family. Each of the brothers is free to fall in love with whomsoever he chooses, even the sister of his "new sister" (his sister-in-law). "Double marriages" and subsequent relationships between relations by marriage sometimes become "substitution incest." (For more on substitution incest, see the story of Guy de Maupassant's conception in Appendix 4.)

Continuing the spiral of relations by marriage

No law forbids two brothers marrying two sisters, or a brother and sister marrying a sister and brother. Freud – who, by the way, does not mention his brothers and sisters in his autobiography with the exception of Anna in passing – and his sister Anna married the sister and brother of the Bernays family.

In 1882, Sigmund Freud (1856–1939) met Martha Bernays (1861–1951). In 1883, his sister Anna Freud (1858–1955) married Eli Bernays (1860–1923), Martha's brother. Then, in 1896, Freud married his "sister-in-law by marriage," Martha Bernays, the sister of the husband of his sister Anna. And each gave the other's name to their daughter. Eli and Anna Bernays named their daughter Martha, and Martha and Sigmund Freud named their daughter Anna (1895–1982).[5]

In certain regions of the world, these double marriages of two brothers marrying two sisters, or cousins marrying cousins has been a traditional – and still current – practice used, for example, to regroup family land. One often notices the transgenerational repetition of these marriages between cousins. Martine Segalen even wrote in 1985 in *Quinze générations de Bas-Bretons*: "Two couples of ancestors exchange their spouses over several generations," revealing this kind of continuation of relations by marriage over the generations.

But many women have a hard time when their sister marries their husband's brother. It is difficult for them to share their new family name with a sister they had hoped to be rid of by leaving their family of origin. Some mothers-in-law cannot share their surname with the "patch" of a new daughter-in-law. Diverse family combinations are possible, sometimes bringing with them problems and even dramatic situations.

False brothers and sisters brought up under the same roof, or, the reconstituted family

Let us take the example of two women, mother and daughter, who marry a father and son and who therefore have the same surname for the second time. They live under the same roof and end up fighting over territory, the kitchen, the house, the land, the heritage – even though it was not large.

In *Précis de psychodrame*, I wrote about Gisèle, a psychotic interned after attempting to kill her mother. Mother and daughter had married father and son, and therefore again had the same surname and lived in the same house. In fact, as the mother had married a widower, Gisèle was raised in the same house with a teenager, the son of her stepfather. The "parents" raised them together, almost like "brother and sister" in a "reconstituted" family. But in fact, the son and Gisèle ended up dating and getting married. After the birth of her child, Gisèle suffered a psychotic decompensation and was interned.

These encounters happen at home and these marriages tend to unite the son and daughter of previous marriages of a remarried couple, in an "extended reconstituted family." Sometimes, it is the stepfather who marries the daughter-in-law. This is also a genealogical incest: confusion of relations and generations – and is not without harmful effects, even if it is not forbidden by law. (See second-type incest, page 162.)

12 Legacy and family structure

When we observe family structures closely, we discover a certain number of "hereditary structures" which include repetitions that have not been consciously decided upon or even noticed.

What seems to be "coincidentally" hereditary, although not clearly defined, can include number of children, time period between having children, even number of marriages, or number of miscarriages and abortions. There are monogamous families, single marriage families, and families with several marriages and remarriages. There are families with one, two, three or four marriages. I have never encountered a five-marriage family, although they can be found, in the United States. There are divorce families and widow families. There are families with suicides, violent deaths, illegitimate children, children from adultery or only legitimate children. There are spending families and frugal families, families that move up or down the social ladder.

It is as though the family composition and structure were repetitive and hereditary, psychologically hereditary, as if there were an unwritten rule followed by the family members, in mind and body.

Certain legacies, certain kinds of "inheritance" could take the form of gifts, like the Bach family's gift for music (Johann Sebastian and Johann Christian). Others inherit qualities like endurance, dexterity, an athletic or artistic spirit, technical know-how or manual skills, etc. But these hereditary structures, stemming more from a psychological or mental inheritance than a biological one and which could be a kind of engram, a sort of bioelectric memory trace left in the brain, are sometimes difficult to understand.

The Mortelacs: child deaths over several generations

This is the story of the Mortelacs, an old, well-known French noble family whose origins can be traced back to the Crusades. Following a conference I gave on "repetitive transgenerational links," a listener offered "to go have a drink together," because he wanted to talk to me about what my approach had reminded him of: dramatic life events reproduced generation after generation. As a child, he experienced the trauma of his younger brother's death. He told me that his name was, say, John de Mortelac (in French, *mort* means "dead" and *lac* means "lake") and that as far back as he knew the family history – over a thousand years – at each generation, a three-year-old or younger child died in water – a lake, a swamp, a pond, etc. This repetitive danger worried him to such a degree that he resolved his problem by not getting married and not having children.

We know that the origin of family names can often be traced back to a form of nickname, linked for example to a location (Worthington, Underhill, Appleby, Ford) or a geographic situation (Sutherland, Delamar, North), to a profession (Miller, Smith, Fisher), to a physical characteristic (Armstrong, Longfellow), or the memory of an event (Boniface, Lependu).

Perhaps the name Mortelac could indicate the occurrence of some dramatic death: the death of an adult or a child in water, in a lake, a swamp, a river, a "dead water," providing a possible explanation of the name's origin.

But why the repetition of the event? What happens so that even now a young child dies in water with each generation? I did not work on their family history, nor draw up their family tree or genosociogram. I simply had a long interview with this young man of the Mortelac family, and then a discussion with one of his cousins who had been born a Mortelac, and who also had lost a younger brother and a child of her own at a young age to accidents. Her mother had also lost a brother and had not told her about it, "for her own good," to protect her.

We should keep in mind that deaths of young children were common in the past, even among kings such as Louis XIV who lost some of his children young. Right up into the nineteenth century, nearly half of the infants born did not reach the age of one. But in this Mortelac family, the children who died were already walking, and they died in water in the thirteenth century, in the sixteenth century, in 1990 and at every generation in between.

There was no family malediction. I do not believe in curses, yet it is tempting to look for an explanation, a "cause." Perhaps this repetition was due to an unconscious "prediction," or an attempt to repair some harm done, or perhaps it served as a reminder, or pinpointed an unspeakable and even unthinkable event.

Predictions and maledictions in history

The history of France is full of predictions of malediction and predictions coming true. King Philip IV (1285–1314) eradicated the Templars in 1312 and sentenced the order's Grand Master, Jacques de Molay, to death. On 13 March 1314, while at the stake, he cried out before dying, "Pope Clement! Knight William! King Philip! Before the year is up, I will call you to appear before the court of God to receive your just punishment. Malediction! Cursed be all through the thirteenth generation of your races!"

During the months that followed, the three people responsible for his unjust judgment had paid for it: the King of France had died, Pope Clement had died, the cardinal who presided over the court had died. Philip IV's son and heir, Louis X, died eighteen months later, in all likelihood assassinated. The line of French kings soon died out. It was the end of the direct Capetian line.

Their cousins, the Valois, succeeded the Capetians in 1328, to be followed by their cousins the Bourbons: Henry IV, 1589 – 1610 – assassinated; Louis XIII, Louis XIV, Louis XV, Louis XVI – guillotined. On his way to the guillotine, Louis XVI left the prison by the same door Jacques de Molay had used four hundred and sixty-seven years earlier. Louis XVI was the thirteenth generation of kings of France since Philip IV.

Can we talk about "divine justice"? We dare not mention malediction: an evil pronounced solemnly which acts on the future. And yet this was the word used by Jacques de Molay at the stake. The facts are there: the stake, a malediction, the king's death, the thirteenth generation. Is it by chance? It is coincidence? Synchronicity over time? A self-fulfilling prophecy?

Of course, Cartesians would say that it is by chance.

Let us look at another historical event in the same family of kings of France. Of course, it is purely by coincidence that two centuries later, on Monday, 30 January 1989, during the bicentennial celebration of the French Revolution, the fifty-two-year-old distant cousin of Louis XVI, Prince Alphonse de Bourbon, Duke of Anjou, president of the Winter Olympic Games committee, "was decapitated" while inspecting the Olympic ski slope at Beaver Creek by a wire forgotten in the field. Although news of his "decapitation" covered the front pages of the French press, the detail itself is false: the Prince died of a skull fracture, even though the death was caused by the wire. For royalists, he was the real "king" of France – Louis XX – and recently had presided over celebrations of the "Capetian millennium." The requiem mass held at the royal basilica of Saint Denis drew crowds to mourn this Duke of Anjou, cousin of Juan Carlos of Spain, distant cousin of Louis XVI. He was fatally injured in the head during the same month and within a few days of the anniversary date of his ancestor Louis XVI's death by guillotine on 21 January 1793.

One month prior to the accident, on 21 December 1988, Alphonse de Bourbon won proceedings brought against him by his cousin, Henry of Orléans, concerning inheritance rights. He had thus been recognized as a true Bourbon, potentially a pretender to the throne of France. As early as 1789, the ambassador of Madrid was claiming the Spanish Bourbons' right to the throne of France, in case something happened to Louis XVI and his descendants. Louis XVI's brothers, Louis XVII and Charles X, succeeded him on the throne, followed by his French cousins (the descendants of Philippe-Egalité who voted Louis XVI's death), and then Louis-Philippe who reigned until 1848.

The effects of "strong words"

Without believing in maledictions, one can wonder about the effects of strong words accompanied by strong emotions, and particularly when they come from an authority figure, a priest, a healer, a parent or a teacher. Because of how predictions affect the unconscious, I remain wary of astrology, divination by cards or palm reading, and clairvoyance. Who knows if a foreseen misfortune, which does sometimes occur, does not stem from the words themselves which allow the ill-fate, death or accident to settle in the person's mind thus making it possible or foreseeable, thus changing the body (space) and the future (time). This could be similar to the "self-fulfilling prophecy" creating a "prophecy stress." Perhaps this explains the "evil eye" we find in numerous tales, legends and stories of witches and ill-fate.

We can wonder about what happened to the Capetians, to the end of their line and the "self-fulfilling prophecy" affecting the various actors in the story and their descendants, but for now, these remain only observations, and our questions remain unanswered. In any case, there can be a "negative prophecy stress," just as there can be an assistance brought by a positive prediction and positive encouragement (the Pygmalion effect).

Delenda – a father's anger and a child's sex: the Cato curse

From my experience with the transgenerational approach, I discovered the *weight of words* – I do not know how to say it otherwise – in a culture other than my own. I have worked on the histories and family trees of families from countries other than France, including Arab families from North Africa, and particularly from Tunisia.

I would like to tell the story of an Arab family, which had a series of daughters: Djamila, Aïcha, Leila, Oriane, Yasmine. A sixth daughter was born, whom the father named Delenda. The following year, "the son," Mohamed, was born, followed by a second son Ali. This occurred in the region of Carthage.

Several times, I observed this same configuration of a succession of daughters, with a Delenda before the first son.

What does "Delenda" mean? Delenda is not an Arabic first name, but a Latin word, coming from Cato the Elder's curse pronounced during the Punic Wars between Rome and Carthage: *Delenda Carthago est* – "Carthage must be destroyed."

In the region of Carthage, when a farmer or a city dweller has "had enough" of a series of daughters, he names the last-born daughter Delenda in an expression of anger: it is the race of girls that will be destroyed. Nothing bad happens to Delenda or to her descendants or the other girls, but the series of daughters comes to an end and sons are born. This tradition has lasted two thousand years in this region. Is it coincidence? There is no explanation. One could call it superstition. But how does this superstition determine a child's sex? Is it the power of words? But how does "the power of words" influence genetics? And if the father were to say, "May a boy be born," or "I want a son," it doesn't work.

The father needs to get angry, to be exasperated after a long series of daughters after the birth of a fifth, sixth or seventh daughter, whom he names Delenda, in order for a son to be born. We find this tradition among the literate as well as among the illiterate who have never heard of the Punic Wars. It has been passed on for two thousand years throughout North Africa.

The priest: strong words misunderstood

Let us examine another family history. In a psychodrama group a few years ago, a woman said, "I'm preoccupied. My young daughter has very bad asthma and I'm afraid she will die from it."

"Why?" I asked.

"Because she's my eldest daughter, she is sick...my eldest sister died...my mother lost her eldest sister...my grandmother lost her eldest

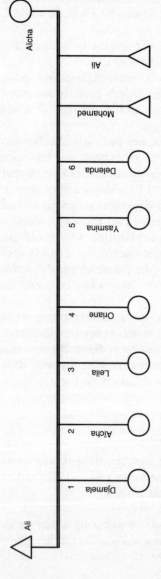

Figure 12.1 Delenda's simplified genosociogram: a series of daughters in a family near Carthage, Tunisia

brother…generations have gone by with the eldest of the children dying young." And she added, "I want to bring an end to this and I can't! I spoke to my doctor and he is also worried about my daughter."

I asked her to speak at length about her family history and as she talked we drew up her psychogenealogy, her genosociogram. We worked on what has happened over several generations and she patiently sought out the significant life events concerning her great-great-grandparents, going back in time, under the Third Republic in France, the Empire, the Revolution – going back seven or eight generations over two centuries.

Her ancestors were peasants of the land who moved little: farmers of the Savoy region, who, during the Terror and the Revolution, hid a priest. After the Terror, the priest came out of hiding, thanked them and said, "As a sign of my gratitude, the eldest of each generation will watch over you." And then, for two centuries, by chance or by accident, the eldest of each generation became "a little angel in heaven" who watched over the family. And this woman experienced the generation after generation of child deaths as a kind of incomprehensible family malediction.

Every system depends on its ecosystem. I therefore thought about this *family's context and frame of reference* – at that time in the past and now in the present. I talked at length with this woman and had her understand that one can hear things differently depending on one's frame of reference; that there is a difference between a benediction and a malediction. The sentence "the eldest of each generation will watch over you" can be interpreted in several ways. As a result, if by chance her daughter became a doctor or a nurse, she could watch over her when she became elderly or ill. There are many ways of watching over a family: by being a care-taker (doctor, nurse, druggist), a useful citizen (baker, farmer, policeman, notary, banker, etc.), a priest, a nun, a psychotherapist, etc.

We therefore *reframed* the sentence…and the prediction. From that moment on, something changed in her perception and experience and the little girl was cured. This little girl did not die, and ten years later she was still doing well. This was the first time since the French Revolution that the eldest child had not died young in this family.

How does an event repeat itself with each generation over two hundred years? Why? What happened? Where is it registered in the personal and family unconscious? How is it passed on? Is it a kind of engram? What meaning does it have? How can one break the chain? Why and how do (therapeutic) words bring it to an end?

What happened in this family so that the eldest child always died? They were serious and responsible people, living in good conditions. They paid attention to their children. What happened so that from the French Revolution through to the present, over seven generations, there was always some slip-up and the eldest child fell ill or was injured and died?

And why, when we bring light to a single sentence, what was said, the injunction, and reframe it in another manner, does it no longer happen?

It is as though somewhere, one did not have the right to know and to speak about it; and at the same time, as if one did not have the right to forget, and all that had had to be known, but not said explicitly, nor known that it was known and passed on: a doubly binding devilishly constraining double bind, a double Gordian knot.

Again, we can identify a characteristic of the secret. The French psychoanalyst Guy Ausloos[1] noted, as we have, that "it is *forbidden to know* and *forbidden not to know.*"

It is as though the unconscious has a good memory, and likes to remind us of events and "mark them," without words or explanations. Yet the way the unconscious pinpoints events also depends on the manner in which the family interprets, understands and reacts to what is happening.

A life can be perceived, read and interpreted in a context, in a given framework. We can take something in one context and put it in another context or another frame, and the same sentence takes on another shade; we can reframe an event: a curse could become a blessing.

We see the same phenomena in terminal cancers. An insurmountable situation can become merely difficult to surmount, or even fascinating to try to surmount. This is the concept of hardiness, as described following interviews with Japanese survivors of war camps.

On genosociograms, it is surprising to note these repetitions generation upon generation, as if something were talking. As Lacan says, quoting Freud and Freud's comment on Fechner about *The Interpretation of Dreams*, "Ça parle sur l'autre scène,"[2] but pulling the red thread brings us further backstage.

Conrad writes in *Typhoon*, "It was enough, when you thought it over, to give you the idea of an immense, potent, and invisible hand thrust into the ant-heap of the earth, laying hold of shoulders, knocking heads together, and setting the unconscious faces of the multitude towards inconceivable goals and in undreamt-of directions." As if an extraordinary force drove us to our destiny.

And when we care for the seriously ill – like cancer patients – we often find repetitions when we draw up an annotated genosociogram, a psychogenealogy, a completed family tree, mentioning given names, who lives with whom, the illnesses, the accidents, the main life events, the important displacements, the estrangements and uprootings, and when we establish the relationships and the significant links.

By pinpointing and bringing to light these repetitions, we allow a subject who is having a difficult experience in a difficult period of increased vulnerability to improve the situation, by reframing it in another manner, by changing the "life script" of illness and death, of multiple accidents, or of failure, into a positive script. The client will be able to become – and become again – a subject and live out his or her own choices – and *live*, finally.

Reframing a terminal illness within a larger repetitive family context gives it another meaning and often changes the course of the illness. I do not mean that it necessarily keeps a death or a series of dramatic accidents from happening. But these events can be experienced differently. Often, things turn around, the subject emerges from his period of vulnerability when he can talk about what has happened, when he can decipher and pull on the red string of the events, when the events are framed and reframed in another manner, when the secret is spoken, when the unsaid is confronted. We can manage to differentiate family love, respect, loyalty from an identification with the Other (invisible family loyalty) so strong as to lead to living another's life and dying for that Other. This often occurs when we pinpoint an anniversary syndrome.

Throughout my therapeutic experience, and particularly since I began using a transgenerational approach, I have seen families who repeat illnesses, accidents or involuntary deaths over one, two or even several generations, without understanding why. We observe it clinically, like a mark on the body or a notch in time.

I have also observed that this work of bringing to the forefront links and repetitions, of decoding, gives meaning to events and provides a hold over them: when we see, when we understand, a meaning emerges, a context is transformed, another form emerges from the depths and things change. The subject can breathe, gets rid of the weight of the past, often his body changes, his life changes. He becomes another person...and (sometimes) in addition is cured of serious or even life-threatening illness.

Van Gogh, Dali and Freud: replacement child and repairing child

We also observe unexplainable events when we encounter what is called a "replacement child," a child conceived to replace a recently deceased young child or other relative, and who often bears the given name of the deceased and/or is born for the anniversary of the death, without the grieving having been accomplished. When this death is overshadowed and the mourning unfinished, the replacement child's life itinerary is not among the happiest.

One of the most striking examples can be found in the life of the painter Vincent Van Gogh, born on 30 March 1852, one year to the day after the death of another Vincent, his elder brother. The family did not want to talk about the deceased child, but gave his first and middle names, Vincent-Wilhelm, to the future painter. Vincent Van Gogh lived a tragic life as if somehow he had been forbidden to exist. He was very close to his "father-like brother," Theo, who had been a loving brother to him. Theo married and named his son Vincent-Wilhelm, out of the love he felt for his brother. Several months later he wrote to his brother the painter about his son, "I hope that this Vincent will be able to live and accomplish something." When Vincent Van Gogh received this letter, he attempted suicide, as if for him there could not be two Vincent Van Goghs living at the same time, as if his brother pinpointed the incompatibility of co-presence.

This is an example of a replacement child who took the place of a deceased person for whom grieving had not been finished, the replacement child not being left the space to live. He was a replacement child who did not even have the possibility of talking about his dead brother and who in a way felt like a "usurper" because he took a place and a name which had not been destined for him.

Salvador Dali, on the other hand, had been able to exorcise his position as a replacement. From his childhood, he knew that another Salvador Dali, the "real" Salvador Dali, had been his elder brother, his "dead brother" on whose tomb his mother cried twice a week. As a result, he decided, he said,[3] to become a clown to differentiate himself from this Salvador Dali who was so good, this little angel who was dead and buried. And Salvador Dali, the replacement child who had decided not to be had, made an obsession of Jean-François Millet's painting *The Angelus*, painting sixty-four different versions of this picture of a farmer and his wife, hands joined, heads lowered, praying in a wheat field over a basket of potatoes.

X-rays of this painting revealed a young child's casket under the basket of potatoes. Millet recounts in his memoirs that when he had wanted to exhibit this painting of a dead child, a friend advised him to change the subject, because it was too sad and it would not sell...so he quickly covered up the casket with a basket of potatoes.

he said, "I always felt the death of a

and in part understood the survival
d:

life.... My brother died...three
leath plunged my father and
.... And in my mother's belly, I
anguish. My fetus swam in a
the persistence of this presence
This dead brother, whose ghost
e that he was named Salvador,
earned to live by filling up the
lly given to me.[4]

I cannot keep myself from
...ade by the Japanese novelist Kenji
Nagakami in an interview in *Le Nouvel Observateur* (25 July 1991) in which he mentions the death of his brother, a violent man he hardly liked:

When he died...I experienced an intense feeling of relief...but his death haunted me, it comes back endlessly in my novels along with my guilt for the joy I had felt then. For a long time, I thought I would die when I reached the age of twenty-four, the age at which my brother killed himself. This date approached, but my son was born – he took the place of this dead brother, and then I knew I would not die.

A child who is born after a death does not necessarily become a replacement child, nor a child of a "dead mother" (that is, a mother depressed and grieving). Sometimes, the child represents a sign that life is coming back with force and joy through the birth of a "repairing child." For example, the young Sigmund Freud was raised as an only cherished child. He was born three months after the death of his grandfather Shlomo Freud (1856). Even the sadness of his younger brother Julius' (1857–8) death and his young uncle Julius' (his mother's brother) death at the age of twenty (also in 1858) did not change his privileged position as the loved child.

But the death of the younger baby while he was still very young perhaps left its mark. We can suppose he alludes to this younger brother as the revenant in the analysis of his dream *Non vixit* : "'No one is irreplaceable!' 'There are nothing but *revenants*: all those we have lost come back!'"[5]

Sigmund Freud spoke about revenants, and Françoise Dolto spoke about the invisible and mentioned Jules Laforgue's frequent reference to Saint Augustine's words: "The dead are invisible, they are not absent." For Dolto, the invisible are present around us and guide us. Dolto's invisibles resemble Socrates' Daimon, and perhaps provide another insight into how events and traumas are transmitted between generations.

Cendrine and a few others: marking the anniversary

In reference to the two brothers Lucien and Bernard, the deceased and the survivor, we already mentioned the anniversary syndrome and the period of increased vulnerability (same age or same time of the year, or even the same date, day for day) to certain difficult events, illnesses, accidents, deaths, being "ill at ease," etc.

"The dead pass down to the living," says the Roman adage – it is as if the death of a child or a teenager "telescopes" the dead child or teenager in a time and generation collapse. This is often the drama experienced by a replacement child that we mentioned.

Gregory Bateson told me in 1976 how much he had been marked by his brother's suicide at the age of twenty-two on 22 April 1922. Martin Bateson committed suicide with a revolver in the middle of London, in Trafalgar Square, on the birthday of his elder brother John (22 April 1898–14 October 1918), who was killed at the end of the First World War.

One of my students, whom I will call Cendrine, while drawing up her genosociogram at the University of Nice, uncovered something similar to a chain reaction in her family. Her mother died of cancer on 12 May. The following year her uncle (her mother's brother) had a fatal accident on 12 May. Later, she started working on the loss of her grandmother, who also died – from natural causes and age – on 12 May. In looking through the family papers, she discovered that her grandfather died of an accident on 12 May and that her grandfather's great-uncle and godfather had been killed during the war on 12 May.

Cendrine herself felt "ill at ease" in springtime, had difficulty breathing and was to be operated on on 12 May, "a date chosen randomly by the surgeon." But too much is too much and after our interview, she changed the date of the operation (which was successful).

After drawing up her genosociogram, Cendrine went on to do some genealogical research in order to go back further than her grandfather's great-uncle, all the way back to the 1789 Revolution in order to understand why and how this date kept coming back to affect the members of her family at different ages, like a recurring milestone throughout their entire family history.

Let us take another example marking an anniversary date of a death that was not in the family, but rather the death of very close friends, intimate loved ones, a chosen family, just as close as blood family. Both are part of what Moreno called the "social atom," a person's emotional circle, those close to an individual through love or hate and who lodge "somewhere" in the unconscious, preconscious and conscious.

One can also add to this family circle, loved pets. We often see this attachment in children who are sometimes marked for life by the tragic loss of a domestic animal whose death was not at all or not sufficiently cried over. This is also often the case for single women for whom a cat, dog or parrot replaces the children she never had or who have left the house. We also see it in some men with regard to their dogs.

These people and things (grandmother, nanny, mothering neighbor, dog, piano, family house, painting) that make up the social atom often need to be included on the genosociogram, but using another color.

Livia and Maria were two best friends who had been very close since they were teenagers. Maria got married and was expecting a child. Livia then decided to have a child also. Maria died during childbirth on 27 December, from a fibrinolysis (a rare accident). Her child survived. The young, single mother Livia gave birth six months later. Maria's child was to have been born for Saint Sylvester's Day and therefore was named Marie-Sylvain, and Livia's child was named Sylvain-Marie. Without talking about predictions, Maria had said that the child she was carrying was "sneaky" and would bring nothing but sadness and problems.

Ten years later, on 27 December, doctors discovered that Livia had cancer and operated on her immediately. She was fine afterwards. The previous year, she had already sprained her ankle on 27 December, seriously enough for her to use crutches for two weeks. The year following her operation (eleven years after Maria's death) she went skiing with her family and had a small accident on 27 December.

Two years later, she "didn't feel well": she was anxious, full of a vague apprehension, as "always" during the holiday season, and she stayed home in bed. Three years later, a few months after an operation, she was in the mountains, where she slipped, fell and hurt her hand just before Christmas and dislocated her shoulder on 27 December. The X-ray showed that she had not broken anything, but she had been frightened, as had her loved ones. So she came to talk to me and we discussed everything, drawing up her complete genosociogram, with her social atom, including her family and close friends. We underlined the dates of important events in red, and the repeating dates and ages. The repetitions jump out at you even more clearly when you draw the links connecting them in red on the chart (sociometric links).

The 27 December repetition appeared obvious along with the connections and links between these accidents and the surgery and the anniversary of the death of her close friend, each time a "hitch" marking the sad and tragic anniversary of this "early and unjust death."

We hoped that after this work revealing how the anniversary was marked, Livia would no longer have accidents on 27 December, and could finally really bury her deceased friend and finish her grieving, which she had now been able to put into words and not only into tears and actions – and even more so because at the time of the death she had had nobody to talk to about it.

Four other examples

The unconscious has its own way of calculating anniversaries and dates, which is not without importance. Here are four short examples.

Let us refer to the major dates of the Crusades and what Amin Maalouf wrote in *The Crusades through Arab Eyes*:

> On Friday 17 June 1291 the Muslim army, now enjoying overwhelming military superiority, finally penetrated the besieged city. King Henry and most of the notables hastily sailed off to take refuge in Cyprus. The other Franj were all captured and killed. The City was razed.
>
> The city of Acre had been reconquered, Abu'l-Fida' explains, at noon on the seventeenth day of the second month of Jumada in the year of the Hegira 690. It was on precisely this day, and at this hour, that the Franj had taken Acre from Saladin in the year of the Hegira 587, capturing and then massacring all the Muslims in the city. A curious coincidence, is it not?

The coincidence is no less astonishing by the Christian calendar, for the victory of the Franj at Acre had occurred in 1191, a hundred years, almost to the day, before the ultimate defeat.[6]

This marked the end of the occupation of Egypt, Syria and Palestine by Crusaders. Nevertheless scores were not yet settled. Eight centuries later, on 13 May 1981, in Rome, the Muslim Ali Agça attempted to shoot Pope Jean-Paul II, injuring the "supreme commander of the Crusades." It would be nothing more than a simplification just to attribute this act to "fanaticism." In fact, despite the many centuries that have gone by, the slate has not been wiped clean, and Muslims still speak of the Crusades as a genocide.

Françoise Dolto-Marette recounts in her memoirs, *Autoportrait d'une psychanalyste*, that her sister Jacqueline was born almost to the day of the anniversary date of her younger brother Jacques' death. Like her brother, she was named in honor of Saint Jacques. Jacqueline also died young.

Our young neighbor Michael was killed in a bicycle accident on Easter Monday on his way to church. When we sought for repetitive events with his family, we found that his grandfather had been injured in an accident that occurred in spring, but on a different date. When we checked, we discovered that date to have been also an Easter Monday. Going back further in the family history, we found that his great-grandfather had been tried for involuntary manslaughter, after having killed a cyclist who had not respected a stop sign and ran into the great-grandfather's car. Verifying the date of movable holidays, we found the accident occurred on an Easter Monday. The great-grandfather was acquitted. Going back even further, we found an ancestor, an artillery man, who involuntarily caused the accidental death of a gunner because he misheard the orders during the battle of Sebastopol.[7]

In my own family, my daughter and her children were all born in October like her father, with the exception of her eldest daughter who was born by chance in mid-January. In searching for Moreno's actual date of birth for one of my books, I confronted changes of the dates of life events due to differences of calendar, after the relatively recent "making up" of lost days on our Gregorian calendar, compensating for the lunar discrepancy in Eastern and Central Europe which occurred in 1917 in the former Soviet Union. This is when I remembered that we celebrate my mother Isabelle's birthday on 25 January, but at the end of her life, she reproached us on 13 January for having forgotten her: she was born in Moscow on 13 January on the "old calendar," but raised in Switzerland, where her birth date changed and had been "caught up" to 25 January. At the end of her life, she confused the two of them. And she had been born on the night between 13 and 14 January 1892, a little before midnight: the thirteenth for her birth certificate, while her mother (my grandmother) was dancing at the ball in honor of Saint Tatiana, the patron saint of Moscow. And my first granddaughter was born within a few hours of the same date, a little after midnight on the night between 14 and 15 January – the fifteenth for her birth certificate. Her name is Aude Isabelle. My daughter did not know the story of the corrected calendar.

Noelle: conflict of habit and food identity

Marital and family conflicts are not always related to intercultural, inter-ethnic or interracial marriages. They can also be connected to differences of social class (related to social class neurosis), differences of political or religious opinions, or simply to customs and everyday life. "Early risers" and "night owls" have problems together; there are conflicts between those who sleep with the window open and those who sleep with the window closed; between those who like to spend and those who are frugal; between athletes and more sedentary types; classical music lover versus rock music lover; even Bach versus Wagner, or opera versus operetta, etc.

Many conflicts are linked to money, to budget and an economic unconscious: who spends and on what, who saves, how the budget is decided upon and who manages it, how things are shared, common accounts and separate accounts. One can use a genosociogram along with role playing to clarify such problems and resolve them.

In this category of ordinary, everyday conflicts, let us look at the example of food-related conflicts, often related to "food identity."

Noelle was a young medical student, French, raised in North African and Spanish ways by her grandmother (cooking with oil) and with roots in the French Alps through her paternal great-grandfather (cooking with butter). She lived with her husband and son in the south of France. She came from a simple family: her father was a professor of mathematics in Algeria and the family had to leave their country in 1962, at the time of the declaration of independence. They moved to the south of France in 1968. As she said, they "either packed their bags or it was the coffin."

Her husband, a doctor, came from the same circle.

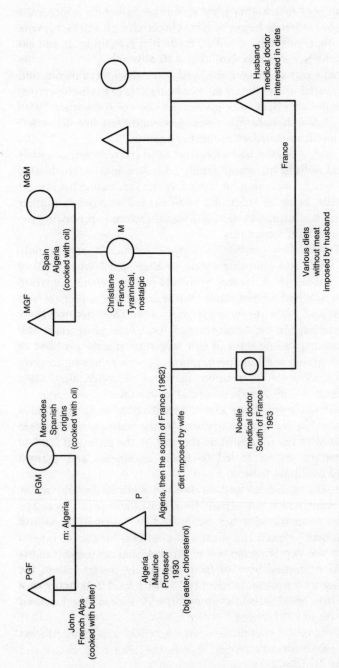

Figure 12.2 Simplified genosociogram of food conflicts

In her family of origin, they liked to eat: her father ate a lot, and a lot of meat, but when he began to have cholesterol problems, his wife (Noelle's mother) put him on a diet, made him give up meat and eat boiled vegetables, sometimes sprinkled with olive oil.

When Noelle was a teenager, she lived in the shackles of dieting and continued to suffer all her life from "not being able to eat like everyone else." Her only escape was to be invited over by her godmother, "who ate normally." She thought that marriage would "free her stomach," and studied medicine in order "to cure her parents."

Her husband, a doctor, had successive food conversions, or rather passions, and obliged his whole family to follow him in his dieting; he was very strict concerning his son's food intake, basing his diet on rice and lentils, being as strict and diet-oriented as Noelle's mother was regarding her husband's diet. She was therefore experiencing the same stress and food constraints.

Her husband's first passion was for "instinctotherapy": only eating raw food, and choosing foods by their smell when you sit down at the table, which creates problems for the person preparing the food, for she had to buy more than was necessary, prepare and present it all and often throw away part of it. Then he took on a conviction and passion for "macrobiotic" food, eating essentially rice and grain sprouts, and no meat or fish, which creates the problem of sprouting the grains and long preparation, as well as having to shop in specialty stores, not to mention questions of conviviality when family or friends – with so-called normal food habits – come over.

Noelle suffered from this social differentiation, which created a social distance. She was also disoriented by the tastes, smells, texture and appearance of the food, just as she was by the style and kind of store she had to go to. It led to many arguments and marital conflicts, and continual tension.

But more serious, hidden and insidious was her husband's violent rejection of meat which cut her off from her family roots, from her food identity, from the idea her father had of "normal" food and what "a real man" should eat: meat and potatoes, for the most part. Her husband was depriving her son of this essential component of his family tradition, cutting him off from his family, his traditions, his "food identity and masculine identity." These food rejections even cut him off from the husband's family, who considered the husband to be a little bit of a "crackpot."

In Noelle's family, it was the woman who chose and imposed food identity; in her husband's family, it was the man who chose and imposed food identity.

13 Conclusion: the human canopy

Considering the current state of scientific knowledge and research, the genosociogram and transgenerational approach can only lead to clinical work that aims at repairing family repetitions in order to bring them to an end where necessary and at repairing the damage done by the unspoken in order to transcend it. This work allows the subject to ask vital questions.

Yet it is obvious that identity is forged from the history belonging to individuals – their family history as well as their individual history, both connected to their historical context. And it is better to be aware of it rather than submit to it passively.

Genealogy is fashionable at this end of the century. We live in a period of radical transformations of our milieu and our way of thinking, the framework of our lives and its context. It is, as Alvin Toffler said, a stress, a kind of "future shock," which many people experience with anxiety. So much is unknown, including whether our culture will survive, and even our planet.

All trainers, therapists and even medical doctors, whatever school they belong to, find themselves confronted by "difficult cases" that classical theories cannot explain. They encounter a "rooting" of the person in their own history, often a secret history, which emerges at specific moments, moments of "flashes," whether it be on the level or words or a manifestation of the "thing" in the body, or even through illness, accident or death.

The therapist's role is to accompany clients by helping them to rediscover their "history" through speaking it, to be able to represent it to themselves in a coherent manner, to be able to see the thread and the meaning. And, when it is a question of a difficult personal history, the stakes include helping clients finally leave the chaos, the unthinkable, the unspeakable, the unspoken – and the repetition – and fully accept and shoulder their family history and their past. One cannot "get a new start" and "turn the page" until the page itself is uncovered and the slate erased, or just about to be erased, or "assimilated." This is the price a man or woman must pay in order to create and invent his or her life.

In the spring of 1963 or 1964, without much thought, I went alone into the Amazon forest in my role as ethnologist. I joined a group of tiger hunters and gold diggers. A small plane piloted by "air cowboys" was to fly us to a place unknown at the time: the Canaima lagoon, on a loop of the Orinoco and the Rio Carrao. Finding our way thanks to the wreckage of lost planes, we landed in a clearing called "Angel's Jump," camped near the huge, 3,000-foot Salto del Angel waterfalls, and slept in hammocks attached to the trees.

I will never forget my awakening in the early morning. It was a miracle of serendipity: it was like the three princes of Serendip who, helped by "good luck", happily discovered what they were not looking for and what they needed or wanted. Serendipity is an expression used by Horace Walpole (1717–97) in a novel based on a tale recounted by a sixteenth-century Venetian writer named Michele Tramezzino, telling the story of the three princes of Serendip who had the faculty of making unanticipated and exciting discoveries by chance. The research psychologist W. B. Cannon used the term in 1945 in reference to scientific discoveries that occur by accident. The term is used by existential psychologists. The Greeks already used the root, "tychè," meaning chance or fortune, in the word meaning "reach a goal," "eutychia."

That morning in the Amazon, below my hammock, I saw an unexpected sight: indigenous people had come out of the forest and were playing with my things, imitating me, trying anti-mosquito spray, my comb, perfume, soap and clothes, without fully understanding their meaning or use. Later, I came down from the hammock and we got to know each other and they invited me to their village, making for one of the most unforgettable encounters of my lifetime.

And up above, high above, existed life even more mysterious and totally unknown, the life in the high branches of the thousand-year-old trees, with a whole world of unknown flora and fauna.

Since that time, explorers, botanists, biologists, zoologists and ethologists have been studying what they call the canopy, the tree tops of the tropical rain forest, using for their research tree top rafts, which they reach by smaller skiffs. The canopy was discovered by certain researchers after the Second World War, at the end of the 1940s, and the most important research was accomplished in the Amazon, in Guyana and Cameroon around 1986 and 1989.

They thus discovered unknown interlacing and links, a whole world of life between the skies and the earth in this interface between the forest and the atmosphere, 100–130 feet above the ground, with vegetation and small animals that live nowhere else.

The canopy makes up a leafy screen for the organisms living at lower levels (on the ground) and could be the solar energy generator which allows for the growth and functioning of the entire forest.

These researchers, ethologists in the large sense of the word, use the canopy to study the origins of life and of humankind, and propose theories concerning the future of our planet.

It seems to me that in the same way, exploring the summits of our family tree and our psychogenealogy, understanding its various interfaces and interlacing, we could unravel the leading thread of our family and personal life, our genosociogram, and understand it. It is a perspective of the "human canopy."

Let us go back to Freud. In *The Interpretation of Dreams*, he speaks of ghosts, "revenants": "I had insisted on their names being chosen, not according to the fashion of the moment, but in memory of people I had been fond of. Their names made the children into revenants."[1]

Remember the psychoanalytical roots of this work, in the lineage of Freud and Sandor Ferenczi. "Family repetitions" – both tragic and happy – had been noted, along with synchronicity of age and date, and anniversary syndromes.

Around thirty years ago, Ivan Boszormenyi-Nagy found "invisible" links and "invisible (family) loyalties" (1973) which bind individuals to their families with a touch of morality, involving justice and balancing family accounts.

Nicolas Abraham and Maria Torok (1975) found themselves confronted by something resembling buried "ghosts" or "phantoms" that from time to time leave the secret family "crypts" and sometimes could haunt the body or mind, not unlike in tales of haunted houses in Scotland or certain Agatha Christie stories.

But how is it possible? Could it be a kind of engram – a hypothetical change in neural tissue postulated in order to account for persistence of memory – that is more psychological than physiological?

If we simplify, we could say that at birth – or even already *in utero* – the child, the person, receives a certain number of messages: one gives him a family name and a first name, a role expectation he will have to fulfill or avoid. It could be positive and/or negative. One projects on to him, for example, that he is "the spitting image of great-uncle Jules" and thinks he will then become an explorer or an adventure-seeker like uncle Jules, and one turns him into a scapegoat or makes him don the clothes of someone deceased he will replace. Like the fairy tale of Sleeping Beauty, one says and foresees things, injunctions, scripts, a future – things said or left unsaid – in a weighty and secret unspoken language: this is what "programs" the child.

Then, the family, those surrounding the child, will ingrain – or engram – this program into the child's mind, a program which includes life and death, marriage or celibacy, profession or vocation. Thus, the future will be entirely based on the full configuration of the family context – both said and unsaid.

But we do not know. Every individual elaborates his or her own system of thought and chooses the school of thought to which he or she adheres.

Among the information we know with certainty, the studies done by Josephne Hilgard reveal that the anniversary syndrome occurs in a statistically significant number of cases. There have been clinical observations of significant synchronicity of birth and death dates in numerous families, incontestable family repetitions.

One thing appears to be more than probable: we are in the domain of *origins*, which, in psychoanalytical terms, would include a kind of founding lapse of memory.

To be more explicit, let us refer to a case cited by the psychoanalyst Sylvana Olindo-Weber, whose research concentrated on somatization, on "the role the unconscious plays on the body."[2] The case relates the story of a woman whose fourth child, a boy, woke up screaming night after night. And then, during this woman's therapy, she remembered that at the age of two, her little brother died one night from "cot death." Two other brothers suffered this same tragic end.

The very same night, after telling her analyst about the memory of these deaths, her child started sleeping calmly. Very similar situations were described in the numerous case studies mentioned by Françoise Dolto in her seminars on her manner of working with babies and children.

Everything that happens in transgenerational therapy is, in my opinion, of the same nature.

Freud, by the way, intuited the importance of transgenerational transmission in *Totem and Taboo*:

> Unless psychical processes were continued from one generation to another, if each generation were obliged to acquire its attitude

to life anew, there would be no progress in this field and next to no development....and what are the ways and means employed by one generation in order to hand on its mental states to the next one? I shall not pretend that these problems are sufficiently explained or that direct communication and tradition – which are the first things that occur to one – are enough to account for the process....Even the most ruthless suppression must leave room for distorted surrogate impulses and for reactions resulting from them.[3]

Without wanting to compare what cannot be compared, for the time being, transmission remains in the domain of the unknown, offering nothing but open-ended questions. Nevertheless, we hope that soon progress in interdisciplinary research that covers at once social sciences, biology, quantum physics, animal and human ethology, along with the study and discovery of new neurotransmitters will allow us to better outline how these transmissions are passed down and communicated between individuals and generations, what Moreno intuited and termed "tele."

Karl Pribram demonstrated that the brain operates like a hologram. The work of Ilia Prigogine, David Bohm, Fritjof Capra on time and the body – space-time – demonstrate that everything is interconnected.

Animal ethology from Darwin to Hinde and Sheldrake has also raised the question of transmission. Rupert Sheldrake[4] explored transmission from the perspective of a sort of "engrammation" in the way that the British bluetits transmitted from generation to generation how to open delivered milk bottles, because it seemed as though they did not have to learn it.

The question of transmission, of origin and of memory lapses perplexed not only Freud[5] and more recently René Kaës.[6] This problem was already raised by Plato in the myth of Er the Pamphylien:[7] Plato describes how souls lose their memory of everything and forget what they had seen before being born. We could say that this forgetting of a former knowledge is what allows us to live here and now, by creating a possible personal future, and thus, in a certain way, delivering us from the weight of the past. If I understand Plato correctly, the Plain of Lethe would refer to a return to the generation.

Over the past several years, psychoanalysts both in the United States – notably Martin Bergmann and Hilton Jacoby who have worked since 1982 on the generation of children of the Holocaust –

and in France – in particular Françoise Dolto, Nicolas Abraham and Maria Torok, and also Didier Dumas and Serge Tisseron – have suggested the hypothesis of a "preservative repression" where what matters is the preservation of a shut-up or excluded reality. For the children who carry the unmentioned and therefore "encrypted" secret, a chain connecting one generation to the next around an unspoken event becomes a suffering they can represent but not speak (mentioning it is forbidden), and which becomes registered, or encrypted, in the unconscious like an internal structure. At the third generation, the unspoken secret, the unspeakable, becomes unthinkable, because it can no longer be represented (a genealogical inconceivable event); it becomes a "ghost" that haunts a person who shows unexplainable symptoms, hinting at a secret a parent unknowingly projected on to him.

In transactional analysis, the psychoanalyst Fanita English goes as far as saying that one passes a "hot potato" from one generation to another to be rid of it, like in a closed system.

For her, in cases of serious difficulties with the parents, a young child builds an "episcript": a story, a secret intrigue based on a magical belief that he himself will avoid a harmful destiny if he manages to transmit it to a sacrificial victim or scapegoat.[8] In "passing on the problem to another" the person gets rid of his own "destructive script."

Montaigne, having lost his friend La Boétie at the age of thirty, spent his life as if haunted by him, trying to make him live again by publishing his writings and speaking about him and about his affection and friendship for La Boétie in his *Essays* (1580–2). Montaigne describes this possession of the soul:

> In the friendship I speak of, our souls mingle and blend with each other so completely that they efface the seam that joined them, and cannot find it again. If you press me to tell why I loved him, I feel that this cannot be expressed, except by answering: Because it was he, because it was I.[9]

La Boétie, in Sainte-Beuve, describes: "Certain souls, once united, nothing can separate them. What united me to you, Oh Montaigne, forever, and whatever may happen, is the force of nature, it is the most pleasant attraction of love, virtue."[10]

For Montaigne, this life-long haunting was conscious. He kept La Boétie alive in his *Essays* and he passed his memory down to us. As a matter of fact, he speaks of a "quintessence of all this blending," which makes it such that we cannot distinguish the thoughts of one from the thoughts of another.

The work of the ghost or phantom in the unconscious described by Nicolas Abraham and Maria Torok is a haunting of this kind, but an unconscious one.

These hypotheses fit into the field of psychoanalytical research, operating with analytical concepts such as projection, incorporation, repression and separation.

But let us not forget that Freud also thought in terms of phylogenetic inheritance as a "biologist of the mind."[11] Freud specifies in *The History of an Infantile Neurosis*: "The first relates to the phylogenetically inherited schemata....I am inclined to take the view that they are precipitates from the history of human civilization,"[12] although this hypothesis has been contested by certain people as a fanciful extrapolation.

We find insight into this phenomenon mentioned in 1991–2 in the periodical *Somatothérapie* by rebirth researchers who observed that already *in utero*, as early as the seventh month of pregnancy, the child begins to dream, and the mother could be transmitting her dreams to her child: if he has the same dreams, he could have access to her unconscious.

This insight joins those of Françoise Dolto, according to whom a mother's and a child's unconscious are linked and the child knows, guesses and feels family events over two or three generations.[13]

In a certain way, these theories join our clinical experience in which reliving birth through psychodrama, an adult takes on the attitudes, lip movements and the voice of a baby (striking in an adult man who takes on a child's unbroken voice) and rediscovers important facts and traumas about their birth or the period prior to birth. In some cases, these discoveries are later verified as true.

Nicolas Abraham and Maria Torok wrote that "The phantom is a formation of the unconscious that has never been conscious – for good reason. It passes – in a way yet to be determined – from the parent's unconscious to the child's."[14]

Socrates already said that he went his way, as he wished, except if the little voice of his "Daimon" – his "inner guide," his "good spirit" or familiar – stopped him and made him go back, according to Plato's *Apology*:

> The reason is a thing you have heard me mention many times in many places, that something divine and godlike comes to me.... I have had it from childhood. It comes as a kind of voice, and

when it comes, it always turns me away from what I am about to do, but never towards it.... My accustomed oracle, which is divine, always came frequently before in everything, opposing me even in trivial matters if I was about to err...[15]

But we do not always have the wisdom or patience to take the time to listen to our inner voice.

It seems to me that, considering the current state of knowledge, it is up to clinicians to try to observe and relate these, to say the least, strange phenomena of transmission from unconscious to unconscious, to accumulate facts and clinical descriptions and publish them, to carry out both clinical and statistical studies (as did Josephine Hilgard for the anniversary syndrome), and then, perhaps soon, an understanding of these "ghosts" of the unconscious, of these repetitions, of the anniversaries, will be added to the knowledge we have of these beings of interaction, intuition and language that we are.

The dead pass down to the living.

Postscript: forms of the unconscious

At the turn of the century, Freud described the individual "unconscious," then Jung defined the "collective unconscious." In the 1940s, J. L. Moreno spoke about the "co-unconscious" and the "family or group co-unconscious" partially shared by members of a given group and stemming from their living together as a group.

As early as 1930, Eric Fromm speaks about a "social unconscious" based on the classical sociological works of Emile Durkheim, Max Weber, Karl Marx and Robert Merton. In 1937, Karen Horney applies the sociological and anthropological concept of "social unconscious" to clinical psychotherapy and D. W. Winnicott seems to have been influenced by this concept when he spoke about "environmental mother"(1965). This idea can be found among many English authors, such as Jane Austen (1811).

A similar concept appears among new Jungian therapists in the "shared unconscious" (Zinkin, 1979), Ethel Spector-Person's "cultural unconscious" (1992) and in the work of Otto Kernberg (1993), Earl Hopper (1996) and René Kaës. Ada Abraham speaks of a "co-self" in referring to the mother–child unit prior to and shortly after birth.

Appendix 1

Definition of the crypt and the phantom according to Nicolas Abraham and Maria Torok

In certain cases such as when there are secrets, everything occurs as if someone who died in dramatic, shameful or unjust circumstances could not move on and remained attached to the family in the form of a ghost or a revenant, hidden or poorly buried in a crypt in the heart of a descendant. This phantom expresses itself from time to time like a ventriloquist and sometimes appears in the form of symptoms – repetitive – which are passed down from a parent's unconscious to a child's unconscious.

> For a crypt to establish itself, the shameful secret must have resulted from an object playing the role of Ego Ideal. It is a question of keeping the secret, of covering up the shame.[1]

The authors define the place held by the tomb in the mental apparatus:

> The crypt marks a definite place in the topography. It is neither the dynamic unconscious nor the ego of introjections. Rather, it is an enclave between the two, a kind of artificial unconscious, lodged in the very midst of the ego....Nothing at all must filter to the outside world. The ego is given the task of a cemetery guard.[2]

According to Abraham and Torok, the building of the crypt stems from a preservative repression as opposed to a constitutive repression (generally termed dynamic repression), which is particularly apparent in hysteria. They define the major difference between these two forms of repression as follows: in hysteria, prohibition gives rise to the desire that seeks a form of expression and finds it in symbolic fulfillment (hysterical conversion); while, on the other hand, ...for

the cryptophore, an already filled desire lies buried – equally inca-
pable of rising or of disintegrating....This past is present in the
subject as a block of reality; it is referred to as such in denials and
disavowals.[3]

To summarize, the crypt would be an inclusion within the ego
itself, the effect of which is a preservative repression. Using the same
vocabulary as the authors, we could say a crypt is a kind of artificial
unconscious lodged within the ego which results in the loss of an
indispensable narcissistic object when this loss cannot even be
acknowledged due to a secret shared between the crypt-carrier (or
cryptophore) and the lost object. The contents of the secret are
considered an unmentionable "crime" stained with shame, which
constitutes the Reality (in the metapsychological sense of the word)
of the crypt-carrying subject.

The phantom's work in the unconscious

> The phantom is a formation of the unconscious that has never
> been conscious – for good reason. It passes – in a way yet to be
> determined – from the parent's unconscious to the child's.[4]

> The phantom is what works in the unconscious from an
> unspeakably shameful secret belonging to another – incest,
> crime, illegitimacy, etc.[5]

> The phantom which returns to haunt bears witness to the exis-
> tence of the dead buried within the other.[6]

> It has no energy of its own.... It pursues its work of unbinding in
> silence. We can add that it is helped by eclipsed words, all invis-
> ible goblins which apply themselves to breaking down the
> coherence of links in the unconscious.[7]

> It is crucial to emphasize that the words giving sustenance to the
> phantom return to haunt from the unconscious. These are often
> the very words that rule an entire family's history and function as
> tokens of pitiable articulations.[8]

> ...They point to a gap, they refer to the unspeakable....The pres-
> ence of the phantom indicates the effects, on the descendants, of

something that had inflicted narcissistic injury or even catastrophe on the parents.[9]

Its manifestation, the haunting, is the phantom's return in the form of bizarre words and actions, in the symptoms...[10]

The phantom's periodic and compulsive return...works like a ventriloquist, like a stranger within the subject's own mental topography.[11]

As a result "haunted" individuals are caught in two inclinations. They must at all costs maintain their ignorance of a loved one's secret; hence the semblance of unawareness (nescience) concerning it. At the same time they must eliminate the state of secrecy; hence the reconstruction of the secret in the form of unconscious knowledge. This twofold movement is manifest in symptoms and gives rise to "gratuitous" or uncalled for acts and words, creating eerie effects: hallucinations and delirium, showing and hiding that which, in the depths of the unconscious, dwells as the living-dead knowledge of someone else's secret.[12]

Dual unity and haunting

Nicolas Abraham and Maria Torok consider that the introduction of dual unity, a genealogical concept par excellence, provides the only tool allowing one to apprehend the phantom and its manifestation, the haunting, as metapsychological facts.

The concept of unity has a fundamental dual nature: the original dual unity is the mother–child relation (or parent–child).

Dual unity is the separated non-separated, or the separation included in the non-separated. The non-separated, the individual, comes to be by the separation that occurs inside.[13]

The concrete nature of this separation is the phylogenetic event of the separation from the mother. As a result:

The disjunction of the *paido-meter* carries in the two partners only the wound of a single lack, that of the mother. In fact, here is the paradox: if the child misses the mother, in turn it is the mother who will again miss her own mother.[14]

As one matures: the mother–child dual unity transforms into an internal dualist union between the unconscious and the ego.[15]

Appendix 2
Josephine Hilgard's (1952–89) statistical research on anniversary syndrome[1]

In a short article published in 1953, Josephine Hilgard describes a few clinical cases of "anniversary reactions" in parents, reactions "precipitated," in the chemical sense of the word, or reactivated by their children being the same age they were when their own parents died or had been interned. Below are two of the cases in question:

> Mary Bancroft, the mother of a six-year-old daughter, Jenny, developed pneumonia, pleurisy, and a psychosis. When she was a child of six, her own father had died of pneumonia and pleurisy, with a terminal meningitis. The possible anniversary nature of Mrs. Bancroft's illness is indicated by the fact that the acute symptoms appeared when her daughter reached the age she had been at the time of her father's death, and by the fact that her pneumonia and pleurisy mirrored the symptoms of her father in his final illness. The psychotic symptoms appeared while she was still in the hospital for pneumonia. The patient announced one morning that she had had a talk with God, and that she was divine and could not be harmed by mortals. She became combative and disorderly, and assumed bizarre postures. She showed a flight of ideas and sang, whistled, and shouted.[2]
>
> The patient's psychosis had continued for a year before I saw her. During this time she had been hospitalized with three courses of electric shock treatment. These resulted twice in temporary mild improvement.[3]

> Early in the course of psychotherapy, Mrs. Bancroft commonly related her daughter's experiences to her own experiences as a child: how Jenny saw her taken away on a stretcher, and how she herself had seen her father taken away on a stretcher; how her mother had rejected her, and how she was now rejecting Jenny

through her absence. Mrs. Bancroft found that she was doing many things that her own mother had done, things that were unlike her usual self. When her present illness was treated as a re-enactment of something she was unable to handle as a child, there were noticeable therapeutic gains. Within two months she had left the sanitarium. She became friendly and more decisive. She is again living with her husband, although they have not yet brought their daughter back to live with them.[4]

James Carson, 34 years old, who was hospitalized on the basis of his complaint that he had had headaches for four years.... Immediately before entry he had attempted suicide by taking 50 phenobarbitol tablets. The acute symptoms had begun when his son was four years old, the age he had been when his own father died suddenly of influenza.[5]

...one finds a startling change of employment for the patient the same year that the son was born. The patient shifted from department store work, in which he had been employed for more than ten years, to become a "criminologist" on a private policing job....When his son was four years old, at the time his severe headaches began, he obtained employment as a special policeman with the railroad for which his father had worked, though he had said earlier that he would never work for the railroad. At this possible anniversary, do we see an unconscious identification with his father?[6]

At the time I first reviewed the case...the situation was considered hopeless. He was subject to delusions and hallucinations, and was on the maximum security ward as both homicidal and suicidal. However, once the working hypothesis of the anniversary nature of the illness was adopted, there were gradual therapeutic gains.... Statements similar to the following were brought out spontaneously and with much feeling: "If my father had lived, I wouldn't be in this spot....Damn it, if my father hadn't died I wouldn't be in this mess....You know it just came to me he had a boy and a girl and I have a boy and a girl.... Somehow I had the feeling that he was me and I was my father."[7]

In the course of therapy, the incorporative aspects of identification with the dead father were manifested symbolically; for instance, in talking about his stomach symptoms he said that he felt bloated and as though there was something inside him like a corpse.[8]

Several years later, in 1989, Hilgard writes with regards to these two cases:

> Before the central theme [anniversary reaction] was discovered, these were among the most baffling of cases. The symptoms seemed to appear with no discernible precipitating cause. After the focal episodes were understood, the rest of the material began to fit into place. One reason that cases such as these often go unrecognized is that the central figure – a young child, with relatively few signs of involvement – provides the clue to the parent's disturbance.[9]

In order to test the anniversary syndrome hypothesis, Josephine Hilgard undertook two systematic studies of admissions to a California hospital for her PhD dissertation in psychology with the support of grants from the National Institute of Mental Health. The studies screened 8,680 patients who were admitted to Agnews State Hospital.

Her team examined the files and case histories of all the admissions to the hospital for nine-month periods during each of the years from 1954 through 1957. They eliminated the cases of patients older than fifty or those diagnosed with alcoholism, an organic disease or psychopathic personalities. The pool was reduced to 2,402 native-born, white patients of which three-fifths were diagnosed as schizophrenic, one-fifth as manic depressive and one-fifth as "psychoneurotic." Among these patients, she further reduced the study to those who were first admitted after marriage and parenthood, and who had lost a parent by death between the ages of two and sixteen, on the condition that the date of the loss of the parent could be firmly established through the interviews, written documents and verification of the hospital records.

Of the 8,680 admissions, reduced to 2,402 by age and parental situation requirements, and further reduced by stricter criteria, only 193 patients remained in the experimental sample, or 8 per cent of the psychotic-neurotic population of 2,402: 40 men and 153 women (49 per cent Protestant, 34 per cent Catholic, 1 per cent Jewish).

> Among the female patients, age coincidences appeared in 14 of 65 women whose mothers had died, but in only 9 of 82 women whose fathers had died. Both groups were large enough to permit statistical study....For each patient two ages were recorded. The first one was the age at first admission to the

hospital and the second one was a hypothetical anniversary age, i.e. the age the patient had to have been at admission *if* her oldest child was to be her age at parent loss. The problem for the statisticians was to determine whether the correspondence between these two ages occurred beyond the frequency expected by chance.[10]

For women who lost mothers, however, there was a significantly greater occurrence of age-coincidences than would be expected by chance, the appropriate test yielding a p-value of .032 (two-sided test). Thus a non-random factor in agreement with the anniversary hypothesis was demonstrated.[11]

Unfortunately, the number of men found using these criteria was too small for a statistical analysis, although it was nevertheless sufficient to indicate a similar tendency among men who had lost their father, although it was not significant for the loss of a parent of the other sex.

We could speculate about this difference between men and women. Hilgard examined an additional group of 930 patients hospitalized for alcoholism, among whom 679 were men.

Based on the hypothesis of a possible "choice" made by the men between psychosis and other pathological problems and the study of coincidences in age and loss in adult male alcoholism, Josephine Hilgard suggests that "A man's role presents alternatives that permit him more flexibility in meeting conflictual feelings brought out by a new baby in the home. Alcoholism is one of these."[12]

One of the important aspects of this study is the discovery of the anniversary syndrome, and the double anniversary – or successive anniversary – which occurs in the case of a mother having two children and who experiences an onset of depression with psychotic periods when each of the children reaches the age she was at her own mother's death. Hilgard provides the case of Martha Newell who was hospitalized when each of her children reached the age of thirteen. Her own mother had died when she was thirteen.

Again, the psychotic onset with hospitalization (internment) is statistically significant (.03) in cases involving a daughter in relation to the loss of her mother (by death or psychosis), and only probable in cases involving the loss of the father, thus happening more frequently and in a significant manner for the loss of a parent of the same sex as the subject. For Hilgard, the fact that there are fewer cases of psychosis in men can be explained by the fact that men have more flexibility in their roles and more role choices than women in society and in life, and more men choose when in difficulty to take refuge "in the bottle," that is, in alcoholism.

Hilgard and Newman provide other case studies in their articles published in 1959 and 1961.

The studies concerning the loss of the mother through psychosis and hospitalization demonstrated the same anniversary phenomenon when the daughter reached the age at which the mother was hospitalized, the daughter experiencing a psychotic episode with hospitalization:

> A detailed account of treatment illustrated clearly the persistence into adult life of a core of confused and unintegrated identifications.... It was only when circumstances of the early trauma were repeated – now she was the mother instead of the child – that the trauma, encapsulated since childhood, was triggered.[13]

When parent loss occurs at a certain age, and when the subject reaches that "critical age," there is a strong probability of the development of a crisis with a psychotic episode at the anniversary age or on the anniversary date, as we see in the double anniversary, each time one of the children reaches the age the subject was at the time of the loss of the parent of the same sex.

This occurs more frequently when the child and the parent have the same position among the siblings and when in some way the family or the person herself foresees this development: it is the "saga of psychosis," similar to what Robert Rosenthal calls "self-fulfilling prophecy" and the "family deck of resemblances" and identifications.

However, many people do not become psychotic or neurotic after losing a parent during their childhood. It is therefore important to understand why the problem arises and determine in what circumstances the death of a parent (father or mother) during childhood can create this increased vulnerability during the anniversary period.

Another study done by Josephine Hilgard covered a community sample of 2,000 homes of people between the ages of nineteen and forty-nine from the normal population in the metropolitan area. This so-called normal population showed fewer incidences of anniversary syndrome than the studied hospital population.

What is the difference between these two populations?

Factors that Protected Those in the Community Sample from Serious Psychological Damage. A stable marriage of the parents prior to a death of one of them augured well for the next generation. Many of the surviving parents under these circumstances were strong enough to keep the family together after the loss.... Within a home feelings of grief and mourning had been acknowledged, shared, and adaptive steps to compensate for the loss had been taken. If networks of family and/or community resources were available, these had provided additional support for the bereaved parent as needed.[14]

Coincidences between patient's age at parent loss and age of oldest child at first admission of patient to a mental hospital: women who lost mothers between the ages of 2–15

	Father loss	Mother loss
Sample size	82	65
Obtained coincidences	9	14
Expected coincidences	10.56	7.98
Standard error	2.99	2.57
Normal deviate*	-.35	2.143
Probability (2-sided)*	NS	.032

* Corrected for continuity

Source: Lincoln E. Moses

Many people experience anxiety when nearing or reaching the age or period marking a major loss, a phenomenon Hilgard referred to as the "mild anniversaries." Hilgard observed that once the year of vulnerability had passed, the people (ex-children become adults) who are the age of the dead or hospitalized parent "manage" better. Some even marry afterwards. In passing, she noted that with the death of a parent, the functioning of a household becomes more difficult and the child must fend for himself and confront more difficulties and the trauma can remain fixed or implanted in the unconscious. It marks a return of the repressed.

For Josephine Hilgard, the psychotherapist's role is to provide support by bringing these events to light at difficult times or during anniversary periods, by integrating past and present, in order better to heal a painful memory. This "support" is very close to what British psychoanalysts call "holding" and "containing."

What was new was the recognition of the specific syndrome created when contextual coincidences resulted in the reinstatement and reliving of early traumas which could lead to severe mental illness.[15]

Appendix 3
On the souls of women

During the sixteenth century, women were turned into diabolical creatures. This has been wrongly attributed to the 325 Council of Nicaea in which mention was made of women's souls being like the souls of animals and flowers.

According to Latin specialists, this was due to an error in translation (later corrected by the Council of Macon in 538) and to a lack of knowledge of Latin. Nevertheless this error and the subsequent prejudices die hard, as we witnessed when the press took them up again in December 1993.

Appendix 4
An example of substitution incest from the literary world

In Rouen, France, during the nineteenth century, the Le Poitevin and the Flaubert families were close friends. The young Mr Le Poitevin married the young Mrs Flaubert's best friend and each became the godparent of the other's son: the surgeon Achille Flaubert (1784–1846) became the godfather of Alfred Le Poitevin (1817–49) and five years later Paul-François Le Poitevin became the godfather of Gustave Flaubert (1821–80). Their children, Alfred Le Poitevin, his sister Laure and Gustave Flaubert developed a close friendship, and the young men decided never to separate and to travel in the Orient together; Laure was their confidante. For various reasons, in 1846 (the year his father died), twenty-nine-year-old Alfred married the sister of another Gustave: Louise de Maupassant. His heartfelt friend Gustave Flaubert almost died of sorrow. Laure Le Poitevin married that other Gustave, her new brother-in-law, Gustave de Maupassant. Alfred died suddenly two years later, in 1849.

One year after Alfred Le Poitevin's unexpected death, his friend Gustave Flaubert, thirty-two at the time, embarked for Egypt on 4 November 1850 with a friend (a substitute?), Maxime du Camp, and at the same time Laure conceived Guy de Maupassant (1850–93) with her husband Gustave. Shortly thereafter, Laure left her husband and raised her son alone.[1]

We can speculate a genealogical incest in this case, or rather, a substitution incest in this double marriage of a brother and a sister, followed by a symbolic conception at a specific moment, an important moment for this brother and sister, and even three-way substitution relations: Alfred who tenderly loves his sister Laure and his friend Gustave, marries the sister of another Gustave, and his sister marries the brother-in-law, and then she conceives a child just when her friend Gustave leaves for Egypt with another friend (a trip substituting for the foreseen trip between Alfred and Gustave?).

Laure de Maupassant-Le Poitevin asked the heartfelt friend of her tenderly loved and deceased brother, Gustave Flaubert, to become "like a father" to her son, which is what Flaubert did. Gustave Flaubert became a well-known author, taught all he knew to Guy de Maupassant and in 1873 introduced the twenty-three-year-old young man to the Parisian literary and mundane world, introducing him to Zola, and having him participate in Parisian literary salons.

In January 1880, at the age of 30, Guy de Maupassant published *Boule de suif*. Flaubert congratulated him in writing, telling him it was a masterpiece and even wrote: "my dear son." Shortly thereafter, Flaubert died suddenly from a stroke at the age of fifty-nine, having, if you will, perfectly fulfilled his work and his mission as a substitute father.

Let us not go too deeply into Flaubert's intimate life, into his confidences: "Mme Bovary is I," or into his losses and regrets. Let us simply take note.

Guy de Maupassant had a series of health accidents, a life that was both joyful, famous and difficult: he learned and inherited a love of life from his uncle Alfred and his friend Gustave Flaubert and tasted, as they did, the pleasures of the flesh. In turn, he paid a high price for his lucidity and his life: he was interned in a psychiatric hospital, probably the aftermath of syphilis, poorly treated at the time, and died young at the age of forty-three, from a venereal disease.

Appendix 5
"I remember": stigmata of family memories and unfinished grieving

The Canadian national motto, "I remember," could be symbolic of the unfinished mourning that we find like stigmata when we examine accidents that repeat from generation to generation, or unnoticed illnesses of a psychological-psychosomatic nature, or families with secrets concerning death, or nightmares in descendants of families traumatized by a horrible or uncertain destiny or death without a burial site (at sea, on the battle field, in concentration camps, by kidnapping or fleeing, the unknown outcome of missing persons), whose family continues to hope for a return, having not seen the body. The scream-sound of London Roy Hart Theater (from the cries of soldiers dying on battlefield transformed by Wolfsohn into a kind of therapy), "primal scream" (named by Janov), psychodrama or other forms of emotional therapy can perhaps be applied to these cases, like the groaning of repetitive nightmares of certain descendants of people missing or traumatized by war.

Appendix 6
Trauma of the "wind of the cannonball"

With the commemoration of the end of the Second World War (1944), the fiftieth anniversary of the Normandy landing (6 June 1944), of the Liberation of France (Paris, 25 August 1944), the liberation of the concentration camps and peace (1945), we saw expressions of a renewed anxiety and terrifying nightmares with vivid images ("as if I were there now") appear among descendants of survivors of those gassed at Ypres during the First World War (1915), at Verdun (1916), descendants of concentration camp prisoners, and even of victims of the Sedan massacre on 2 September 1870 (125 years later), or the French Revolution of 1789 – with various manifestations such as coughing, asthma-like symptoms, "fatal cold", similar to "anxiety of near-death," a brush with the wings of death, the "deadly wind of the cannonball" which killed a brother in arms.

Brought up to date, replaced in the historical and family context, expelled and then "contained" by the attentive listening, the "holding" of a therapist who understands the context, these manifestations diminish and/or cease in adults and even in the children (the fourth generation after Verdun).

We explain these phenomena as the involuntary and unconscious legacy of traumatic, "horrible" events. These events were too terrible to speak – too terrible or terrifying to be mentioned, like Hiroshima or Verdun, the Armenian massacres or torture. These unspoken traumas, "shattering" events, were left unelaborated by words, unassimilated, and then became "unthinkable". Yet, they manifest in a psychosomatic manner, through "memories of traumas one did not experience," traumas that nevertheless filtered through, oozing from generation to generation, and which we can overcome through expressing them (psychotherapy, dreams, drawings, even chants and "lamentations") and by framing them in a transgenerational manner.

For example, at the time of the fiftieth commemoration of the

Normandy landing, Barbara had nightmares in August and the beginning of September 1994 in which she "saw" vague forms that tumbled down onto her. She described and drew images like men on horseback "with a kind of round pot on the head, with a pointed 'thing' on the top." I observed attentively and said, "The Prussians?" And she cried out with terror and panic, "Oh! The Uhlans!" Inquiring into her distant family, she discovered that her grandfather's father was six years old when he saw the Sedan massacre, where thousands of men and horses died in torment and screaming – and Barbara's nightmares ended (125 years later). We played out the terrible Sedan battle in a therapeutic psychodrama. She drew her nightmares, we analyzed her dreams: she is better now.

A three-and-a-half-year-old girl named Nathalie had repetitive nightmares which woke her up every night, screaming, suffocating (asthma-like) since she was born. I attempted to come up with a working hypothesis and asked her mother (a medical doctor) if any members of her family had been at Ypres or Verdun. She answered, "I don't know if they were gassed, but my grandfather's family lived near Ypres." That night, the little girl did not have her asthma attack, but one month later, the night before my monthly meeting with her mother, it came back. Her mother talked to me about it, and I suggested she have the little girl draw her nightmares. She drew the "beast" of her nights and represented a gas mask which, having never seen, she called "a diver's mask with an elephant's trunk." Following an enquiry into the French army archives, we discovered that her great-uncle had been gassed at Ypres and her great-grandfather wounded and decorated at Verdun in 1916. Once it had been spoken about in the family, the nightmares ended and the coughing ceased, and a year later had not returned. The little girl had been born on 26 April, the date of the last gas attack on Ypres.

Appendix 7
Incest and second-type incest

In the usual sense of the word, incest applies essentially to taboo relations (sexual or almost sexual) between blood-related family members: father–daughter, grandfather–granddaughter, uncle–niece, brother–sister, mother–son, sometimes father-in-law–daughter-in-law, etc.

Dr Ghislain Devroede, university professor of surgery at Sherbrooke, Canada uses a clinical test (related to the work done by Arnold and Denis) to bring to light and heal incest trauma and sexual abuse (or the shock of sexual harassment) often connected to serious constipation (consequence of "anisme").

In 1994, Professor Françoise Héritier demonstrated (*Les Deux Soeurs et leur mère*) how the family relationship that had been taboo for a long time between relatives by marriage could be almost incestuous through a third party: the sisters and the mother of a woman are taboo for the husband – as is his father's second wife – because of a "contamination" by the "feminine fluids," which make a couple "of the same flesh." For a long time these relationships were forbidden by the Christian Church and by law, until only recently, although they were common practice in biblical times (with a near-obligation to marry one's brother's widow, as Jacob married two sisters, Rachel and Leah) and in many rural areas.

American and French civil laws no longer forbid marriage between ex-brother-in-laws and sister-in-laws or with a son-in-law or daughter-in-law (although the problem was raised for Woody Allen in 1994 concerning his relations with the adoptive daughter of an ex-companion). Many popular American B-films and television programs, aired in France between 1992–8, recount these various marriages and remarriages between relatives and relatives by marriage.

Appendix 8
The anniversary syndrome

The human being has an "elephant's memory," and marriage customs, number of children, and often even age at death or choice of profession are passed down from generation to generation (intergenerational links) in a conscious and spoken manner. One often becomes a farmer, engineer, doctor, teacher, notary, baker or military officer from father to son, and without knowing it, we often get married and die at the same age, sometimes at the same period or date. Many people do so either consciously as part of a project, or by some prediction, unconsciously through an "invisible family loyalty" and "transgenerational transmission."

Only recently (since Josephine Hilgard's research on adult psychosis in the United States and my own work on cancer (*Vouloir guérir*, 1985), car accidents, and the somatic consequences of war traumas in descendants (1994)) has the anniversary syndrome been revealed in certain illnesses of a psychosomatic-somatopsychic nature, or "mind-body" in a single hyphened word, as Ernest Rossi indicates.

Recent studies have brought to the fore vivid nightmares with near photographic memory or terrible, unspeakable war traumas in descendants of survivors over several generations, among survivors of concentration camps (Judith Kestenberg, Nathalie Zaijdé), genocide, various massacres, horrible wars like among the descendants of those gassed at Ypres (1915) and Verdun (1916), traumatized at Sedan (1870) (Anne Ancelin Schützenberger, 1985, 1994), with various symptoms of constriction or inflammation of the mouth and throat zone (cough, spitting, scratchy throat, frequent bronchitis, "asthma," etc.).

One could ask how this kind of transgenerational* transmission works. How this unconscious and involuntary transmission passes down, "punctuating" certain periods and historical or family dates, revitalized by anniversaries or commemorations.

We could speak about, as Moreno did, the family or group co-conscious and family or group co-unconscious, of the *in utero* mother–child dual unity (Torok), of memory impregnation between father and son, or grandfather and grandson, of co-self (Ada Abraham), of the "phantom and the crypt" (Abraham and Torok), following a parental secret or unspoken event, of "invisible loyalties" (Boszormenyi-Nagy). On this subject, many clinical observations have been made of these transmissions and a few statistical studies (Hilgard). However, the neurological or genetic means of transmission of acquired characteristics and factors of transmission remain to be elucidated, despite the discovery of many new neurotransmitters.

When we allow people to express themselves, and we help them to speak, have them draw, replay scenes in psychodrama, the symptoms often cease in the patient and even in their children, when they are "listened to and heard" by an understanding person, a holding psychotherapist.

---

*   One should not confuse conscious *intergenerational transmission* with unconscious identification, unconscious "invisible family loyalty" and unconscious *transgenerational transmission* (secret, unspoken, hidden, quieted, unthought) which often speaks through symptoms.

Appendix 9
Two case studies of the anniversary syndrome

The following case studies were given to me by Dr Ghislain Devroede, university professor of surgery at Sherbrooke, Canada. The case studies will be presented in further detail in Montreal from 23–28 September 1998 at the first international conference on pelvic floor questions: front, middle, rear.

Myriam or the materialization of a family unconscious

Myriam was thirteen years old when she accidentally impaled herself on an iron bar that marked a road in Quebec. It was winter, a little before Christmas. In between delivering newspapers, she was playing on some banks of accumulated snow. She jumped, lost her step and slid past the bottom of the snow bank and fell on one of the bars stuck deep in the ground to mark the road.

The bar was frozen in the ground and the ambulance workers were unable to take the foreign object with the victim and had to disimpale her before taking her to the hospital. The teenager was breathing with difficulty due to a right pneumothorax, for which a thoracic drain was placed.

She survived the accident, despite the 50% risk of death that accompanies a double perforation of the duodenum. In fact, the only damage caused by the metal bar was a ruptured hymen, double perforation of the duodenum and the perforation of the diaphragm on the right which caused the pneumothorax. All her other organs were intact, although the object passed within millimeters of several of them. It even passed through that virtual space separating the rectum and the vagina without perforating one or the other. Ten days later Myriam was back home.

In the weeks following the accident, she was very agitated, slept poorly, remembering the conversations of the ambulance workers who had removed her from the bar. She drew a cartoon of the accident, with the goal of "producing" a concrete object to manifest her anxiety in a non-verbal way. The image in which she is impaled shows a very phallic lamp-post ejaculating rays of light from its tip. She subtitled it "sur une pine de métal" ("on a metal prick"), using a popular Quebecois expression for metal bar. In the image where she is removed from the bar, the lamp-post is limp.

During the accident, Myriam's father, much older than his wife, kept a distance. He rarely came to follow-up appointments. Myriam's mother was very present during the intensive care, coming to the clinic at each visit. She kept rocking herself back and forth. When asked why, she didn't have time to respond before Myriam says: "She's always rocking back and forth." And the mother said, "Wouldn't Myriam like to know my big secret."

As it turns out, the victim's mother had been raped by two men at exactly the same age that her daughter impaled herself, and the mother had never talked about it to anyone.

Myriam integrated this discovery with what she herself lived. She spoke about the relationship between her parents, which was getting worse, and she predicted their separation. She deduced that her mother's rape was not the only one in the family. Suspecting a similar misfortune had befallen her maternal grandmother, she investigated, and the grandmother told her granddaughter that she had also been raped at the age of thirteen, by one man, and at the age of eleven had already been raped. She had not spoken about it to anyone either.

Myriam recovered well physically. She continues to experience perineal hypersensitivity at the slightest examination, which is unusual and could foreshadow sexual difficulties. She continues to come to the hospital regularly to talk about her family. Signs of a masked existential depression are beginning to appear. She is becoming aware of the fact that she often "made as if" and wore a mask in public.

Noëlla or lonely birthdays with the scalpel

Noëlla was a constipated old spinster, hospitalized to have a full colonectomy with re-anastomosis of the rectum in order to relieve a severe transit problem. The surgeon was not enthusiastic about doing this operation, but declared he had no alternative. He nevertheless asked for a second opinion from a colleague, who concluded without any doubt that psychotherapy and not surgery was necessary.

The patient categorically refused the idea that she could be "crazy," refused psychotherapy, preferred surgery and underwent the colonectomy.

Ten years later she died. In between times, she was hospitalized every year around her birthday. Three of these hospitalizations led to surgery. In retrospect, it was revealed that the total colonectomy was performed on her birthday.

(Dr Ghislain Devroede, 13 December 1997)

Appendix 10

A few historical dates (a reminder)*

1096–99   First Crusade.

1492   Christopher Columbus (1451–1506), departure after the Inquisition, which was followed by the expulsion of the Jews and Moors from Spain (and discovery of America).

13 March 1313   Philippe the Beautiful (1284–1314) orders the Templars burned.   Jacques de Molay curses him while at the stake; followed by the beginning of the Hundred Years War between England (Edward III, his grandson by female line) and France (Philippe VI, Valois, his nephew by male line). France reinforces the "Salic law" ruling on the primogeniture of males, and Joan of Arc helps the "kind prince" be crowned in Reims King Charles VII of France; cf. lineage of French kings – Capetiens, Valois, Bourbons.

21 February 1916   Beginning of the German offensive at Verdun.

25 February 1916   Seizing of the Douaumont Fort (Verdun).

22–5 April 1915   Gas at Verdun.

24 April 1915   Genocide of Armenians, and battle of Gallipoli, Dardanelles.

6 June 1944   Normandy landing.

8 June 1945   German capitulation.

18 June 1855   Defeat of Malakoff (near Sebastopol, Crimean War).

18 June 1940   Call by General de Gaulle.

---

*   Dates are listed by month, using the Gregorian calendar

118 June 1389   Battle of Kosovo Fields (currently ex-Yugoslavia); defeat of Serbs by Ottomans.

28 June 1914   Archduke Franz Ferdinand enters Sarajevo and is assassinated by a Serb activist, starting the First World War (1914–18)

28 June 1989   Slobodan Milosevic, Serbian leader, gives a speech on Kosovo Fields recalling the historical defeat by the Turks in 1389.

4 July 1776   American Declaration of Independence; American national holiday; and death of second and third American presidents, Jefferson and Adams, for the fiftieth anniversary.

14 July 1789   Taking of the Bastille; French national holiday (beginnings of French Revolution).

4 August 1789   Abolition of privileges (the night of 4 August).

4 August 1870   Wissembourg defeat (Franco-Prussian War), MacMahon beaten by Bismarck's Prussians.

24 August 1572 The Saint Bartholomew massacre of the Huguenots (Protestants) by the Catholics, the killing of Admiral Coligny, 5000 dead in Paris, Henry IV saved (24 August 1997, Pope Jean Paul II came to Paris to celebrate mass for young people).

1–2 September 1870   Sedan massacre (Franco-Prussian War, abdication of Napoleon III). The Germans create the *Sedantag* (Sedan holiday).

5–10 September 1914   Battle of the Marne.

7 September 1812   Napoleon enters Moscow, 14 September (and Moscow fire on 12 September, ordered by Governor Rostopchine).

19 September 1870   Siege of Paris by Prussians (cf. Paris Commune, 26 March–28 May 1871).

19 October 1812   Beginning of the French retreat from Russia (of Emperor Napoleon I).

24 October 1916   Recapture of the Douaumont Fort (500,000 dead, wounded, missing without burial at Verdun).

24–5 October 1917 October Revolution in Petrograd/Saint Petersburg (beginning of the Russian Revolution).

9 November 1799 (18 Brumaire, year VIII)   Napoléon Bonaparte takes power. He returned riding flat out on 18 December 1812 to save his throne.

11 November 1918   Armistice (First World War).

November 1812   French retreat from Russia (Napoleon I's troops).

22 November 1963   Assassination of President Kennedy.

27 November 1812   Passage of the Beresina by the French, during retreat.

6 December   Saint Nicolas's Day.

13 December   Santa Lucia, Festival of Lights.

25 December   Christmas Day.

6 January   Epiphany - celebration of the Three Kings.

13–25 January   Saint Tatiana Day (patron saint of Moscow).

21 January 1793   Louis XVI guillotined.

* * *

The French have experienced three major wars against the Germans in the last 150 years, as important and vivid in their minds as the War of Independence for the Americans. They are present not only in family memories, on monuments, in lullabies and songs, but also – now – in the latest generation of children's nightmares.

The Franco-Prussian War (1870–1) included the human losses of the battle of Sedan, which was followed by the French territorial loss of Alsace-Lorraine.

The First World War (1914–18) included the long battles of Verdun (trenches, gas. 800,000 killed); the unsuccessful Gallipoli landing; the epidemic of Spanish flu which killed 22 million in Western Europe between 1918–20. After the war, France regained Alsace-Lorraine.

The Second World War (1939–45) featured the defeat of the French; General de Gaulle's call on 18 June 1940 to resist the Germans; and the Resistance Movement. Following the 6 June 1944 Normandy landings by the Allies, the war lasted until the capitulation of Germany on 8 June 1945.

Notes

1 A genealogy of transgenerational therapy

1 Theodor Reik, *Listening with the Third Ear* (New York: Farrar, Strauss and Company, 1983).
2 Eric de Rosny, *Les Yeux de ma chèvre* (Paris: Plon, 1981); *Healers in the Night of the Duala* (New York: Orbis Books, 1985).
3 Peter Gay, *Freud: A Life for Our Time* (New York: Norton, 1988).
4 Sigmund Freud, *The Interpretation of Dreams* (1900), in *The Complete Psychological Works of Sigmund Freud* (London: The Hogarth Press, 1953), vol. 5, 487.
5 Sigmund Freud, *Moses and Monotheism* (1939), in *The Complete Psychological Works of Sigmund Freud* (London: The Hogarth Press, 1953), vol. 23, 99.
6 Sigmund Freud, *Totem and Taboo* (1913), in *The Complete Psychological Works of Sigmund Freud* (London: The Hogarth Press, 1953), vol. 13, 157–158.
7 For more on the history of psychoanalysis, see Reuben Fine, *A History of Psychoanalysis* (Northvale, NJ: Crossroad Publishing, 1990); Marthe Robert, *La Révolution psychanalytique* (Paris: Petite Bibliothèque Payot, 1989); and Elisabeth Roudinesco, *Histoire de la psychanalyse* (Paris: Le Seuil, 1986).
8 C. G. Jung, *On The Psychology of the Unconscious* and *The Relations Between the Ego and the Unconscious* in *Two Essays on Analytical Psychology*, 2nd edition, translated by R. F. Hull (New York: Pantheon Books, 1966).
9 I recall reading in an American newsletter published in the 1980s an article by Bruno Bettelheim in which he discussed the "real" ethical reasons for the estrangement between Freud and Jung and the investigation of the complaints by traumatized patients – notably Sabina Spielrein: Freud did not approve of a therapist "going out" with his young patients, reproaches Jung apparently did not take well. For more on this subject, see the commentaries by Sabina Spielrein, discovered by Aldo Carotenuto and Carlo Trombetta in *Entre Freud et Jung*, translated into French by Michel Guibal and Jacques Nobecourt (Paris: Aubier, 1980).

10 See *La Famille: l'individu plus un* (Marseille: Hommes & Perspectives, 1991). In this book rich in teachings on the psychoanalytical approach and the systems approach to family therapy, Robert Pessler states: "Psychoanalysts and systems therapists resemble each other (without being exactly the same) in their approach to the family in clinical practice....Clinical practice should bypass polarization and mutual exclusion."

11 See Richard Bandler and John Grinder, *Frog into Prince: Neurolinguistic Programming* (Utah: Real People Press, 1979).

12 In 1934, students of George Herbert Mead published his courses after his death and at the same time Moreno published *Who Shall Survive?*, both postulating a "role theory" to explain human behavior.

13 For more details, see René Marineau, *J.L. Moreno, ou la troisième révolution psychiatrique* (Paris: A.M. Métaillé, 1989) and *Jacob Levy Moreno, 1889–1974: Father of Psychodrama, Sociometry and Group Therapy* (London: Routledge, 1989)

14 Henri Collomb, "La Mort en tant qu'organisateur de syndromes psycho-somatiques en Afrique," *Psychopathologie africaine*, XII, 2 (1977), 137–147. Also personal communication, Nice, 1978.

15 Sigmund Freud, "The Uncanny" (1919), in *The Complete Psychological Works of Sigmund Freud* (London: The Hogarth Press, 1953), vol. 17, 220.

16 Ibid., 240.

17 Ibid., 219.

2 Family therapy and the genogram/genosociogram

1 Dr Frieda Fromm-Reichmann worked with J.L. Moreno and together they edited *Progress in Psychotherapy* (New York: Grune & Stratton, 1956). She was the "Dr. Fried" in the autobiographical novel by Hanna Green, *I Never Promised You a Rose Garden* (New York: Holt, Rinehart & Winston, 1964) which was later published under her real name, Joanne Greenberg, by Signet Books (New York, 1989). This novel, and the film drawn from it, retrace the therapy of a patient labeled as schizophrenic. Frieda Fromm-Reichmann spent a year at Stanford in 1955–6 at the Center for Advanced Study in Behavioral Sciences, and worked for many years at the famous psychiatric and psychoanalytical clinic Chestnut Lodge, where she worked with Harry Stack Sullivan and supervised Josephine Hilgard. She was also the one who, in 1956 in Palo Alto, suggested that anthropologists and psychiatrists film the interaction of families of schizophrenics, from which sprang Gregory Bateson's "double bind" and the research on non-verbal communication.

2 Gregory Bateson, *Perceval's Narrative, A Patient's Account of His Psychosis, 1830–1832* (Stanford, California: Stanford University Press, 1961).

3 Jay Haley, *Power Tactics of Jesus Christ and Other Essays* (New York: Norton, 1989).

4 Paul Watzlawick and Jackson Beavin, *Pragmatics of Human Communication: A Study of Interactional Patterns, Pathologies and Paradoxes* (New York: Norton, 1969).

5 Virginia Satir, *Helping Families Change* (New York: Jason Aronson, 1982), and all her work.
6 See "The Grandmother's Ghost" in Augustus Napier, Carl Whitaker, *The Family Crucible* (Glenville, Illinois: Harper and Collins, 1978).
7 Cf. Erving Goffman, *Asylums: Essays on the Social Situation of Mental Patients and Other Inmates* (NewYork: Doubleday, 1968), *Presentation of Self in Everyday Life* (New York: Doubleday, 1959) and *Stigmates* (London: Pelican, 1963).
8 Salvador Minuchin, *Families and Family Therapy* (Cambridge, MASS.: Harvard University Press, 1974).
9 It is worth mentioning that Nathan Ackerman worked in psychodrama with J.L. Moreno, who had been treating couples and families with psychodrama and group therapy since 1930.

3 Invisible loyalties

1 See Ivan Boszormenyi-Nagy and Geraldine M. Spark, *Invisible Loyalties* (New York: Brunner/Mazel Publishers, 1973/1984). Some Europeans such as Magda Heireman (*Du côté de chez soi: la thérapie contextuelle d'Ivan Boszormenyi-Nagy*, Paris: ESF, 1989) have popularized his ideas with a simple and clear presentation.
2 I am not a student of Ivan Boszormenyi-Nagy, and I only met him once, very briefly in 1994.
3 Boszormenyi-Nagy, op. cit., 14.
4 Gwen Raverat, *Period Piece: A Cambridge Childhood* (London and Boston: Faber & Faber, 1952/1987), 122.
5 For more on this concept of "resentment", read O. Carl Simonton, Stephanie Matthews-Simonton and James Creighton, *Getting Well Again* (Los Angeles: J. P. Tarcher, 1978) and Anne Ancelin Schützenberger, *Vouloir guérir* (Toulouse: Erès; Paris: La Méridienne, 1985; Epi/La Méridienne, 1993; DDB, 1996) – and also Ivan Boszormenyi-Nagy on justice, "giving and receiving" and "family book-keeping."

4 Psychosomatic/somatopsychic

1 *Psychoneuroimmunology* (New York: Academic Press, 1981; second edition completed 1991).
2 "Time collapse" is defined thus by Vamik Volkan in his book *Bloodlines* (1997: p.35): "In 'time collapse'...the interpretations, fantasies, and feelings about the past shared traumas commingle with those pertaining to a current situation. Under the influence of time collapse people may intellectually separate the past event from the present one but, emotionally, the two events are merged."

This concept is close to Haydée Faimberg's "téléscopage des générations" (see Faimberg 1993) and to the "anniversary syndrome" of Josephine Hilgard. It also has links with the author's (1993) clinical work with anniversary nightmares and with Nathalie Zaijdé's findings concerning third-generation descendants of Holocaust victims.
3 Boszormenyi-Nagy, 1973, 37.

4 Father of transactional analysis, Eric Berne described the three "states of me" (child, adult, parent), along with transactions, "games" and "scenarios." Cf. *Games People Play: The Psychology of Human Relations* (New York: Grove Press, 1964).

5 Boszormenyi-Nagy, op. cit., 37–38.

6 *A Theory of Cognitive Dissonance* (New York: Evanston, Row, Peterson, 1957).

7 Boszormenyi-Nagy, op. cit., 39–40.

8 On the subject of gifts, there are "gifts with teeth," there is the gift and the counter-gift and there is what we call the "potlatch," which is a gift-exchanging custom in certain regions where a great feast or banquet is offered with the expected return of another great banquet. In certain regions of Melanesia, this custom has led to the total impoverishment of the population, because if the first gives, let us say, five cattle and thirty goats for the first banquet, the next feels compelled to provide ten cattle and sixty goats, etc. and in the end there is nothing left to eat. Through this potlatch custom, the riches of the region disappeared.

9 Françoise Dolto, *La Cause des enfants* (Paris: Laffont, 1985), 446.

10 Ibid., 421.

11 In 1992, at the Cannes Film Festival, Francis Ford Coppola, director of *Dracula,* declared that vampires symbolize for him the anguish felt by children who had been victims of incest: a way of expressing nocturnal fears, a visit or contact during sleep, a mixture of pleasure, disgust and something mortal, which destroys life.

12 It is interesting to note that the comparatively recent modernized implementation of the Julian calendar, which takes the lunar cycle into account, moved 13 December to 25 December (Christmas), but that the festival of light continued to be celebrated on 13 December. Also, our current Western calendar derives from the Roman calendar, reformed in AD 46 by Julius Caesar (Julian Calendar) and then again in 1582 by Pope Gregory XIII (Gregorian Calendar), which had to "catch up" in order to avoid the "astronomical gap" of ten days (twelve in the nineteenth century): the 13 December of old now corresponds to the current 25 December. Some European countries only accomplished this "catching-up" in the twentieth century. For example, the former USSR implemented this new mandatory calendar in 1917. The Nordic countries have kept the Saint Lucia (the primitive feast of lights) on 13 December, the date around which the Nobel prize is awarded in Scandinavia (10 December).

13 See also: Jean Oury, Félix Guattari and Maurice Vigneux, *Pratique institutionnelle et politique* (Paris: Editions Matrice, 1985), et "Le vécu de la fin du monde dans la folie," in the French research and teaching association journal, *Journal de l'association pour la recherche, l'enseignement, la formation et la pratique de la psychiatrie* (and François Tosquelles, private discussions, 1968).

14 Cf. Pierre Verdier and Michel Soulé, *Le Secret sur les origines* (Paris: ESF, 1986), 64, and Martine Lani, *A la recherche de la génération perdue* (Marseille: Hommes et Perspectives, 1990).

15 Cf. *Growing Up in New Guinea* (New York: William Morrow, 1975).

16 See Emmanuel Todd, *L'Invention de l'Europe* (Paris: Le Seuil, 1990) for implicit rules in French and western European families and their archaic origins, as well as their traditional geographic distribution, and what rules family habitat and its sharing.
17 Vincent de Gaulejac, *La Névrose de classe* (Paris: Hommes & Groupes, 1987).

5 The crypt and the phantom

1 Nicolas Abraham and Maria Torok, *L'Ecorce et le noyau* (Paris: Aubier-Flammarion, 1978), translated by Nicolas T. Rand, *The Shell and the Kernel: Renewals of Psychoanalysis* (Chicago: University of Chicago Press, 1994).
2 Cf. *Cahiers internes du symbolisme*, no. 6, 196.
3 Abraham and Torok, op. cit., 429; in English translation, 173.
4 Ibid., 391.
5 Ibid., 427; in English translation, 171.
6 Ibid., 449; in English translation, 189.
7 Ibid., 391.
8 Ibid., 431; in English translation, 175.
9 Ibid., 439; in English translation, 181.

6 Origin and death

1 Serge Tisseron, *Tintin chez le psychanalyste* (Paris: Aubier-Archimbaud, 1985) and *Tintin et les secrets de famille* (Paris: Librairie Séguier, 1990). Also private conversations, 1988, 1990.
2 Claudine Vegh, *Je ne lui ai pas dit au-revoir* (Paris: Gallimard, 1980). Translated into English: *I Didn't Say Goodbye: Interviews with Children of the Holocaust* (New York: Dutton, 1985).
3 Vegh (1979), op. cit.
4 Amin Maalouf, *Les Croisades vues par les Arabes* (Paris: Lattès, 1983, second edition, "J'ai Lu", 1985), 304. Translated into English by Jon Rothschild, *The Crusades through Arab Eyes* (New York: Schocken Books, 1984), 265–266.

7 The genosociogram and the anniversary syndrome

1 I sought a more general, less technical term for genosociogram. I recently learned that the term "psychogenealogy" had been used in France by an artist who employed it in a totally different context with a different interpretation. Alexandre Jodorovsky ("Jodo") is a Chilean film maker and director of Russian origin who lived and worked in Mexico, then the United States and France. In the 1980s, he apparently worked with a kind of "psycho-sorcery" (in the Mexican sense of the term), or intuitive reading of family genealogy using the Tarot, which, after one of his students heard me on the subject, he baptized "psychogenealogy." As of 1991–2, he had not published anything on the subject because his manuscript had apparently disappeared from his car during his holidays. Was this a whim of the unconscious? He no longer works in this area, or

only occasionally staging public theatrical demonstrations. I do not know him.

Regarding coincidences, it is amusing to note that I also used this term during the 1980s. I published leaflets and articles on this subject, but when I came to write an entire book about it, my typist's machine apparently "swallowed" the typed manuscript of my book. Neither the notes nor the original were returned to me, slowing publication by two years. I rewrote the book, with modifications and fewer references, making it perhaps a little more readable. What a strange coincidence, those two manuscripts disappearing, his and mine.

2 In private conversations in 1990 and 1992, Rupert Sheldrake mentioned to me that the American psychologist Josephine Hilgard had written about the anniversary syndrome. I was not able to find her articles at the time I wrote my first manuscript, although I finally found her studies in 1991–2, after her death. I have summarized them in Appendix 2. Although Sheldrake (1988) speaks about the "presence of the past," he found no relationship between my work – which does interest him – and his research or Basarab Nicolescu's "time ropes" (as if what is acquired by one were transmitted to others).

3 André Green, "La Mère morte" in *Narcissisme de vie, narcissisme de mort* (Paris: Minuit, 1983).

8 How to build your genosociogram

1 Cf. C. Himmelman, *A Family Tree: From Adam to Jesus,* Israel, Bethlehem, The 3 Arches, republished in the 1980s.

2 Jean Guyotat, *Psychanalyse à l'Université*, 1979, vol. IV, no. 16, 652.

3 Jacques Dupâquier, in *Le Temps des Jules*, studied the frequency by region of given names used in France in the nineteenth century: Jean (7,222), Pierre (3,141), Louis (2,969), François (2,511), Joseph (2,279), Jules (sixth position in 1860 – with Joseph and Marie as middle names for boys. Marie (12,661), Jeanne (2,408), Louis (1,466), Anne (1,434), Marguerite (1,163), for girls. This study was based on a survey of descendants of 3,000 couples married between 1803 and 1832, whose names began with "Tra" (such as Travers or Trabut), and 92,700 birth certificates.

9 My transgenerational clinical practice

1 I consider astrology, tarot and various forms of clairvoyance to be arts or pastimes, but not science or psychology.

2 André Green, "La Mère morte," in *Narcissisme de vie, narcissisme de mort* (Paris: Minuit, 1983).

3 Sigmund Freud, "Letter 69," in *The Complete Psychological Works of Sigmund Freud* (London: The Hogarth Press, 1953), vol. 1, 259.

4 Ibid., "Draft L," 248.

5 Ibid., "Draft M," 252.

6 J. L. Donnet and A. Green, *L'Enfant et le ça* (Paris: Editions de Minuit, 1973).

7 I have deliberately chosen not to mention the work of Szondi, because I do not believe in destiny, but in the possibility of making choices and changing your life, which is why I am a therapist, trainer, professor and do "Action Research." In addition, in a series of studies done with Dr Marcel-Paul Schützenberger from 1950–4 in Paris, and done again in the United States with Ardie Lubin, it was shown that Szondi had proven nothing (cf. A. A. Schützenberger, "L'Attirance au premier regard," in *Contributions à l'étude de la communication non-verbale*, 1976, and A. E. Ancelin, Henri Duchêne and M. P. Schützenberger, 1949, "Etude clinique et statistique du test de Szondi - à partir de 500 cas étudiés," Berne, Congrès International de Psychologie Appliquée – Actes. Revised and reprinted in the *Spanish Review of Psychology*, Madrid, 1950).

10 Anniversary syndrome and invisible family loyalty

1 See Anne Ancelin Schützenberger, *Vouloir guérir* (Toulouse: Erès/La Méridienne, 1985; revised Paris: Epi/La Méridienne D.D.B., 1991 /1993/1996).

11 Family configuration and the double anniversary syndrome

1 Didier Dumas, *L'Ange et le fantôme* (Paris: Editions de Minuit, 1985).
2 Catherine Mesnard, 1986, Master's Degree Thesis, Nice University, 115–116.
3 Dumas, op. cit., 80.
4 Laurence LeShan, *You Can Fight for Your Life: Emotional Factors in Causation of Cancer* (New York: M. Evans, 1977).
5 This favorite daughter of Freud's worked with him and became a psychoanalyst. Note that the following year, 1896, Freud's sister-in-law, Minna Bernays (1865–1941), came to live with Freud and that she had to go through the Freuds' bedroom to get to her own. The Freuds put an end to their sexual relations. Shortly thereafter, still in 1896, Freud's father Jacob died and Freud began his self-analysis. Note also that Freud seemed to have been a little traumatized by the death of his youngest brother Julius at the age of nine months, the same year that his uncle Julius died at the age of 20. Julius was the younger brother of his mother Amalia, but had kept his privileged position as eldest son. Sigmund Freud and Anna Freud-Bernays were the only two of their sibling group to emigrate and avoid being killed during the Second World War.

12 Legacy and family structure

1 Guy Ausloos, "Les Secrets de famille," in *Annales de psychothérapie: changements systémiques en thérapie familiale* (Paris: ESF, 1980), 62–80.
2 Freud took G. T. Fechner's (1889, *Elements of Physics*) expression of another, different scene ("Szene") to describe the unconscious (*The Interpretation of Dreams* (Freud, *Standard Edition*, vol. 4, 48). (G.W. I.II, 541 *et seq.*.). This "other" scene has been discussed and commented on widely since, especially by Jaques Lacan (private communications

1954–67, Paris), P. Kauffmann, in *L'Apport freudien* (Paris: Bordas, 1993, 603), Joyce MacDougall in *Plaidoyer pour une certaine anormalité* (Paris: Gallimard, 1978), and Octave Mannoni, in *Clefs pour l'Imaginaire, ou l'Autre Scène* (Paris: Seuil, 1985, 8, 99, 107, 112–113. Thus "Ça parle sur l'autre scène" has become a classic quotation to express the difficulty of seeing and understanding the unconscious.

3 Interview on tape at Centre Pompidou during a Dali exhibit during the 1980s in Paris, and autobiography, *Comment on devient Dali.*

4 Salvador Dali, *Comment on devient Dali*, 12–13.

5 Sigmund Freud, *The Interpretation of Dreams*, in *The Complete Psychological Works of Sigmund Freud* (London: The Hogarth Press, 1953), vol. 5, 486.

6 Amin Maalouf, *Les Croisades vues par les Arabes* (Paris: Lattès, 1983, second edition, "J'ai Lu", 1985), 249. Translated into English by Jon Rothschild, *The Crusades Through Arab Eyes* (New York: Schocken Books, 1984), 258–259.

7 Many interesting things could be said about this Sebastopol battle (27 March 1854–September 1855), which began due to tensions between the Czar defending the Orthodox and the Emperor defending the Catholics over holy places, and a hesitant recognition of Napoleon III by the Czar Nicholas in May 1851 (Crimean War, 1853–5). An unexpected alliance between the French and the English, against the Russians, led the Englishman Raglan and the Frenchman Pelissier to choose 18 June (anniversary of Waterloo) in order to attack Malakoff – and this would be a tragic defeat, following which Raglan died of cholera on 28 June and Pelissier took Malakoff on 8 September 1855 – which brought peace (Lavisse, 1989, *Histoire générale*, v. X).

13 Conclusion

1 Sigmund Freud, *The Interpretation of Dreams*, in *The Complete Psychological Works of Sigmund Freud* (London: Hogarth Press, 1953), vol. 5, 487.

2 Sylvana Olindo-Weber and V. Mazeran, "A l'écoute du corps souffrant," in *Journal des psychologues*, September 1991.

3 Sigmund Freud,*Totem and Taboo*, in *The Complete Psychological Works of Sigmund Freud* (London: The Hogarth Press, 1953), vol. 13, 158–159.

4 Rupert Sheldrake, *A New Science of Life: The Hypothesis of Formative Causation* (London: Blond and Briggs, 1981, second edn 1985), *Rebirth of Nature* (London: Rider, 1990), *The Presence of the Past: Morphic Resonance and the Habit of Nature* (London: Collins, 1988) in which Sheldrake refers to Fisher and Hinde, 1949, on bluetits and delivered milk bottles in Great Britain. And private communication, 1991/1992.

5 Sigmund Freud (1915) *Metapsychology*, in *The Complete Psychological Works of Sigmund Freud* (London: The Hogarth Press, 1953), vol. 14; "Repression," 141; "The Unconscious," 159.

6 René Kaës, "L'Invention psychanalytique du groupe; hommage à Didier Anzieu," *Portrait d'Anzieu avec groupe*, Marseille, Hommes et Perspectives, 1992.

7 Plato, translated by Francis MacDonald Cornford, *The Republic of Plato* (New York and London: Oxford University Press, 1941, 1945, 1967), 351 ff.
8 See Fanita English, "Episcript and the 'Hot Potato Game'," *TA Bulletin VIII*, October 1969, 77–82.
9 Montaigne, translated by Donald M. Frame, *The Complete Works of Montaigne* (Stanford, California: Stanford University Press, 1957), 139.
10 Sainte-Beuve (1857), *Causerie du Lundi*, vol. IX (Paris: Garnier).
11 Frank Sulloway, *Freud, Biologist of the Mind* (New York: Basic Books, 1979).
12 Sigmund Freud, *The History of an Infantile Neurosis* (1915) in *The Complete Psychological Works of Sigmund Freud* (London: The Hogarth Press, 1953), vol. 17, 119.
13 Françoise Dolto-Marette (1908–1988), all her works and private communication (1953–88).
14 Abraham and Torok, op. cit., 429, in English translation, 173.
15 Plato, *Apology*, 31d, 40a, 40b, translated by R. E. Allen, *The Dialogues of Plato* (New Haven/London: Yale University Press, 1984), 94, 103.

Appendix 1

1 Nicolas Abraham and Maria Torok, *L'Ecorce et le noyau* (Paris: Aubier-Flammarion, 1978). In English: *The Shell and the Kernel: Renewals of Psychoanalysis* (Chicago: University of Chicago Press, 1994).
2 Abraham and Torok, op. cit., 254–255, in English translation, 159.
3 Abraham and Torok, op. cit., 255, in English version, 159.
4 Abraham and Torok, op. cit., 429, in English version, 173.
5 Ibid., 391.
6 Ibid., 431, in English translation, 175.
7 Ibid., 421.
8 Ibid., in English translation, 176.
9 Ibid., in English translation, 174.
10 Ibid., 449, in English translation, 189.
11 Ibid., in English translation, 173.
12 Ibid., 391.
13 Ibid., 397.
14 Ibid., 396.
15 Ibid., 399.

Appendix 2

1 I would like to thank Professor Ernest R. Hilgard of the University of Stanford for sending me the documents concerning his wife's work and his kind authorization to cite them.
2 Josephine Hilgard, "Anniversary Reactions in Parents Precipitated by Children," *Psychiatry*, vol. 16, 73.
3 Ibid.
4 Ibid., 74.
5 Ibid., 74.
6 Ibid., 75.

7 Ibid., 75.
8 Ibid., 77.
9 Josephine Hilgard, "Anniversary Syndrome as Related to Late-Appearing Mental Illnesses in Hospitalized Patients," in A. L. S. Silver, ed., *Psychoanalysis and Psychosis* (Madison, Conn.: International Universities Press, 1989), 235.
10 Ibid., 237.
11 Josephine Hilgard and Martha F. Newman, "Evidence for Functional Genesis in Mental Illness: Schizophrenia, Depressive Psychoses and Psychoneurosis," *The Journal of Nervous and Mental Disease*, vol. 132, no. 1 (1961), 15.
12 Hilgard, 1989, op. cit., 238. Cf. Hilgard and Newman, 1961 and "Anniversaries in Mental Illness," *Psychiatry* vol. 22 (1959).
13 Ibid., 240. Cf. Hilgard and Fisk, "Disruption of Adult Ego Identity as Related to Childhood Loss of a Mother Through Hospitalization for Psychosis," *The Journal of Nervous and Mental Disease*, vol. 131, no. 1 (1960).
14 Ibid., 243.
15 Ibid., 247.
16 Hilgard and Newman, 1961, op. cit., 12.

Appendix 4

1 For more details, see the *Correspondance de Gustave Flaubert* (1887–93); selected, edited and translated by Francis Steegmuller, *The Letters of Gustave Flaubert* (Cambridge, Mass.: Harvard University Press, 1980–2); *Souvenirs intimes* by Mrs Commanville, his niece, and the research by Pierre-Marc de Biasi and his *Carnets de travail de Flaubert* (Paris: Balland, 1992).

Bibliography

Abraham, Nicolas and Maria Torok. 1967. *Le Verbier de l'homme aux loups*. Paris: Aubier Flammarion. Translated by Nicolas Rand, *The Wolfman's Magic Word: A Cryptonomy*. Minneapolis: University of Minnesota Press, 1987.

—— 1978. *L'Ecorce et le noyau*. Paris: Aubier Flammarion. Revised edition, 1987. Edited and translated by Nicolas Rand, *The Shell and the Kernel*, vol. 1. Chicago and London: Chicago University Press, 1994.

Acrement, Germaine. 1991. *Ces dames aux chapeaux verts*. Paris: Editions Miroir.

Ancelin Schützenberger, Anne. 1966. *Précis de psychodrame*. Paris: Editions Universitaires. Second edition, 1970.

—— 1971. *La Sociométrie*. Paris: Editions Universitaires.

—— 1973. *L'Observation*. Paris: Epi.

—— 1975. "Psychodrama and role-playing," in S. Jennings (ed.) *Therapy and Creativity*, London: Pittman.

—— 1976. *Contributions à l'étude de la communication non-verbale*. Paris: Service de publication des thèses, University of Lille III and Librairie Champion.

—— 1979. "Nonverbal communication," in S. Weitz (ed.) *Nonverbal Communication*, 2nd edn., New York: Oxford University Press

—— 1980. "Corps et identité," in Pierre Tapp et al. *Identité nouvelle et personnalisation*, 305–12. Toulouse: Privat.

—— 1981. *Le Jeu de rôle*. Revised edition. Paris: ESF, 1990.

—— 1984. "Psychodrame, roman familial, génosociogramme et formation," in *L'Homme et ses potentialités*, 109–122. Paris: ESF.

—— 1985. "Diagnostic et pronostic d'une maladie fatale terminale," in Jean Guyotat and Pierre Fedida, *Evènement et psychopathologie*, 124–126, SIMEP.

—— 1985. "La Vie, la mort dans l'imaginaire familial: réflexions et cas cliniques," in *Psychoses, famille, culture*, edited by E. Jeddi et al., 404–415. Paris: L'Harmattan.

—— 1985. *Vouloir guérir*. Tenth revised edition, Paris: DDB, 1997.

—— 1986. "Stress, cancer, liens transgénérationnels," in *Questions de: Médecines nouvelles et psychologies transpersonnelles*, special edition, Albin Michel, number 64 (March): 77–101.

—— 1986. "Forme européenne inconsciente du chamanisme: la 'réalisation automatique des prédictions'," in *Transe, chamanisme et possession*, Papers, Second International Meeting on Festivities and Communication, 81–87. Nice: Serres.

1987. "Vouloir guérir," in *Les Médecines, les psychologies et leurs images de l'homme*. Saint-Baume: Editions de l'Ouvert.

—— 1987. "L'Inconscient a bonne mémoire," *Journal des psychologues* 48. Marseille.

—— 1988. *Le Dit et le non-dit, les secrets de famille et leur influence sur les maladies, les accidents, les morts, les professions, le nombre d'enfants*. Paris: Le Corps à Vivre.

—— 1994. "Vie transgénérationnelle et maladie," in *Le Processus de guérison, par-delà la souffrance et la mort*, 57–70. Quebec: Les Ateliers de Montreal, MNH, 3947 Chabanel, Beauport, GIE 4M7.

—— 1995. "L'Enfant de remplacement et l'enfant réparateur," in *Le Deuil comme processus de guérison*. Montreal: MNH.

—— 1995. "Le Cancer en cascade et en ressac, example de syndrome d'anniversaire," in *Le Deuil comme processus de guérison*. Montreal: MNH.

—— 1996. "Transmission de l'angoisse indicible et transgénérationnelle. L' angoisse d'un traumatisme qu'on n'a pas vécu," in "Mélanges en hommage au professeur Juliette Favez-Boutonier," *Bulletin de psychologie* LIX, 423 (April). Paris: Sorbonne.

—— 1996. "La Serendipity. Coïncidences et synchronicité," in "Hommages au doyen J. P. Weiss," *Annales de la Faculté des Lettres de l'Université de Nice* (June).

—— 1996. "Phénomènes transgénérationnels et crises de la société et de la famille," in *Ecrits*. Nice.

—— 1997. "Transgenerational Psychotherapy. Health and Death. Family Links through the Family Tree" *Caduceus* (March).

—— 1998. "De génération en génération. Liens transgénérationnels," in *Hommage à Ada Abraham*. Montreal.

—— 1998. "Epilogue about psychodrama," in P. Holmes, M. Karp and K. Tauvon (eds), *The Handbook of Psychodrama*, London and New York: Routledge.

Antonovsky, Aaron. 1985. *Health, Stress and Coping*. San Francisco: Jossey Bass, Inc.

Ansky, S. 1917–22. *Dybbuk and Other Writings*. New York: Schocken Books, 1992.

Anzieu, Didier. 1968. *La Dynamique des groupes restreints*. Paris: PUF.

—— 1985. *Le Moi-peau*. Paris: Dunod. Translated, *Thought: From the Skin to the Thinking Ego*. London: Karnac, 1996.

—— 1987. *Les Enveloppes psychiques*. Paris: Dunod. Translated by D. Briggs, *Psychic Envelopes*. London: Karnac Books, 1990.

—— 1993. "La Fonction contenante et la peau, du moi et de la pensée: conteneur, contenant, contenir," *Les Contenants de la pensée*, 15–40. Paris: Dunod.

Anzieu, Didier, Serge Tisseron, et al. 1993. *Les Contenants de la pensée*. Paris: Dunod.

Assoun, Jacques. 1994. *Questions d'enfance. Les contrebandiers de la mémoire*. Paris: Syros.

Attali, Jacques. 1991. *1492*. Paris: Fayard.

Aulagnier, Piera. 1975. *Sur le fantasme originaire*. Private interview.

—— 1975. *La Violence de l'interprétation: du pictogramme à l'énoncé*. Paris: PUF.

1984. "Le Droit au secret," in *L'apprenti historien et le maître sorcier*. Paris: PUF.

Ausloos, Guy. 1980. "Secrets de famille," in *Annales de psychothérapie: changements sytémiques en thérapie familiale*, 62–80. Paris: ESF.

Balmary, Marie. 1975. *Psychoanalyzing Psychoanalysis: Freud and the Hidden Fault of the Father*. Reprint. Ann Arbor: Books on Demand. French trans. *L'Homme aux statues, Freud et la faute cachée du père*, 1975, Paris: Grasset.

Bandler, Richard and John Grinder. 1975. *The Structure of Magic*. Palo Alto: Science and Behavior Books.

—— 1979. *Frog into Prince: Introduction to Neurolinguistic Programming*. Moab, Utah: Real People Press.

Bartlett, F. C. 1992. *Remembering*. Cambridge: Cambridge University Press.

Bateson, Gregory. 1961. *Perceval's Narrative, A Patient's Account of His Psychosis, 1830–1832*. Stanford, California: Stanford University Press.

—— 1972. *Steps to an Ecology of Mind*. New York: Dutton.

Bateson, Gregory, Don Jackson and J. Haley. 1956. "Toward a Theory of Schizophrenia," *Behavior Science* 1: 251–264.

Bergson, Henri. 1946. *Matière et mémoire*. Paris: PUF. Translated by N. M. Paul and W. S. Palmer, *Matter and Memory*. Cambridge: Zone Books, 1988.

Bernard, Jean. 1992. *Le Syndrome du colonel Chabert ou le vivant mort*. Paris: Buchet-Chastel.

Berne, Eric. 1964. *Games People Play*. New York: Grove Press. Reprint. New York: Ballantine Books, 1985.

—— 1975. *What Do You Say After You Say Hello?* New York: Grove Press.

—— 1976. *Beyond Games and Scripts*. New York: Grove Press.

Bettelheim, Bruno. 1969. *Children of the Dream*. London: Thames and Hudson.

Bion, W. R. 1958. "On Hallucination," in *Second Thoughts*. London: Heinemann.

Blanchard, François. 1995. "Pour un autre regard sur la démence." *Gérontologie et société* 72: 156-166.

Bohm, David. 1980. *Wholeness and the Implicate Order*. London: Routledge and Kegan Paul.

Bollas, C. 1987. *The Shadow of the Object*. London: Free Association Books.

Boszormenyi-Nagy, Ivan and Geraldine M. Spark. 1973. *Invisible Loyalties*. New York: Harper and Row. Reprint. New York: Brunner/Mazel, 1984.

Boszormenyi-Nagy, Ivan and J. L. Framo, eds. 1965. *Psychothérapies familiales*. Paris: PUF. Translated from the American 1980.

—— 1985. *Intensive Family Therapy: Theoretical and Practical Aspects*. New York: Brunner/Mazel.

Bourguignon, Odile. 1984. *Mort des enfants et structures familiales*. Paris: PUF.

Bowen, Murray. 1978. *Family Therapy in Clinical Practice*. New York: Jason Aronson.

—— 1978. *La différentiation du soi*. Paris:ESF. Translated from the American 1984.

Bowlby, John. 1969. *Attachment and Loss*. London: Penguin Books, 1991.

Brossard, A., J. Cosnier, et al. 1984. *La Communication non-verbale*. Neuchâtel and Paris: Delachaux-Niestlé.

Buber, Martin. 1957. *I and Thou*. New York: Scribners.

Cannon, W. B. 1945. *The Way of an Investigator*. New York: Norton.

Capra, Fritjof. 1975. *The Tao of Physics*, third edition. Boston: Shambhala. 1991.

Cardinal, Marie. 1983. *The Words To Say It: An Autobiographical Novel*. Translated by Par Goodheart. Cambridge, MA: VanVector and Goodheart.

Carlier, Emile. 1995. *Mort, pas encore*. Verdun: Société archéologique du Nord, Douai.

Carter, E. A. and M. McGoldrick, eds. 1980. *The Family Life Cycle: A Framework for Family Therapy*. New York: Gardner Press.

Ciavaldini, A. 1989. "L'Etre d'exil ou les traces immémoriales de l'oubli," in A. Yahyaoui, *Corps, espace-temps et traces de l'exil*.

Cohen, Lawrence H., ed. 1988. *Life Events and Psychological Functioning: Theoretical and Methodological Issues*. London: Sage.

"Confidence et secret," Special Issue of *Le Groupe familial* 132 (July 1991).

Collomb, Henri. 1977. "La Mort en tant qu'organisateur de syndromes psychosomatiques en Afrique," *Psychopathologie Africaine* 12(2): 137–147.

Colte, Thomas. 1995. *Enfants prisonniers d'un secret de famille*. Paris: Laffont.

Costa de Beauregard, Olivier. 1963. *Le Second Principe de la science du temps*. Paris: Seuil.

—— 1987. *Time, the Physical Magnitude*. New York: Reidel Publishing Co.

Couvert, Barbara. 1997. "Introduction au secret de famille." Dissertation, University of Paris VII. For publication in 1999 by DDB, Paris.

Crouch, Michael and Robert Leonard, eds. 1987. *The Family in Medical Practice: A Family System Primer*. New York: Springer.

Cyrulnick, Boris. 1983. *Mémoire de singe et paroles d'homme*. Paris: Hachette.

—— 1989. *Sous le signe du lien*. Paris: Hachette.

—— 1991. *De la parole comme d'une molécule*. Paris: Eshel. Reprint, Paris: Seuil, 1995.

—— 1991. *La Naissance du sens*. Paris: Hachette.

—— 1993. *Les Nourritures affectives*. Paris: Odile Jacob.

—— 1997. *L'Ensorcellement du monde*. Paris: Odile Jacob.

Dali, Salvador. 1973. *Comment on devient Dali: les aveux inavouables de Salvador Dali*. Paris: R. Laffont.

Davis, J. 1984. *The Kennedys: Dynasty and Disaster 1848–1983*.New York: McGraw Hill.

Delassus, Claire. 1993. *Le Secret ou l'intelligence interdite*. Paris: Hommes et Perspectives.

"Deuils dans la famille." *Groupal* 1 (1995). Paris.

Dolto-Marette, Françoise. 1971. *Le Cas Dominique*. Paris: Seuil. Reprint. "Point," 1974.

—— 1985. *La Cause des enfants*. Paris: Laffont. 196–197, 287–291, 419–424, 446–448.

—— 1988. *Inconscient et destin*. Paris: Le Seuil.

Donnet, J. L. and André Green. 1973. *L'Enfant et le ça*. Paris: Editions de Minuit.

Dumas, Didier. 1985. *L'Ange et le fantôme: introduction à la clinique de l'impensé généalogique*. Paris: Minuit. Preface by Françoise Dolto.

—— 1985. "Le Généalogique dans l'histoire et la pensée freudienne," in *Patio, Psychanalyse* 4: 201–218. Paris: L'Eclat.

—— 1989. *Hantise et clinique de l'Autre*. Paris: Aubier.

Dunbar, Florence. 1954. *Emotions and Bodily Change: A Survey of Literature, Psychosomatic Interrelationship, 1910–1953*. New York: Columbia University Press.

"Du Secret," *Nouvelle revue de psychanalyse* 14. 1975.

Eiger, A. 1983. *Un divan pour la fmille*. Paris: Dunod.

Eiger, A. 1997. *Le Générationnel: approche en thérapie familiale psychanalytique*. Paris: Dunod.

Eliade, Mircea. 1957. *Mythes, rêves et mystères*. Paris: Gallimard. Translated, *Myths, Dreams and Mysteries: The Encounter between Contemporary Faiths and Archaic Realities*. New York: Harper Collins, 1979.

Engel, G. 1975. "The Death of a Twin: Mourning and Anniversary Reactions: Fragments of 10 Years of Self Analysis," *International Journal of Psycho-Analysis* 56(1): 23–140.

English, Fanita. 1969. "Episcript and the 'Hot Potato Game'," *Transactional Analysis Bulletin* VIII (October), 77–82.

186   *Bibliography*

Faimberg, Haydée. 1993. "Le téléscopage des générations, à propos de la généalogie des certaines identifications," in R. Kaës and H. Faimberg. *Transmission de la vie psychique entre générations*. Paris: Dunod.

Fedida, Pierre, Jean Guyotat, et al. 1986–7. *Actualités transgénérationnelles en psychopathologie*. Paris: Echo Centurion.

Ferenczi, Sandor. 1909. "Transfert et introjection," in *Oeuvres complètes*, vol. 1. Paris: Payot, 1982.

Festinger, Leon. 1957. *A Theory of Cognitive Dissonance*. New York: Evanston: Row, Peterson.

Fine, Reuben. 1990. *A History of Psychoanalysis*. London: Crossroad Publishing.

Fisher, J. and R.A. Hinde. 1949. "The Opening of Milk Bottles by Birds," *British Birds* 42: 347–357.

"Les Fixations précoces et leur devenir," Special Issue of *Groupal* 10 (1994). Paris.

Forrester Viviane. 1983. *Vincent Van Gogh ou l'enterrement dans les blés*. Paris: Le Seuil.

Foulkes, S. H. 1964. *Therapeutic Group Analysis*. London: Allen and Unwin.

Framo, James. 1992. *Family-of-Origin Therapy: An Intergenerational Approach*. New York: Brunner/Mazel.

Freud, Sigmund. 1897. "Drafts L and M", in *The Complete Psychological Works of Sigmund Freud*, vol. 1, 248–249, 250–252. London: Hogarth Press, 1953.

—— 1900. *The Interpretation of Dreams*, in *The Complete Psychological Works of Sigmund Freud*, vols 4 and 5. London: Hogarth Press. 1953.

—— 1909. *Family Romances*, in *The Complete Psychological Works of Sigmund Freud*, vol. 9, 235–244. London: Hogarth Press, 1953.

—— 1910. *Five Lectures on Psychoanalysis*, in *The Complete Psychological Works of Sigmund Freud*, vol. 11, 1–55. London: Hogarth Press, 1953.

—— 1913. *Totem and Taboo*, in *The Complete Psychological Works of Sigmund Freud*, vol. 13. London: Hogarth Press, 1953.

—— 1914. *On Narcissism: An Introduction*, in *The Complete Psychological Works of Sigmund Freud*, vol. 14, 67–104. London: Hogarth Press, 1953.

—— 1917. *Mourning and Melancholia*, in *The Complete Psychological Works of Sigmund Freud*, vol. 14, 237–258. London: Hogarth Press, 1953.

—— 1916-17. *Introductory Lectures on Pschoanalysis*, in *The Complete Psychological Works of Sigmund Freud*, vols 15–16. London: Hogarth Press, 1953.

—— 1919. *The Uncanny*, in *The Complete Psychological Works of Sigmund Freud*, vol. 17, 217–252. London: Hogarth Press, 1953.

—— 1920. *Beyond the Pleasure Principle*, in *The Complete Psychological Works of Sigmund Freud*, vol. 18, 1–64. London: Hogarth Press, 1953.

—— 1933. *New Introductory Lectures on Psychoanalysis*, in *The Complete Psychological Works of Sigmund Freud*, vol. 22, 1–182. London: Hogarth Press, 1953.

—— 1939. *Moses and Monotheism*, in *The Complete Psychological Works of Sigmund Freud*, vol. 23. London: Hogarth Press, 1953.

Fromm, Eric. 1962. "The Social Unconscious," in *Beyond the Chains of Illusion: My Encounter with Marx and Freud*. New York: Simon and Schuster.

Garland, C. 1980. *The Proceedings of the Survivor Syndrome Workshop*. London: Institute of Group Analysis.

Gaulejac, Vincent de. 1987. *La Névrose de classe*. Paris: Hommes et Groupes.

—— 1996. *Les Sources de la honte*. Paris: DDB.

Gaulejac, Vincent and Isabel Taboada Leonetti. 1994. *La Lutte des places, insertion et désinsertion*. Paris: DDB and Hommes et Perspectives.

Gay, Peter. 1988. *Freud: A Life for Our Time*. New York: Norton.

Goffman, Ervin. 1959. *Presentation of Self in Everyday Life*. New York: Doubleday.

—— 1963. *Stigma: Notes on the Management of Spoiled Identity*. Indianapolis, Ind: Macmillan.

—— 1986. *Frame Analysis: An Essay on the Organization of Experience*. Boston, Mass: Northeastern University Press.

—— 1990. *Asylums: Essays on the Social Situation of Mental Patients and Other Inmates*. New York: Doubleday.

Grandjon, Evelyne and Jean Guyotat (eds). 1985. *Rencontres cliniques d'Arles*.

Green, André. 1983. "La Mère morte," in *Narcissisme de vie, narcissisme de mort*. Paris: Minuit.

GREPS. 1986. "Le Phénomène psychosomatique et la psychanalyse", in *Analytica*. Paris: Editions Navarin.

Groddeck, Georg. W. 1923. *The Book of It*. Vision Press. 1979.

"Le Groupe familial en psychothérapie," *Revue de psychothérapie psychanalytique de groupe* 22 (March 1994 Congress, Paris.)

Guir, Jean. 1983. *Psychosomatique et cancer*. Paris: Points Hors Lignes.

Guyotat, Jean. 1980. *Mort, naissance et filiation: études de psychopathologie sur le lien de filiation*. Paris: Masson.

—— 1980. "Filiation et généalogie," in *Psychanalyse à l'université* 5(18).

—— 1982. "Recherches psychopathologiques sur les coïncidences mort-naissance," in *Psychanalyse à l'université* 27–8 (September).

Guyotat, Jean and Pierre Fedida. 1986. "Mémoire, transmission psychique," in *Psychanalyse à l'université* (January).

Haley, Jay. 1989. *Power Tactics of Jesus Christ and Other Essays*. New York: Norton.

Heireman, Magda. 1989. *Du côté de chez soi: la thérapie contextuelle d'Ivan Boszormenyi-Nagy*. Paris: ESF.

Hergé, 1946. *Les Aventures de Tintin. Le secret de la licorne.* Paris: Cast-
erman.

Héritier, Françoise. 1994. *Les Deux Soeurs et la mère.* Paris: Odile Jacob.

Hilgard, Josephine R. 1953. "Anniversary Reactions in Parents Precipitated
by Children," *Psychiatry* 16: 73–80.

—— 1989. "The Anniversary Syndrome as Related to Late-Appearing
Mental Illnesses in Hospitalized Patients," in A. L. S. Silver, ed. *Psychoanalysis and Psychosis.* Madison, Conn: International University Press.

Hilgard, Josephine R. and Martha F. Newman. 1959. "Anniversaries in
Mental Illness," *Psychiatry* 22: 113–121.

—— 1961. "Evidence for Functional Genesis in Mental Illness:
Schizophrenia, Depressive Psychoses and Psychoneuroses," *Journal of
Nervous and Mental Disease* 132(1): 3–16.

—— 1963. "Parental Loss by Death in Childhood as an Etiological Factor
among Schizophrenic and Alcoholic Patients Compared with a Non-
Patient Community Sample," *Journal of Nervous and Mental Disease*
137: 14–28.

Hilgard, Josephine R. and Fern Fisk. 1960. "Disruption of Adult Ego Identity as Related to Childhood Loss of a Mother through Hospitalization
for Psychosis," *Journal of Nervous and Mental Disease* 131(1).

Holmes, T.H. and M. Masuda. 1974. "Life Change and Illness Suscepti-
bility," in B. S. Dohrenwend and B. P. Dohrenwend, eds. *Stressful Life
Events: Their Nature and Effect.* New York: Wiley.

Hopper, Earl. 1981. "A Comment on Pr. M. Jahoda's 'Individual and the
Group'" in M. Pines and L. Rafaelson, eds. *The Proceedings of the VII
International Congress of Group Psychotherapy.* London: Plenum.

—— 1996. 'The social unconscious in clinical work,' in *Group*, 20, 1, 7–42
(UK).

Horney, Karen. 1937. *The Neurotic Personality of our Time.* Norton: New
York.

Houzel, D. 1985. "L'Evolution du concept d'espace psychique dans l'oeuvre
de Mélanie Klein et de ses successeurs," in J. Gammil, et al. *Mélanie Klein
aujourd'hui.* Lyon: Cesura.

Jung, Carl Gustav. 1952. *Synchronicity: An Acausal Connecting Principle*, in
Collected Works of C. G. Jung, vol. 8, 417–432. Princeton, New Jersey:
Princeton University Press. 1969/1981.

—— "On the Psychology of the Unconscious" and "The Relations Between
the Ego and the Unconscious," in *Two Essays on Analytical Psychology*,
second edition. Translated by R.F. Hull. New York: Pantheon Books,
1966.

Kaës, René and Haydée Faimberg, eds. 1993. *Transmission de la vie
psychique entre générations.* Paris: Dunod.

Kernberg, Otto. 1993. "The Couple's Constructive and Destructive Superego
Functions," *Journal of the American Psychoanalytic Association* 41:
653–677.

Kobasa, Suzan et al. 1982. "The Hardy Personality: Toward a Social Psychology of Stress and Health," in S. Sulls and G. Sanders, eds. *Social Psychology of Health and Illness*, 3–33. Hillsdale, New Jersey: Erlbaum.

Lani, Martine. 1990. *A la recherche de la génération perdue*. Paris: *Le Journal des psychologues* and Hommes et Perspectives.

Laplanche, J. and J.B. Pontalis. 1985. *Fantasme originaire, fantasme des origines, origines du fantasme*. Paris: Hachette.

Lavallée, Guy. 1993. "La boucle contenante et subjectivante de la vision," in D. Anzieu and S. Tisseron, *Les Contenants de la pensée*. Paris: Dunod. 87–126.

Lavisse, Ernest and A. Rambeau. 1892–1901. *Histoire générale du IVe siècle à nos jours*. Paris: A. Colin.

Legendre, Pierre. 1985. *L'Inestimable objet de la transmission. Etudes sur le principe généalogique en Occident*. Paris: Fayard.

Legrand, Michel. 1993. *L'Approche biographique*. Paris: Epi, DDB.

Maalouf, Amin. 1983. *Les Croisades vues par les Arabes*. Paris: Lattès. Translated by Jon Rothschild. *The Crusades through Arab Eyes*. New York: Schocken Books. 1984.

Marineau, René. 1989. *J. L. Moreno ou la troisième révolution psychiatrique*. Paris: A. M. Métaillé. Translated, *Jacob Levy Moreno, 1889–1974: Father of Psychodrama, Sociometry and Group Therapy*. London: Routledge.

Martensen-Larsen, Oluf. 1989. *Familiemonsten*. Denmark: Hekla.

Marty, P. 1980. *L'Ordre psychosomatique*. Paris: Payot.

Maslow, Abraham. 1954. "The Instinctoid Nature of Basic Needs," *Journal of Personality* 22: 340–1.

Masson, Odette. 1983. "Les Personnes et leurs rôles dans les systèmes familiaux morphostatiques," *Bulletin de psychologie* 6(36): 360. Special edition.

May, Rollo. 1950. *The Meaning of Anxiety*. New York: Ronald Press.

—— 1983.*The Discovery of Being, Writings in Existential Psychology*. New York: Norton. 1986/1994.

—— 1988. *Paul Tillich as Spiritual Teacher*. New York: Say Book. (And private communications, Barcelona 1976; Formentor 1978.)

—— 1991. *The Cry for Myth*. New York: Norton.

May, Rollo, Ernest Angel, Henri Ellenberger, eds. 1958. *Existence: A New Dimension in Psychiatry and Psychology*. New York: Basic Books. Reprint. New York: Jason Aronson, 1994.

McGoldrick, Monica and Tandy Gerson. 1985. *Genograms in Family Assessment*. New York: Norton.

—— 1994. *You Can Go Home Again*. New York: Norton.

Mead, Margaret. 1975. *Growing Up in New Guinea*. New York: William Morrow.

Mead, George Herbert. 1982. *The Individual and the Social Self: Unpublished Work of George Herbert Mead*. David L. Miller, ed. Chicago: Chicago University Press.

Mendel, Gérard. 1979. *Quand plus rien ne va de soi: apprendre à vivre avec l'incertitude*. Paris: Laffont.

Mercier, Evelyne-Sarrah, ed. 1993. *La Mort transfigurée*. Paris: International Association for Near Death Studies (IANDS France).

Mijolla, Alain de. 1981. *Les Visiteurs du moi*. Paris: Belles Lettres.

Miller, Alice. 1988. *Banished Knowledge: Facing Childhood Injuries*. London: Virago, 1991. New York: Doubleday, 1991.

—— 1984. *For Your Own Good: Hidden Cruelty in Childhood and the Roots of Violence*. London: Virago, 1987. New York: Farrar, Strauss and Giroux, 1990.

Minc, Alain. 1993. *Le Nouveau Moyen Age*. Paris: Gallimard.

Minuchin, Salvador. 1974. *Families and Family Therapy*. Cambridge, Mass. Harvard University Press.

Morel Denise. 1984. *Cancer et psychanalyse*. Paris: Belfont.

—— 1991. *Qui est vivant?* Paris: Editions Universitaires.

Moreno, J.L. 1934. *Who Shall Survive? A New Approach to the Problem of Human Relations*. Washington, DC: NMD Pub. Co. New edn. 1953.

—— 1956. *Sociometry and the Science of Man*. Beacon, New York: Beacon House.

—— 1959. *Psychodrama, Second Volume: The Foundations of Psychotherapy*. Beacon, New York: Beacon House.

—— 1987. *The Essential Moreno: Writings on Psychodrama, Group Method and Spontaneity*. New York: Springer Publishing Co.

Morris, Desmond. 1979. *Manwatching*. New York: Harry N. Abrams. 1985.

M'Uzan, Michel de. 1994. In P. Marty, M. M'Uzan and C. Daid, *L'investigation psychosomatique*, Paris: PUF.

Nachin, Claude. 1989. *Le Deuil d'amour*. Paris: Editions Universitaires.

—— 1993. *Les Fantômes de l'âme. A propos des héritages psychiques*. Paris: L'Armattan.

Napier, Augustus and Carl Whitaker. 1978. *The Family Crucible*. Glenville, Illinois: Harper and Collins.

Nardone, Giorgio and Paul Watzlawick. 1993. *The Art of Change*. San Francisco: Jossey Bass.

Nathan, N. 1985. "L'Enfant ancêtre," *Nouvelle revue d'ethno-psychiatrie* 4 (December). Paris: La Pensée Sauvage.

Nathan, Toby. *L'Influence qui guérit*. Paris: Odile Jacob.

Offroy, Jean-Gabriel. 1993. *Le Choix du prénom*. Marseille: Hommes et Perspectives.

Olindo-Weber, Sylvana and V. Mazeran. 1991. "A l'écoute du corps souffrant," *Journal des psychologues* (September).

Pankow, Gisela. 1969. *L'Homme et sa psychose*. Paris: Aubier-Montaigne.

Penfield, Wilder. 1975. *The Mystery of the Mind*. Princeton, NJ: Princeton University Press.

Perrot, Jean. 1985. "L'Enfant ancêtre." *Nouvelle revue d'ethnopsychiatrie* 4 (December). Paris: La Pensée Sauvage.

Pessler, Robert. 1991. *La Famille: l'individu plus un*. Marseille: Hommes et Perspectives.

Poe, Edgar Allan. 1857. "The Purloined Letter," in *The Complete Stories*. New York: Alfred A. Knopf, 1992.

Pribram, Karl. 1971. *Languages of the Brain*. Englecliffs, New Jersey: Prentice Hall. (And private communication, New York 1989, Cannes 1991.)

Prigogine, Ilya and Isabelle Stengers. 1988. *Entre le temps et l'éternité*. Paris: Fayard. Translated, *The Birth of Time and Eternity*. Boston, Mass: Shambhala, 1988.

Racamier, Paul-Claude. 1992. *Le Génie des origines, psychanalyse et psychoses*. Paris: Payot.

—— 1995. *L'Inceste et l'incestuel*. Paris: Les Editions du Collège.

Reik, Theodor. 1983. *Listening with the Third Ear*. New York: Farrar, Strauss and Co.

Rank, Otto. 1954. *The Myth of the Birth of the Hero and Other Writings*. Philip Freund, ed. New York: Vintage Books.

Rinpoche, Sogyl, ed. 1992. *The Tibetan Book of Living and Dying*. San Francisco: Harper, 1994.

Robert, Marthe. 1989. *La Révolution psychanalytique*. Paris: Petite Bibliothèque Payot.

Rosenthal, Robert and L. Jacobson. 1971. *Pygmalion in the Classroom*. Reprint. New York: Irvington. 1986/1996.

Rosny, Eric de. 1981. *Les Yeux de ma chèvre*. Paris: Plon. *Healers in the Night of the Duala*. New York: Orbis Books, 1985.

Rossi, Ernest and David Cheek. 1988. *Mind–Body Therapy*. New York: Norton.

Roudinesco, Elisabeth. 1986. *Histoire de la psychanalyse*. Paris: Le Seuil.

Ruffiot, André, et al. 1981. *La Thérapie familiale psychanalytique*. Paris: Dunod.

Sami Ali, M. 1990. *Le Corps, l'espace et le temps*. Paris: Dunod.

Satir, Virginia. 1964. *Conjoint Family Therapy*. Palo Alto, California: Science and Behavior Books. London: Condor Books, 1978.

—— 1982. *Helping Families Change*. New York: Jason Aronson.

Schneider, Michel. 1980. *Blessures de mémoire*. Paris: Gallimard.

"Le Secret," *Connexions* 60. Eres, 1992.

Ségalen Martine, Françoise Zonabend, Anne Burguière and Christine Klapisch-Zuber. 1986. *Histoire de la famille*, 2 vols. Paris: Armand Collin. Translated, *A History of the Family*. Cambridge, Mass.: Harvard University Press.

Selous, E. 1931. "Thought Transference or What?" in *Birds*. London: Constable.

Sheldrake, Rupert. 1981. *A New Science of Life: The Hypothesis of Formative Causation*. London: Blond and Briggs. Second edition, 1985.

—— 1988. *The Presence of the Past: Morphic Resonance and the Habits of Nature*. New York: Random House, 1989. Inner Traditions, 1995.

—— 1990. *The Rebirth of Nature*. London: Rider.

Siebert, Lawrence Q. 1983. "The Survivor Personality," paper presented at the Western Association of Psychology Convention. Cited by Siegel (1989) (See section below On terminal illnesses).

Soulé, Michel, ed. 1979. *Les Grands-parents dans la dynamique psychique de l'enfant*. Paris: ESF.

—— ed. 1984. "On te le dira quand tu seras grand," in *Le Nouveau Roman familial*. 110–126. Paris: ESF.

—— et al. 1995. "Origines, identités, destinés: que dire à un enfant qui s'inquiète de son origine?" Annual Day for the Centre for Child Guidance. (March), 111–120, 121–133. Paris: ESF.

Stierlin, H. 1977. *Le Premier Entretien familial*. Paris: Delarge. Translated from the American 1979.

Sulloway, Frank. 1979. *Freud, Biologist of the Mind*. New York: Basic Books.

Sutter, Jean. 1995. "L'Anticipation dans l'impasse dépressive," in *L'Anticipation, clef du temps du déprimé*. Collection Scientifique Survector.

Sztulman, Henri, André Barbier and Jacques Cain. 1986. *Les Fantasmes originaires*. Toulouse: Privat.

Tap, Pierre, ed. 1979. *Identité individuelle et personnalisation*. Toulouse: Privat.

—— 1980. *Identité nouvelle et personnalisation*. Toulouse: Privat.

Tholet, Claude. 1984. *Tel père, tel fils*. Paris: Dunod.

Tillich, Paul. 1952. *The Courage to Be*. New Haven, Conn.: Yale University Press.

Tisseron, Serge. 1985. *Tintin chez le psychanalyste*. Paris: Aubier-Archimbaud.

—— 1986. "Honte, affiliation et généalogie," *Les Temps Modernes* (February).

—— 1990. *Tintin et les secrets de famille*. Paris: Séguier. Reprint Paris: Aubier, 1992.

—— 1992. *La Honte: psychanalyse d'un lien social*. Paris: Dunod.

—— 1996. *Secrets de famille, mode d'emploi*. Paris: Ramsey.

Tisseron, Serge, Maria Torok, Nicolas Rand, et al. 1995. *Le Psychisme à l'épreuve des générations. Clinique du fantôme*. Paris: Dunod.

Todd, Emmanuel. 1990. *Invention de l'Europe*. Paris: Le Seuil.

Toffler, Alvin. 1970. *Future Shock*. New York: Random House.

Torok, Maria. 1989. Preface in Nicolas Rand, *Le Cryptage et la vie des oeuvres*. Paris: Aubier.

Toubiana, Eric. 1988. *L'Héritage et sa psychopathologie*. Paris: PUF.

Vegh, Claudine. 1979. *Je ne lui ai pas dit au revoir: des enfants de déportés parlent.* Paris: Gallimard. Translated, *I Didn't Say Goodbye: Interviews with Children of the Holocaust.* New York: Dutton, 1985.

Verdier, Pierre and Michel Soulé. 1986. *Le Secret sur les origines, problèmes psychologiques.* Paris: ESF.

Vigouroux, Françoise. 1993. *Le Secret de famille.* Paris: PUF.

Vincent, Jean-Didier. 1997. *La Chair et le diable.* Paris: Odile Jacob.

Volkan, Vamik. 1997. *Bloodlines: From Ethnic Pride to Ethnic Terrorism.* New York: Farrar, Strauss and Giroux.

Walsh, S. 1975. "Living for the Dead? Schizophrenia and Three Generations of Family Relations," Abstract from paper presented at the thirty-eighth annual meeting of the American Psychological Association.

Watzlawick, Paul and Jackson Beavin. 1969. *Pragmatics of Human Communication: A Study of Interactional Patterns, Pathologies and Paradoxes.* New York: Norton.

Weber, Max. 1947. In Talcott Parsons, ed. *The Theory of Social and Economic Organization.* New York: Oxford University Press.

Webster, Harriet. 1993. *Family Secrets: How Telling and Not Telling Affect Our Children, Our Relationships, Our Lives.* Reading, Mass.: Addison Wesley Longman.

Winkin, Yves. 1981. *La Nouvelle Communication.* Paris: Le Seuil.

Winnicott, D.W. 1951–3. "Transitional Objects and Transitional Phenomena," in *Through Paediatrics to Psychoanalysis.* London: Karnac Books, 1992. New York: Brunner/Mazel, 1992.

—— 1957. *The Child, the Family and the Outside World.* Harmondsworth: Penguin, 1992.

—— 1965. *The Maturational Processes and the Facilitating Environment.* New York: International University Press.

—— 1971. *Playing and Reality.* London: Routledge, 1982.

Zaijde, Nathalie. 1993. *Souffle sur tous ces morts et qu'ils vivent! La transmission du traumatisme chez les enfants de l'extermination nazie.* Paris: La Pensée Sauvage.

Zeigarnik, Bluma. 1928. "On Unfinished Tasks," in *Deutsche Psykologiske Fohrshung* Germany: Forsch, pp. 1–85.

Zinkin, L. 1979. "The Collective and the Personal," *Journal of Analytical Psychology* 24 (3): 227–250.

Zuili, Nadine and Claude Nachin. 1983. "Le Travail du fantôme au sein de l'inconscient et de la clinique psychosomatique à propos du psoriasis," *Ann. Med. Psy* 141(9): 1022–1028.

See also: *Dialogue* (published by the French Association of Marriage Counseling Centers (AFCCC), 44 Rue Danton, Galerie Damoiselles, 94270 Kremlin-Bicetre. Telephone: (1)46.70.88.44.) (AFCCC 1980) "Les Secrets de famille," No. 70.

—— (1984) "Mythes familiaux," No. 84.

—— (1985) "Héritages et filiations," No. 89.
—— (1985) "Généalogie et fantômes," No. 90.
—— (1986) "Les Rites familiaux," No. 91.
—— (1987) "La Présence de l'absent," No. 98.
—— (1988) "Détruire ceux que l'on aime," No. 99.
—— (1988) "Le Dialogue et le secret," No. 100.
—— (1990) "Dettes et cadeaux dans la famille," No. 110.
—— (1991) "Loyautés familiales et désir d'enfant," No. 111.
—— (1992) "Le Sacrifice dans la famille," No. 116.
—— (1994) "Construire la parenté," No. 126.
—— (1995) "Rites et marques de passage," No. 127.
—— (1996) "Couples et secrets de famille," No. 134.

On terminal illnesses

Ader, Robert. 1981. *Psycho-neuro-immunology*. New York: Academic Press. Revised edition, 1991.

Ancelin Schützenberger, Anne. 1984. "Retrouver des raisons de vivre et d'espérer, le malade cancéreux soigné comme un homme total," *Symbiose* (special edition on alternative medicine.)

—— 1985. *Vouloir guérir, l'aide au malade atteint d'un cancer*. Toulouse: Erès Méridienne. Revised editions 1991, 1993. Paris: DDB-La Méridienne, 1996.

—— 1991. "The Drama of the Seriously Ill Patient: Fifteen Years Experience of Psychodrama and Cancer," in *Psychodrama: Inspiration and Technique*, edited by Paul Holmes and Marcia Karp, 103–205. London and New York: Routledge/Tavistock.

Ariès, Philippe, Françoise Dolto, Ginette Raimbault, Léon Schwartzenberg and F. Marty. 1983. *La Mort en face*. Toulouse: Privat. Translated by Helen Weaver. *The Hour of Our Death*. Oxford: Oxford University Press, 1991.

Barash, Marc Ian. (1993) *The Healing Path*, New York: Arkana, Penguin.

Cousins, Norman. 1989. *Head First: The Biology of Hope*. New York: Norton.

Kübler-Ross, Elisabeth. 1976. *La Mort, dernière étape de la croissance*. Ottawa: Ed. Québec-Amérique. Monaco: Le Rocher. *Death: The Final Stage*. New York: Simon and Schuster.

—— 1982. *Living with Death and Dying*. New York: Macmillan.

LeShan, Lawrence. 1977. *You Can Fight For Your Life*. New York: M. Evans.

Matthews-Simonton, Stephanie and Robert L. Shook. 1989. *The Healing Family: The Simonton Approach for Families Facing Illness*. New York: Bantam Books.

Orr, Emda and Mina Westman. 1990. "Does Hardiness Moderate Stress and How? A Review," in Michael Rosenbaum, ed. 1990, *Learned Resourcefulness: On Coping Skills, Self Control, and Adaptive Behavior*. New York: Springer.

Raimbault, Ginette. 1975. *L'Enfant et la mort*. Toulouse: Privat.

—— 1982. *Clinique du réel*. Paris: Le Seuil.

Siegel, Bernie. 1986. *Love, Medicine and Miracle*. New York: Dutton.

—— *Peace, Love and Healing*. 1989. New York: Harper and Row.

Simonton, Carl, Stephanie Matthews-Simonton and James Creighton. 1979. *Getting Well Again*. Los Angeles: J.P. Tarcher.

Spiegel, David. 1993. *Living Beyond Limits*. New York: Times Books.

Stierlin, H. 1977. *Le Premier Entretien familial*. Paris: Delarge. Translated from the American 1979.

Tavernier, Monique. 1991. *Les Soins palliatifs*. Paris: PUF, Que sais-je?

Yohyaoui, Adel Ssalen, ed. 1989. *Le Corps, espace-temps et traces de l'exil: incidences cliniques*. Grenoble: APAM/La Pensée Sauvage.

Novels, short stories, plays, autobiographies, essays

Anet, Claude. 1919. *Ariane, jeune fille russe*. Paris: Grasset. Translated by Guy Chap, *Ariane*. New York: A. Knopf, 1927.

Balzac, Honoré de. 1832. *Colonel Chabert*. Translated by Carol Cosman, New Directions, 1997.

Beddock, Francine. 1988. *L'Héritage de l'oubli: de Freud à Claude Lanzmann*. Nice: Transes, 1991.

Bernard, Jean. 1992. *Le Syndrome du colonel Chabert ou le vivant mort*. Paris: Buchet-Chastel.

Clairier C., A. M. Gauch, M. Traiblin and Y. Clavier. 1992. *Objectifs calcul: nouveau programmes de maths CE2*. Paris: Hatier.

Dolto, Françoise. 1986. *Enfances*. Paris: Le Seuil.

Dumas, Alexandre, fils. 1986. La *Dame aux camélias*. New York: Oxford University Press.

Duperey, Anny. 1992. *Le Voile noir*. Paris: Le Seuil.

Ferenczi, Sandor. 1932. *The Clinical Diary of Sandor Ferenczi*. Cambridge, Mass.: Harvard University Press, 1988.

Flaubert, Gustave. 1887–93. *Correspondance de Gustave Flaubert*. Translated and edited by Francis Steegmuller, *The Letters of Gustave Flaubert*. Cambridge, Mass.: Harvard University Press, 1980–2.

Fynn. 1974. *Mr. God, This is Anna*. Reissue Edition. London: Ballantine Books, 1996.

Green, Hanna. 1964. *I Never Promised You a Rose Garden*. New York: Holt, Rinehart and Winston. Under the name Joanne Greenberg: New York: Signet Books, 1989.

Goethe, J. W. von *From My Life: Poetry and Truth*. International Book Import, 1987.

Haley, Alex. 1977. *Roots*. London: Picador. New York: Dell.

Hoff, Benjamin. 1946. *The Tao of Pooh*. New York: Dutton. 1982.

Leclaire, Serge. 1975. *On tue un enfant*. Paris: Seuil, 1981.

Montaigne, Michel de. 1595. *Complete Essays*. Harmondsworth: Penguin, 1991.

——— 1595. *The Complete Works of Montaigne*. Stanford, California: Stanford University Press, 1957.

Musil, Robert. 1953. *The Man without Qualities*. London: Secker and Warburg.

Plato. 427–347. "Apology," in *The Dialogues of Plato*. New Haven/London: Yale University Press, 1984.

——— "The Myth of Er," in *The Republic*. New York: Norton, 1996.

"Récits de vie et travail social." *Cahiers de la dépendance* 7. 1987.

Raverat, Gwen. 1952. *Period Piece: A Cambridge Childhood*. London and Boston, Mass.: Faber. Reprint, 1987.

Sainte-Beuve. 1857. *Causerie du lundi*. Paris: Garnier.

Segalen, Martine. 1985. *Quinze générations de Bas-Bretons: parenté et société dans le pays bigouden-sud*. Paris: PUF.

Semprun, Jorge. 1994. *Literature or Life*. Viking Penguin, 1997.

Stéphane, Roger. 1986. *Autour de Montaigne*. Paris: Stock.

Walpole, Horace. 1778. "The Three Princes of Serendip," in *Complete Works of Walpole*. London: British Library and Library of Congress.

Index